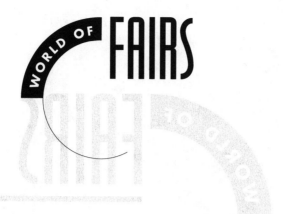

WORLD OF FAIRS

The Century-of-Progress
Expositions

ROBERT W. RYDELL

The University of Chicago Press
Chicago and London

WORLD OF FAIRS

The Century-of-Progress
Expositions

ROBERT W. RYDELL

The University of Chicago Press
Chicago and London

Robert W. Rydell is a professor in the Department of History and Philosophy at Montana State University. He is the author of *All the World's a Fair* (1984), also published by the University of Chicago Press.

The University of Chicago Press, Chicago 60637
The University of Chicago Press, Ltd., London
© 1993 by The University of Chicago
All rights reserved. Published 1993
Printed in the United States of America
02 01 00 99 98 97 96 95 94 93   1 2 3 4 5
ISBN: 0-226-73236-3 (cloth)
       0-226-73237-1 (paper)

Library of Congress Cataloging-in-Publication Data

Rydell, Robert W.
    World of fairs : the century-of-progress expositions / Robert W. Rydell.
        p.   cm.
    Includes bibliographical references and index.
    1. Exhibitions—United States—History—20th century.
    2. Exhibitions—History—20th century.   I. Title.
    T395.5.U6R94   1993
    973.9′074—dc20   92-45690
                                                                                          CIP

⊛ The paper used in this publication meets the minimum requirements of the American National Standard for Information Sciences—Permanence of Paper for Printed Library Materials, ANSI Z39.48-1984.

To Kiki Leigh, Claire, and Johanna Rydell
and
Alex and Trudy Saxton

CONTENTS

CONTENTS

ACKNOWLEDGMENTS

Support from many individuals and institutions made this book possible. A fellowship at the National Museum of American History and a MONTS grant from Montana State University helped lay the groundwork for this study. A Fulbright appointment at the University of Amsterdam provided an opportunity to raise the scaffolding, and a fellowship at the Netherlands Institute for Advanced Studies gave me the opportunity to bring this project to conclusion. I am grateful to G. Terry Sharrer, Rob Kroes, and my colleagues at the Netherlands Institute for Advanced Study in the Humanities and Social Sciences, especially the research group exploring the reception of American mass culture in Europe, for constantly challenging me with their ideas about the ways history matters.

It is difficult to know where to begin to thank the following scholars for their constructive criticism. George Cotkin, Mick Gidley, David Johnson, Jonathan McLeod, Mary Murphy, David Nye, and Alexander Saxton read much of this manuscript and improved it at every turn. David Hollinger and James Gilbert asked excellent questions and made me rethink many of my assumptions. I am also grateful to Burton Benedict and Brigitte Schroeder-Gudehus for sharing their vast knowledge about world's fairs. During the early stages of this project, Brett Gary served as my research assistant and did a tremendous job.

The research requirements for this study put immense pressures on librarians, archivists, and museum curators on both sides of the Atlantic. Several individuals—Mary Ann Bamburger, George Gurney, Charles F. McGovern, Ronald Mahoney, William Massa, Melissa Miller-Quinlan, Helen W. Samuels, and Jon Zachman—went out of their way to help me sort through materials that are often unprocessed and difficult to use. Nancy E. Gwinn of the Smithsonian Institution Libraries has also supported this project through her sustained interest in preserving world's fair publications. I am also aware of the burden I have placed on the interlibrary loan department at my own university and am grateful to Kay Carey, Bette Mongold, and Susan Lessley for their assistance.

ACKNOWLEDGMENTS

Many of the ideas presented here were initially explored in courses offered at the University of Amsterdam, the University of Michigan, and Montana State University. I am grateful to my students for their good questions and for sharing their thoughts about the world of fairs.

At the University of Chicago Press, Douglas Mitchell provided support when it mattered most, and Philip Perry sharpened my prose. I am also grateful to the Winterthur Museum as well as the editors of *Isis* and *European Contributions to American Studies* for permission to publish material originally presented to them.

In ways that are indescribable, I have relied on friends and family for support for a project that required more travel than I ever anticipated when my research first began. From the bottom of my heart, I thank my family and my wife's family for their love and support, my friends and colleagues at Montana State University for their generosity and patience, Jonathan McLeod and George Cotkin for their abiding faith and steady encouragement, and many friends in the Netherlands for helping me see America from another shore.

Finally, I dedicate this book to my wife, Kiki Leigh Rydell, who helped with the research and improved many drafts of this manuscript; to my daughters, Claire and Johanna, who, along with Kiki, so enrich my life; and to Alex and Trudy Saxton, who have been a constant source of inspiration, courage, and friendship.

Bozeman, Montana

INTRODUCTION

San Diegans dared to have faith in the future when clouds still obscured prosperity's horizon, and it was that faith that broke down barriers of pessimism to build an exposition which is recognized as yesterday's beginnings of tomorrow's greater prosperity.
—Frank Merriam, Governor of California, 1936[1]

During the Great Depression, just when the future seemed so bleak, nearly one hundred million Americans visited the 1933–34 Chicago Century of Progress Exposition, the 1935–36 San Diego California Pacific Exposition, the 1936 Dallas Texas Centennial Exposition, the 1937 Cleveland Great Lakes and International Exposition, the 1939–40 San Francisco Golden Gate International Exposition, and the 1939–40 New York World's Fair. These fairs took the nation by storm, firing the imaginations of countless ordinary Americans, including those who saw world's fair newsreels in local movie houses (the New York World's Fair alone generated 236 newsreels that reached an estimated 220 million people), read stories about world's fairs in local newspapers, participated in world's fair contests, and reveled in live radio broadcasts from the expositions. Rivaling the popularity of earlier, Victorian-era expositions that included the 1876 Philadelphia Centennial Exhibition, the 1893 Chicago World's Columbian Exposition, the 1904 St. Louis Louisiana Purchase Exposition, the 1915 San Francisco Panama–Pacific International Exposition, and the 1915–16 San Diego Panama California Exposition, America's depression-era world's fairs similarly became cultural icons for the nation's hopes and future.[2]

I write, in part, from experience—the experience of listening to my father's stories about his youthful adventures at the futuristic Century of Progress Exposition. My father's stories always turned on two exhibits, the television display and Sally Rand's display of, well, as my father recalled, herself. Only later, in the course of researching this book, did I come across a relative who worked at that same fair and claimed, with thousands of other Chicagoans, that it was the employment provided

1

Site of the Century of Progress Exposition, Chicago. Courtesy of the Library of Congress, Prints and Photographs Division.

by the fair, not government programs, that put bread on the table during the depression.

My family was not alone in attributing lasting significance to the world's fairs held during the depression. One former fairgoer recalled visiting the Century of Progress fair at every opportunity, sometimes once a week, scrimping and saving to come up with the fifty cents required for admission to the grounds. "My girlfriend and I were thrilled at each visit and you put that into your book," she emphasized. The 1939–40 New York World's Fair, which cost seventy-five cents to enter, generated a similar hold on visitors' memories. Writing in *Esquire* on the occasion of the 1964 New York World's Fair, Brock Brower recalled the importance of the fair for his childhood education: "Naturally we couldn't have the fair as just our amusement. It was more or less our chief study for two whole grades. During Art, we spent hours trying to carve the Trylon and Perisphere. . . . During Arithmetic, we drew them on the plane as triangles and circles. And I hate to think how hopeless we would've been in Geography without the Lagoon of Nations." On the occasion of an exhibit organized in 1989 to commemorate the fiftieth anniversary of the fair, the Museum of the City of New York compiled the recollections of many fairgoers who had left the fair wearing souvenir "I have seen the future" buttons. "I remember the Fair of 1939," one museum-goer reflected, adding as an afterthought: "I wish I could go back." "I visited the Fair as often as my pocketbook permitted," another noted. Novelist E. L. Doctorow captured precisely these sentiments in *World's Fair*—a novel that turned the New York World's Fair into a structuring metaphor for his generation.[3]

World's fairs were also important for a generation, or what was left of one, of Europeans who had survived the devastation of the First World War. The 1924–25 British Empire Exhibition, despite financial difficulties, rekindled the British world's fair tradition that had begun with the 1851 Crystal Palace Exhibition. Like its more successful predecessor, the British Empire Exhibition stimulated a rapid-fire succession of fairs across Europe: the 1925 Paris Exposition Internationale des Arts Décoratifs et Industriels Modernes; the 1929 Barcelona Exposición Internacional; the 1930 Seville Exposición Ibero-Americana; the 1930 Antwerp Exposition Internationale, Coloniale, Maritime et d'Art Flamand; the 1930 Liège Exposition Internationale de la Grande Industrie, Science, et Application d'Art Wallon; the 1931 Paris Exposition Coloniale Internationale; the 1935 Brussels Exposition Universelle et Internationale; the 1937 Paris Exposition Internationale des Arts et Techniques dans la Vie Moderne; the 1938 Glasgow British Empire Exhibition; and plans by Benito Mussolini to organize a world's fair in 1942 to celebrate the triumphs of fascism.

Europe's fairs attracted tens of millions of visitors. The three Paris expositions alone welcomed over seventy million. And like their American counterparts, several of Europe's fairs have become larger-than-life metaphors for late twentieth-century writers trying to give shape and meaning to human experience as it unfolded in the twentieth century. In Erik Orsenna's best-selling *L'Exposition Coloniale* and Eduardo Mendoza's *La Ciudad de los Prodigios*, the authors give testimony to the enduring presence of the Paris and Barcelona expositions in French and Spanish cultures.[4]

Why was the interwar period on both sides of the Atlantic a world of fairs? Why would national governments and private corporations spend millions of dollars on expositions? And, given massive unem-

EXPOSITION INTERNATIONALE
PARIS 1937

*The Russian and German pavilions, Paris,
1937. Courtesy of the Smithsonian
Institution, National Museum of American
History, Larry Zim World's Fair Collection.*

EXPOSICIÓN INTERNACIONAL DE BARCELONA, 1929

*The Barcelona International Exposition,
1929. Courtesy of the Smithsonian
Institution, National Museum of American
History, Larry Zim World's Fair Collection.*

ployment, growing political instability, and dizzying swings between anxiety and depression, why would so many people pay money to visit something so seemingly ephemeral as a fair?

Answers to these questions turn on recognizing the historical role played by expositions in industrial societies. Ever since London's 1851 Great Exhibition of the Works of Industry of All Nations, expositions have reflected profound concerns about the future and deflected criticism of the established political and social order. The Crystal Palace took form against the backdrop of democratic upheavals on the continent and challenges to prevailing British authorities by the Chartist Movement, while American international fairs, beginning in 1876, were developed as organized responses to class conflict in the aftermath of industrial depressions that occurred with alarming frequency between 1873 and the onset of the First World War.[5]

In the aftermath of the First World War's devastation, traditional promoters of international expositions, including government officials, industrial leaders, and leading intellectuals once again turned to the world's fair medium for buttressing their own authority and for giving ordinary citizens direction through the turbulent seas of the postwar period.

The first efforts to jump start the old exposition movement in Great Britain and the United States were not altogether successful. First proposed in 1915 as a way to build popular support for British imperial policies, but actually held in 1924–25, the British Empire Exhibition at Wembley had to be held over a second season to help promoters recover their losses. And America's lone international exposition of the 1920s, the Philadelphia Sesquicentennial Exposition of 1926, first proposed in 1916 by merchant-prince John Wanamaker, one of the original promoters of the 1876 Centennial Exhibition, turned into the single worst financial disaster in American international exhibition history. What went wrong? Exposition organizers in both Wembley and Philadelphia blamed the historicist architectural forms that characterized their fairs for lacking popular appeal. Some critics, on the other hand, believed that the era of great world's fairs had simply gone the way of dinosaurs. "The big exposition is a failure today because the American people have an exposition before their eyes all the time," a Philadelphia newspaper concluded. Between department stores, radio, movies, and tourism, the newspaper critic continued, there simply was no room left for world's fairs. The Philadelphia fair, the newspaper reported, "may prove to be the last of its particular tribe of Mohican. There

The Golden Gate International Exposition,
San Francisco, 1939. Courtesy of the Library
of Congress, Prints and Photographs
Division.

would seem to be no place for more like it in this complex and highly exciting age."[6]

What those critics failed to appreciate was the depth and breadth of exhibition culture in the 1920s—a culture that included department stores, museums, and local fairs—and the commitment by powerful interests to the world's fair medium as a proven means for lending legitimacy to their positions of authority. When the American and European economies crashed at the end of the 1920s, businessmen, politicians, and intellectuals, inspired by the 1925 Paris Exposition Internationale des Arts Décoratifs et Industriels Modernes, recast the medium of the world's fair in modernistic architectural forms and restored fairs to their former level of popularity by offering millions of people the prospect of salvation from the depression.

Exact formulas for salvation varied. European and British world's fair promoters, usually national governments, tended to stress the de-

Constitution Mall, New York World's Fair;
Trylon and Perisphere in background.
Courtesy of the Hall of History Foundation

velopment of empire as the key ingredient for national recovery, while American exposition promoters, usually industrialists and local civic leaders acting with federal government sponsorship, tended to place more weight on the marriage of science and technology to the modern corporation as the blueprint for building a better tomorrow. Imperial dreams, however, were never far removed from the consciousness of America's exposition organizers. By the close of the 1930s, with another world war threatening the stability of existing colonial arrangements, the U.S. government together with San Francisco civic and business leaders, had recast the imperial visions of Victorian-era exposition builders into a "coloniale moderne" exposition on Treasure Island in San Francisco Bay. The Golden Gate International Exposition not only served as America's counterpart to European colonial fairs of the period, but made clear that the world of tomorrow would be shaped as much by America's long-standing imperial ambitions as by its devel-

*Skyride and Hall of Science, Century of
Progress Exposition, 1933. Courtesy of the
University of Illinois at Chicago, University
Library, A Century of Progress Records.*

oping science-based, machine-age techniques, which permeated the
New York World's Fair.

All of the interwar expositions deserve further study. To date, there
is no modern history of the Belgian and Spanish fairs of this period and
British and French fairs are only beginning to receive their due.[7] My
focus is on American fairs because, despite an upsurge of interest in
American culture between the wars that has resulted in compelling
studies of radio, film, photography, theater, and public art, little has
been written about the significance of America's depression-era expositions for a "culture in crisis," steeped in what historian Warren Susman described as "pervasive feelings of shame, embarrassment, or even
humiliation."[8] Only the 1936 Texas Centennial Exposition has been the
subject of a monograph by a historian. The New York fair has inspired
numerous essays, including several brilliant pieces by Susman, and a
doctoral dissertation by one of his students. Too often, however, the
New York fair has been studied in isolation from its predecessors and

8

from its San Francisco counterpart, thus imbalancing the historical record by simultaneously overvaluing the symbolic grandeur of the New York fair and underestimating the source of its cultural power in the cumulative strength of the century-of-progress exposition movement. Strangely, no scholar has yet published a book-length study of the 1933–34 Chicago Century of Progress Exposition, although it was every bit as important as the New York World's Fair for rebuilding confidence in the nation's future.[9]

Like my earlier book on America's Victorian-era fairs, this book is both more and less than an institutional history of these fairs. I am less interested in the paraphernalia and many functions of each fair than in unshuttering their collective significance and cumulative impact as ideological constructs. In the midst of America's worst crisis since the Civil War, these fairs were designed to restore popular faith in the vitality of the nation's economic and political system and, more specifically, in the ability of government, business, scientific, and intellectual leaders to lead the country out of the depression to a new, racially exclusive, promised land of material abundance. In other words, for all of their modernistic architectural forms, risqué fan dances, and technological marvels, the fairs of the 1930s, far from signaling a complete break with the past, provided an important measure of cultural continuity. Even the New York World's Fair, animated as it was by the drive to sell the world of tomorrow, celebrated the 150th anniversary of George Washington's inauguration as president and featured James Earle Fraser's sixty-foot statue of Washington along with the futuristic abstractions of a Trylon and Perisphere—cultural icons that apparently were inspired by the Eiffel Tower and Celestial Globe built for the 1889 Paris Exposition.[10] At all of the century-of-progress expositions, the footings for the modernistic designs of the world of tomorrow were sunk deeply in an ideological cement that stressed America's historical progress towards becoming a promised land of abundance. To put this argument in slightly different terms, if America's Victorian-era fairs represented an effort to make America modern, America's depression-era fairs represented a drive to modernize America by making it an ever more perfect realization of an imperial dream world of abundance, consumption, and social hierarchy based on the reproduction of existing power relations premised on categories of race and gender. As G. Aubrey Davidson, president of San Diego's 1915 fair, declared about that city's 1935 exposition: "The Exposition of 1935 represents the full flowering of the ideas which motivated our earlier effort."[11]

Therein lay the genius of America's depression-era exposition builders. Their fairs were exercises in cultural and ideological repair and renewal that simultaneously encouraged Americans to share in highly controlled fantasies about modernizing the present in order to attain, as California Governor Frank Merriam put it, "tomorrow's greater prosperity." The century-of-progress expositions were part of a depression-era world that historian Lawrence W. Levine describes as filled with "conflicting urges: a world that looked to the past even as it began to assume the contours of the future; a world in which a crisis in values accompanied the crisis in the economy; a world of special interest to historians because the normal process of cumulative and barely perceptible change was expedited and made more visible by the presence of prolonged crisis." [12] World's fairs certainly highlighted these conflicting tendencies in American culture; they also spoke volumes about the drive by national elites to sustain asymmetrical power relations in American society as a whole and about the efforts of some people in positions of relative powerlessness, especially African Americans, to contest the efforts of world's fair authorities to perpetuate dominant social relations. [13]

World of Fairs is divided into two parts. Part one, "An Exhibitionary Culture," draws on the insights of Tony Bennett about the role of exhibitions in "forming a complex of disciplinary and power relations" and opens with a chapter that examines the roots of the century-of-progress expositions in America's Victorian-era exposition movement. The second chapter, "Fitter Families for Future Firesides," explores a key facet of the national exhibition culture of the 1920s, the eugenics exhibitions, and examines their influence on the world's fairs of the interwar era. Part two, "The Century-of-Progress Expositions," focuses more precisely on America's depression-era fairs and on their historical significance as sites for advancing several specific projects. Chapter three, entitled "Coloniale Moderne" examines one of these projects: the drive by American political and business leaders to revitalize earlier visions of an American empire through modernistic designs inspired less by the 1925 decorative arts exposition in Paris than by contemporary British and European colonial expositions. [14] Chapter four, "The Empire of Science," turns to the campaign by American scientists to popularize science through the expositions and to the deep involvement by scientists in shaping the ideological content of the fairs. Chapter five, "Future Perfect," emphasizes that the future perfect world forecast at the fairs was a conditional construct; conditional, that is, on popular acceptance of the modernizing strategies proposed by exposition planners. This chapter examines the collaboration of architects, industrial designers, leaders of American business, and New Deal planners in laying the groundwork for a world of tomorrow transformed into a corporation-led, consumption-oriented welfare state that, at its core, depended upon dramatizing women as sexual commodities. Chapter six, "African Americans in the World of Tomorrow," examines the fairs from a different perspective: the efforts by African Americans to convert what were intended as vehicles of social and racial control into arenas for resisting dominant white supremacist values. The seventh and final chapter of *World of Fairs* turns to the legacy of the century-of-progress expositions as revealed in the U.S. government's effort to organize an American pavilion to represent American culture at the 1958 Brussels world's fair. The result, a pleasure dome that simultaneously mirrored the contradictions in cold war America and served as a front for U.S. intelligence-gathering activities and national security operations against enemies abroad and dissidents at home, made the world of tomorrow forecast by America's depression-era fairs seem remarkably prescient while simultaneously hastening its realization.[15]

What kept America from collapsing under the weight of the Great Depression? While it would be silly to reduce the answer to world's fairs, it would be equally foolish to ignore their effect. The century-of-progress expositions were theaters of power. They were also what anthropologist Sidney Mintz calls "webs of signification" that served the purpose of "endowing reality with meaning."[16] In the midst of a massive economic depression, that was no small accomplishment and one that would reverberate throughout the culture of twentieth-century America.

PART ONE

*An
Exhibitionary
Culture*

PART ONE

An
Exhibitionary
Culture

CHAPTER ONE
Forerunners of the Century-of-Progress Expositions

Expositions are the timekeepers of progress.
—William McKinley, 1901

The [1893 Chicago World's Columbian Exposition], like all exhibitions, is a striking example of imprudence and hypocrisy: everything is done for profit and amusement—from boredom— but noble aims of the people are ascribed to it. Orgies are better.
—Leo Tolstoy, 1893[1]

The century-of-progress expositions that ringed the United States between the world wars did not emerge out of thin air. They continued— "reinvented" may be a better term—a tradition of world's fairs that dated to London's 1851 Great Exhibition of the Works of Industry of All Nations and continued through San Francisco's 1915 Panama– Pacific International Exposition. Because these Victorian-era fairs played such an important role in shaping the contours of the modern world, they have attracted increasing scholarly attention, much of which turns on the insights that cultural critic Walter Benjamin provided a half century ago. "World exhibitions," Benjamin declared about nineteenth-century international expositions, "are the sites of pilgrimages to the commodity fetish." Over the past two decades, scholars from a variety of disciplines have built on Benjamin's ideas and focused on the connection between international exhibitions and the values of an emerging mass consumer society. Neil Harris has drawn attention to the close relationship between fairs and the rise of department stores and art museums, while Rosalind Williams describes fairs as fountainheads for the "dream world of mass consumption." Umberto Eco has called the world's fair medium the "Missa Solemnis of capitalist culture." More recently, Burton Benedict and Warren Susman have addressed the ritualistic nature of fairs. Benedict, following the lead of Mary Douglas, likens fairs to potlatches—ritualistic displays of goods and power. Susman, drawing on Victor Turner's ideas about liminality, argues that fairs "were rites of passage for American society which made possible the full acceptance of a new way of life, new values, and

Sculpture for Panama-Pacific International Exposition, San Francisco, 1915. Courtesy of the Hall of History Foundation.

World's Columbian Exposition, 1893. From Hubert H. Bancroft, The Book of the Fair *(1894), vol. 1, p. 71.*

Prospectus for the 1899 Omaha Greater
America Exposition. Courtesy of California
State University, Fresno, Henry Madden
Library, Department of Special Collections.

a new social organization." Meanwhile, Alan Trachtenberg, reflecting on the 1893 Chicago World's Columbian Exposition, has underscored the significance of that fair as "an ideal shape of an incorporated America," and James Gilbert has pinpointed the same fair as a pivotal event for the development of a commercial culture.[2]

While agreeing with many of these assessments, I want to offer a caveat. In the rush to consider America's turn-of-the-century fairs as central to the growth of a consumer culture, it is important not to lose sight of a significant—perhaps overriding—characteristic of fairs so often associated with the dawn of the modern era. Victorian-era fairs certainly promised material abundance, but they did so in contexts that elaborated visions of empire as well. In the worldview projected by America's turn-of-the-century fairs, it seemed that becoming a "people of plenty" would mean that Americans would have to accept "empire as a way of life."[3]

To get this idea across, the upper-class underwriters of America's fairs, with the active cooperation of the federal government, turned their enterprises into powerful organizing processes. In the first place, exposition authorities organized themselves and modeled their enterprises after corporations. Second, they set up departments of publicity and promotion to keep information about the fairs in the national press. Simultaneously, exposition sponsors turned to a cadre of exhibition specialists, oftentimes trained scientists, to develop exhibit classifications for the tons of anticipated exhibit materials. Within the taxonomies of racial and material progress that scientists and businessmen created for the fairs, particular displays of "things" and people—including exhibits assembled for midway shows—were developed to give visual evidence to the equation of abundance and empire. Equally important, the process of organization spiraled down from exposition headquarters into the hands of state and local committees in communities as far away as Montana. (In important ways, President William McKinley, who was assassinated at the 1901 Buffalo fair, was right: expositions—and not just souvenirs—entered the home.) Finally, the material basis for the vision of the good life projected by the fairs did not vanish at the close of the expositions. In addition to much-discussed architectural forms and city beautiful plans that framed the urban and suburban landscape of America, fairs generated tons of exhibit materials that found a permanent home in museums. One such museum, the now-forgotten Philadelphia Commercial Museum, was founded to institutionalize and perpetuate the gospel of empire and abundance promulgated at the World's Columbian Exposition and subsequent international fairs. Organized against the backdrop of depressions and industrial violence, America's fairs, like the corporations they were modeled after, moved vertically and horizontally, in the effort to incorporate America.

A common misperception of America's turn-of-the-century international fairs is that they exhibited only such commodities as dynamos, reapers, corn palaces, guns, and household furnishings and such eye-catchers as a state seal made of beans, a California mission built with oranges, or the Brooklyn Bridge constructed from soap. To be sure, these and similar items were on display and did impress visitors, but spectacles of gigantic Vulcans superintending a mining operation and examples of flush toilets, floral tea trays, and woolens existed as part of a broader universe of exhibits that included human beings. In fact, woven into the dream world of goods was a hierarchical continuum of material and racial progress that signified nothing so much as the distance travelled from "savagery" to "civilization." And, in a world alive with social-Darwinian ideas of evolution, displays of material and natural abundance became an outward sign of inward racial "fitness" and culture.[4]

This facet of the bourgeois fantasy world, apparent at all American fairs clustered around the century's turn, came into particularly sharp focus at the 1904 St. Louis Louisiana Purchase Exposition. Occupying an acreage larger than any world's fair before or since, the St. Louis exposition boasted the usual array of goods on display. We know that visitors took notes as they walked—or were wheeled in roller chairs—along miles of exhibit cases filled with commodities. We also know these exhibits, however well attended, were not necessarily the most popular. That distinction fell to the Philippines Reservation, an exhibit of 1,200 Filipinos living at the center of the fairgrounds. Henry Adams may have been bewitched by the machines he saw in Machinery Hall, but oral histories conducted by the Missouri Historical Society suggest that many fairgoers were transfixed by the Filipinos, especially the scantily clad Igorots.[5]

The Philippines Reservation, organized by the U.S. government and located immediately adjacent to the American Indian Reservation, signaled the arrival of the United States as a world imperial power and

ll-known decorative

rian
the
uild-

c | BROOKLYN BRIDGE IN SOAPS

Brooklyn Bridge built of soap. From Hubert Bancroft, The Book of the Fair *(1894), vol. 1, p. 164.*

indicated a willingness by the federal government to compete with the colonial displays that European powers had been building into European fairs since the 1851 London Crystal Palace Exhibition. The magnitude of the St. Louis exhibit—one of its organizers, William P. Wilson, termed it "the largest and finest colonial exhibit ever made by any Government"—exalted American imperial prowess, while the juxtaposition of the reservation to Native Americans underlined continuities with America's expansionist past and with the national experience of subduing "savage" populations. Many of the same officers and soldiers involved in conquering the Philippines had fought in the nation's recently concluded Indian wars. By giving the exhibit of Filipinos a central location within the broader world of goods displayed at the fair, the exhibit's organizers created the impression that Filipinos would not only be producers and consumers in the American empire, but could be regarded and manipulated as commodities themselves. By objectifying the Filipinos, this exhibit also had the effect of confirming in white Americans a sense of their own racial and cultural superiority.[6]

Nonwhites on display at America's turn-of-the-century fairs were linked most closely to the natural world and were displayed as natural

Philippines Reservation, Louisiana Purchase
International Exposition, St. Louis, 1904.
Courtesy of California State University,
Fresno, Henry Madden Library, Department
of Special Collections.

resources to be exploited as readily as mineral deposits. Banners above the U.S. government exhibit at the 1909 Seattle fair made that connection explicit. Under the general heading "The Philippine Islands," two subgroups were arranged. One pointed to "The Natural Resources and the Primitive Peoples," while the other emphasized "The Development of the Natural Resources Under Native Initiative." Depicted as resource-rich and lacking the material goods that anthropologists equated with civilization, "primitive" cultures on display at the fairs had the effect of underwriting the predictions of a bountiful future for the culture of imperial abundance.[7]

It is important to emphasize that Filipino exhibits at the St. Louis and Seattle fairs were not unique. Beginning with the 1893 Chicago World's Columbian Exposition, every American international fair held through World War I included ethnological villages sanctioned by prominent anthropologists who occasionally organized university summer school courses around these displays. Whether one turns to the Seattle fair, where schoolchildren poked Igorot women with straw, or the Omaha, Buffalo, and St. Louis fairs, where Geronimo sold his autograph for ten cents, the expositions, and especially the midways, gave

21

millions of Americans first-hand experience with treating nonwhites from around the world as commodities.[8]

The midways, so important for introducing mass audiences to "junk food," "strip architecture," and to an array of entertainments that would fuel the development of amusement parks also gave world's fair audiences direct experience with that "evolving set of different relationships between advanced industrial societies and the rest of the world" that William Appleman Williams aptly targets as central to imperialism.[9] Displayed alongside mechanical entertainments, wild animals, thrill rides and the like, the midways' ethnological villages gave the impression that empire-building could be fun. Set against displays of foodstuffs, clothing, and machine tools, the exhibits of "anthropology live" with "natives" working primitive handicrafts also created a powerful impression of foreign markets for American surplus production. To create that impression at the Buffalo fair, the managers of the Filipino village concession included several thatched roof huts with "comfortable chairs and tables and even modern cooking stoves." Visitors could peer through the window of one hut and see a Filipino woman at work with a sewing machine.[10] Through such displays, the commodity fetish became an imperial fetish as well.

If the "culture of abundance" imagined by exposition promoters pivoted on dreams of empire, the success of the expositions hinged on attracting visitors and on informing the public generally about the view of the world on display at the fairs. Exposition organizers were up to the task. They established departments of publicity and promotion, usually staffed by newspaper reporters, that flooded the nation with publicity releases, billboards, traveling shows, and speakers. The department of publicity and promotion at the World's Columbian Exposition, in fact, was modeled after a newspaper office and run by newspaper publisher Moses P. Handy, who hired a managing editor and a staff of trained reporters and translators to generate copy for publications in America and foreign countries. As evidence of their importance, Handy's staff could point with pride to the fact that of the 5,314,000 words published about the fair before it opened, nearly half had come from their pens. Furthermore, Handy satisfied the demand by newspaper and magazine editors around the world for pictures. Reproductions of architectural plans and finished buildings were distributed to

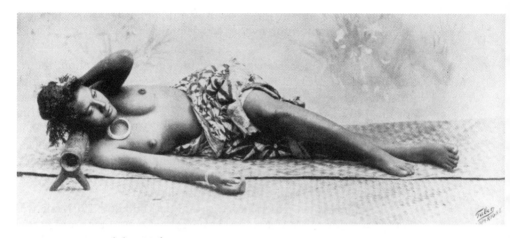

*Samoan women exhibit, Midwinter
Exposition, San Francisco, 1894.*

newspapers and magazines around the world. Most importantly, Handy sponsored a competition for a bird's-eye view of the exposition grounds. Charles Graham's watercolor won the prize and one hundred thousand reproductions along with newspaper copy were sent around the world, surprising travelers who allegedly discovered them in villages on the edge of the Sahara Desert.[11]

By the time of the St. Louis fair, the "press exploitation" bureau actually included two divisions, one devoted to domestic and the other to foreign promotion. The domestic bureau alone employed 76 persons, including 26 full-time reporters and editors, 6 stenographers, and numerous clerks. The director of the bureau, W. A. Kelso, summed up the scope of the bureau's activities:

We furnished the press with from 10,000 to 20,000 words of reading matter daily, the average probably being 15,000 words, equivalent to over eight columns of solid non-pareil in one of our large daily papers. Mr. Stiffelmann, who had charge of the work of marking, cutting, and classifying what the domestic and foreign press had to say about our World's Fair, reports that he has filled 77 scrapbooks with clippings and partly filled 55 others, the amount of reading-matter pasted being 1,075,616 inches, or over 16 miles. Adding the loose clippings not yet pasted, we have a total of 2,009,106 inches, or nearly 32 miles of reading-matter about the World's Fair. Estimating eight lines to the inch and seven words to the line, we have 16,072,84 [sic] lines and 112,509,936 words. This record, as great as it is, represents only a very small portion of the newspaper publicity given the Exposition by the outside press.[12]

When exposition managers tried to skimp on promotion, the results could be devastating. In the early stages of planning for Seattle's Alaska-Yukon-Pacific Exposition, fair managers contacted the directors of the 1907 Jamestown Tercentennial fair and discovered that the indebtedness of the Jamestown corporation was $500,000—a sum greater than had been publicly announced. The source of the problem, they decided, had been advertising. The publicity office for the Jamestown fair had employed only a dozen press agents and had relied on five circus-style railroad cars to advertise the fair.[13]

The Jamestown experience was unusual. Buffalo's 1901 fair was advertised through a stereopticon concession at Atlantic City and by numerous seventy-five-by-sixteen-foot billboards located along railroad tracks in the vicinity of Buffalo. In 1909, the number of billboards on vacant lots in Seattle became so great that residents complained to city officials. To drum up support for the 1897 Nashville fair, the promotion department arranged for an exposition train to tour Tennessee with some of the Chinese from the Chinese Village concession. The directors of the 1905 Portland fair hired a special agent to travel around the West promoting the Lewis and Clark Centennial. As one historian of the Portland fair described the "boomer's" job: "he shared worn-down hotels with traveling salesmen, showed lantern slides to the chambers of commerce, and glad-handed editors of the weekly papers." Exposition organizers also enlisted the support of the federal government. For the 1893 Chicago fair, the U.S. Treasury Department issued a special commemorative half-dollar, while for most of the expositions the postal service issued special commemorative stamps. Portland fair promoters even convinced the local post office to postmark outgoing mail with "World's Fair 1905." Commenting on the value of the Post Office's stamp of approval for its 1898 fair, an Omaha newspaper declared: "The issue will be not only valuable as a medium of advertising the exposition of 1898, but it gives to the project the prestige of government recognition and support." [14]

The concern for "prestige" helps to explain the peculiar relationship that developed between world's fairs and advertising. All the fairs, as Susman observed, were "great advertisements." It is, after all, "characteristic of the culture of abundance that many things and institutions are in fact turned into advertisements." Yet, if on the one hand exposition managers, acting as tough-minded businessmen, engaged in intensive and expensive efforts to promote their expositions, on the other hand world's fair managers also regarded their expositions as "meccas" and "universities" and saw themselves less as businessmen than as curates and educators who stood above the rough-and-tumble world of profit seeking. As late as 1911, Frederick J. V. Skiff, head of the Field Museum of Natural History and the "oracle" of fin de siècle world's fair authorities, could advise the organizers of San Francisco's Panama–Pacific International Exposition to proceed with great caution concerning advertising. "I do not think straight advertising does the Exposition much good," Skiff told San Francisco's world's fair directors. "It is not like what the merchant would do, or what the theaters would do in the way of advertising." Far better than direct advertising, in Skiff's eyes, was unprepared advertising that gave the exposition notice in important places. For example, an article about the exposition president in *The Saturday Evening Post,* "where the advertisement of the Exposition was indirect and incidental," was worth its weight in gold. The key, according to Skiff, involved persuading newspapers and magazines "to recognize that [the exposition] is a national thing." Once that was established, Skiff told fair planners that the press would "help it out as they would any other effort that all the people were concerned in." Skiff's uneasiness about prepared advertising stemmed from his conviction that the exposition, "to reach its highest position . . . should be purely educational in its character." [15]

Such uncertainty about advertising is hardly surprising. Raymond Williams and Roland Marchand have discovered that "psychological advertising" is a post–World War I phenomenon. And, as Marchand has recently observed, doubts about the economic value of advertising persisted through the First World War. Most importantly, advertisers, according to Marchand, had a problem with their image. In the popular imagination, advertisers still reeked of Barnum's smoke and conjured up images of patent medicine scams. [16] For exposition planners, given their notions of expositions as bearers of civilization, advertising—however attractive as a medium for catching the public's attention—had to be treated gingerly lest it create the impression that expositions were mere business enterprises.

Throughout the fin de siècle period, Skiff's ideas about advertising the fairs prevailed. Manufacturers might advertise particular products and even allude to the fact that items had been on display at a fair. Prize-winning companies might, and did, invoke the authority of the fairs in promoting "gold medal" products. And manufacturers like the Singer Sewing Machine Company actually incorporated the ethos of imperial abundance into their advertising. But the directors of fairs held before World War I did not accord advertisers full partnership in the drive to design American culture. That recognition would have to await a generation of interwar fairs, especially the fairs of the 1930s when corporate advertising and world's fairs became inseparable. What stands out in the relationship between advertising and the fairs held before World War I, is that manufacturers sought to derive legitimacy from the fairs, not the other way around. Ironically, the seeds of change were being sown at the San Francisco fair. Before the fair opened, the directors agreed to proposals by several Hollywood studios to show newsreel footage of the exposition in hundreds of movie theaters around the nation.[17]

While recognizing the exposition management's ambivalence about advertising, it is important not to overstate it. One contemporary of the Buffalo fair could give a knowing wink and suggest that "an exhibition of this sort is not solely for a glorification of art and the humanities for their own sake, but is a business proposition as well, and a grand advertising scheme." [18] Businessmen in a world's fair community certainly regarded their particular fair as a golden opportunity to advertise the resources of their area to prospective settlers. "The Lewis and Clark Exposition could not have come at a more opportune time," declared one of Portland's urban boosters. "It will reinforce the advertising that commercial bodies are doing or propose to do, and it will be the climax of the whole plan of attracting settlers and building up the country." [19] Embossed with the imprimatur of a world's fair, the advertisement of urban development schemes—and the advertising business itself— could shift into high gear and give the impression that civic improvement and advertising meant the same thing.

World's fairs accustomed fairgoers to thinking of advertising as integral to the city beautiful. At the Omaha fair, on Children's Day, advertisers loaded down the children with business cards, product literature, pins, and badges.[20] Despite the directors' ambivalence, fairs had the effect of making advertising seem as "true and natural" to the American way of life as midway exhibits of roller coasters and Ferris Wheels and ethnological ghettos of Africans, Asians, Latin Americans, and American Indians.

Perhaps the best evidence of the influence of America's world's fairs on American culture is the fact that one did not have to attend a fair to be affected by the world's fair movement. Local newspaper stories along with regional and national magazine articles, often generated by world's fair publicity bureaus, together with merchandise advertising, carried the gospel of imperial abundance beyond the fairgrounds to a national audience. As important as these promotional campaigns were, there was another, sometimes forgotten, activity that involved men, women, and children in the process of creating and identifying with world's fairs. To secure exhibits from various states and territories and to augment planned artistic, manufacturing, agricultural, and mineralogical displays, world's fair authorities depended upon state legislatures to appoint state world's fair boards comprised of locally prominent men and women. Headed by a commissioner, these boards superintended the collection, identification, and classification of exhibit materials according to the categories provided in the guidelines world's fair managers sent to each state commission. State boards, with the invaluable assistance of women's auxiliary committees, established a network of county committees that involved countless adults and children in the task of promoting the economic and cultural development of their state within the framework developed by world's fair authorities.[21] Promotional activities in Montana were typical.

When the World's Columbian Exposition was formally established by an act of Congress in 1890, Montana's state legislature quickly organized the Montana Board of World's Fair Managers with Missoula businessman Walter Bickford as executive commissioner. Bickford wasted no time soliciting exhibits that emphasized the richness of natural resources—especially the mineral wealth—of the state. He took responsibility for generating two articles a week for newspapers around the state. On top of that, he agreed to an idea proposed by Chicago business interests—and guaranteed by a $35,000 personal bond from banker Lyman Gage—for a silver statue depicting "Justice." With the "silver issue" dominating national politics, the silver-statue "gimmick" was a stroke of Barnum-like genius.[22]

Almost immediately upon announcing the idea to the press, the statue became a rallying point for the state. Even when it became clear that Bickford had misled people into believing that the model for the statue would be selected from Montana women who would compete for the honor—when, in fact, the sculptor, nationally-renowned Richard Henry Park, had contracted with the famous actress, Ada Rehan, to be his model—the ensuing controversy kept the fair idea in the local press for months.[23]

While Bickford publicized the fair and negotiated with Helena

Montana mining exhibit, World's Columbian Exposition, 1893. From Hubert Bancroft, The Book of the Fair (1894), vol. 2, p. 481.

banker Samuel Hauser and Butte "Copper King" William A. Clark for a loan of twenty-four thousand ounces of silver for the statue of Justice, the Montana Board of Lady Managers concentrated their efforts on securing exhibits for the buildings devoted to women's and children's displays. Headed by Eliza Rickards, wife of Montana's governor, and made up of five equally prominent women from around the state, the board organized county committees to translate interest in the fair into actual exhibit material. "The importance of these local committees and the responsibilities assumed by the women appointed to preside over the same is apparent," state board member and mine owner Clara L. McAdow declared. "They are the medium through which must be disseminated in every city, town, village and community all essential information relative to women's work at the Columbian exposition." Once they were in place, county committees in turn organized local world's fair clubs, so-called Columbia Clubs, that met as often as every two weeks to spur local involvement in the fair.[24]

This intensive local campaigning generated a groundswell of interest in the fair—and not only among adults. Children were a particular concern of national and state world's fair officials. Once Chicago fair organizers agreed to construct a Children's Building, state and local committees launched drives to collect money from school children to defray costs. They were so successful in their fund-raising efforts and appeals to state pride that Montana children actually contributed double the amount requested by the Chicago Board of Lady Managers. Like their peers around the country, Montana children also served as the focal point for another campaign: the introduction of the pledge of allegiance in the nation's schools as part of Columbus Day activities organized nationwide in conjunction with the dedication ceremonies for the fair in Chicago. With children generating a whirlwind of excitement, little wonder that Columbia Clubs had little difficulty securing exhibit material—much of it "tasty and elegant bric-a-brac"—for the Montana State Building and for Montana displays in buildings devoted to metallurgy, horticulture, and women.[25]

The significance of these activities can be simply stated. Long before the fair opened, the World's Columbian Exposition had become an object of immense local interest. To the extent that interest became pride, the process of generating exhibits for the fair not only facilitated popular identification with and acceptance of the directions being given to American culture at the Chicago fair by nationally prominent elites, but it augmented the cultural authority of local political elites in their efforts to provide a blueprint for the economic and cultural development of Montana.

That the visions of national and state world's fair directorates coalesced is clear from ceremonies that unveiled the silver statue of Justice to the public. When the silver was cast in a south-side Chicago foundry, numerous dignitaries from the fair as well as from Montana's exposition delegation attended to underscore the value of the statue to the overall aims of the fair. Exactly what those aims were became clear at the public unveiling of six-foot statue standing on a solid gold plinth valued at nearly $250,000. At the public ceremonies, Eliza Rickards called attention to this "silver sentiment crystalized into art." "Its artistic contours," she added, "are mutely eloquent with the aspirations of our people. They seem to speak of the unrevealed wealth of our virgin mountains. They attest to the magnitude of an industry that has linked Montana with the financial interests of the world. They invite to an empire of resources the brain and brawn of the union." When Rickards tugged the cord that removed the red, white, and blue bunting from the statue, Montana took its place in the galaxy of world's fair states as a resource-rich internal colony that eagerly proffered the development of its natural resources in the service of enriching the imperial republic. Back home, Montanans read Commissioner Bickford's understated evaluation: "We could not get the same amount of advertising for the State of Montana for a million dollars in cash."[26]

In return for their exhibit, Montanans received plenty of advertising. The silver in the statue, however, never returned to the state. After the close of the exposition, "Justice" hit the road and was displayed at a series of county fairs around the nation before being reduced to bullion by an Omaha smelter in 1903.[27] What Montanans did receive was an amusement park—Columbia Gardens—that bore a strong resemblance to the Midway Plaisance.

The story of the transformation of Butte's Columbia Gardens from a working-class resort into an amusement park dedicated to children is the story of the sudden rise of mass entertainment to respectability. Staked out in 1876 as a mining claim, the twenty-one acre site became a picnic area during the 1880s before it was sold to entrepreneurs who developed it into a resort for Butte's working class. Throughout much of the 1890s, the Columbia Gardens resort resembled nothing so much as a preindustrial pleasure garden. That dramatically changed in 1899 when, in the midst of the fabled "War of the Copper Kings," William A. Clark, mining investor and former commissioner to the World's Columbian Exposition, purchased the Gardens and converted them into an amusement park for workers and especially for their children. Spending over $100,000 per year on improving his gift, Clark turned the Gardens into a small-scale Midway complete with restaurants, dance hall, zoo, and Shoot-the-Chutes. On one level, Clark's investment represented a bread-and-circus operation. At the very moment he made his bequest, Clark was fighting to regain a U.S. Senate seat that had been denied him by a Senate committee after investigating charges of corruption. On another level, however, Columbia Gardens represented less an effort to win votes than to influence leisure. Like the Midway Plaisance and Coney Island, Columbia Gardens equated fun with spending money and stood in the vanguard of national efforts to disseminate a new vision of society—one based, according to John Kasson, on "consumption and leisure," not on the producer-ethic of republican America.[28]

The World's Columbian Exposition alone left a significant legacy in Montana. But the force of the world's fair movement was deeply felt because it was cumulative. In 1884, while still a territory, Montana's agricultural and mineral resources had been represented at the New

Orleans World's Industrial and Cotton Exposition. Then, at the 1904 St. Louis fair, the Montana Building again housed exhibits designed to attract investment capital and settlers to the state. By the turn of the century, in sum, world's fairs had involved countless Montanans—and Americans generally—in the process of reexamining themselves in the context of the "dream worlds" of imperial abundance woven at the fairs. The result, even in hotbeds of labor agitation like Butte, was to blunt, not obliterate, the jagged edge of class conflict.[29]

Through organizing activities like those in Montana, through saturation media campaigns, including contests for free round-trip excursions to the fairs, launched by publicity bureaus at the fairs, and through keepsakes such as postcards, souvenir albums, spoons, table settings and the like brought home by actual exposition-goers, the festivities associated with fairs (and it is important that these activities were repeated in most states for all of the fairs held between 1876 and 1916) acquired a momentum that swept the country. The message of the fairs, however, not only persisted through memories of hands-on experience in organizing displays or from memories of actually visiting an exposition. Selected exhibits from the fairs were institutionalized in museums around the country.

No systematic study exists of the relationship between world's fairs and museums, but when that story is told it will shed additional light on the lasting importance of fairs for American culture. Such museums as the Museum of Man in San Diego, the Field Museum of Natural History and later the Museum of Science and Industry in Chicago, the Commercial Museum in Philadelphia, and many of the Smithsonian Institution's museums, derived substantial portions of their collections from—and sometimes owed their existence to—world's fairs. These museums helped sustain the ideology of imperial abundance and, in turn, became founts of exposition wisdom as scientists like the Field Museum's F. J. V. Skiff, the Commercial Museum's William P. Wilson, and the Smithsonian Institution's William P. Blake and G. Brown Goode helped develop exhibit classification schemes for the fairs held between the end of Reconstruction and the First World War.[30] At the end of the century, a good example of this symbiotic relationship between fairs and museums could be found in the Philadelphia Commercial Museum.

The Philadelphia Commercial Museum was the brainchild of Uni-

*Philadelphia Commercial Museum. Courtesy
of the Smithsonian Institution, National
Museum of American History, Larry Zim
World's Fair Collection.*

versity of Pennsylvania plant pathologist William P. Wilson. The idea
to organize the museum came to him while visiting the World's Columbian Exposition. When he learned that many of the natural history exhibits on display at the fair would form the nucleus of the Field Museum's collections, he pondered the fate of the countless commerical
exhibits and rushed back to Philadelphia with a proposal to organize a
museum around those commercial and natural resource exhibits on display at Chicago. Fired with enthusiasm, Wilson persuaded Philadelphia
politicians and businessmen to support his plan for "a great group of
Museums, General, Scientific, Economic, Educational and Commercial." More specifically, this museum was intended to institutionalize
one of the central lessons of the Chicago fair, namely the need to dom-
inate foreign markets and to acquire overseas supplies of natural resources. By developing a museum that operated as a clearing house for
information about foreign commerce and as an educational institution,

Wilson saw himself as placing the gospel of imperial abundance on a scientific footing.[31]

Wilson quickly set his plans in motion. He returned to the fair and filled twenty-four railroad box cars with exhibit material that he shipped promptly to Philadelphia. This was only the beginning. Over the next twenty years, Wilson not only obtained tons of exhibit material from American and foreign fairs, he employed world's fair specialists to work at the museum. By 1899, when the permanent buildings opened on a seventeen-acre site between the Pennsylvania Railroad tracks and the University of Pennsylvania, the museum had become nothing less than a permanent world's fair. As President McKinley declared at the museum's dedication: "The Columbian World's Exhibition [sic] at Chicago, glorious testimonial as it was to the world's progress, was the forerunner of this less general but more permanent institution for the world's economic advance." [32]

Once the museum opened, it combined world's fair displays with operations that would be assumed a decade later by the U.S. Department of Commerce. Exhibits consisted of ethnological groups and "the most extensive collections of natural products in existence in any country." What made the displays unique was their arrangement. According to William Pepper, provost of the University of Pennsylvania and chairman of the board of trustees of the Commercial Museum: "[Our collections] are displayed so as to enable manufacturers or traders to study them to the best advantage, and gain the information to make the selections needed for their special interests." With this well-stocked library constantly updated with American consular reports from around the world, it is little wonder that Pepper could boast that the museum "contains the fullest, freshest, and most exact data on all trade conditions which can be obtained." The most distinctive feature of the museum, however, was its scientific laboratory which tested new products, estimated yields of agricultural crops, and provided information about potential markets for agricultural and manufactured products. "It is the earnest aim of this department," declared one of the museum's biologists, "to put the international commerce in raw products on a scientific basis, and to most successfully aid, with exact data, information, and investigation, international trade and industry." In theory, the museum provided information to manufacturers and agriculturists around the world. But as one of the museum's publications made clear: "The object of the institution is to aid in the building up of the foreign trade of America." [33]

Until William P. Wilson's death in 1927, the Commercial Museum continued to add to its collection from world's fairs held around the world. Its agents secured displays from major European fairs, including the 1896 Budapest Millennial Exhibition and the Paris Universal Exposition of 1900. Museum staff, moreover, contributed expert advice to European governments, especially to the French, on organizing colonial exhibitions. And two of its scientists, Wilson and botanist Gustavo Niederlein, bore chief responsibility for developing exhibits for the Philippines Reservation at the St. Louis fair. Rivaled only by the Field Museum and Smithsonian Institution, the Philadelphia Commercial Museum, born of a world's fair, became one of the sources for expertise on international expositions.[34]

The tongue-and-groove relationship between fairs and the Commercial Museum was further evidenced by Wilson's decision to arrange an international exhibition that would draw attention to the museum. With its five miles of aisles lined with such displays as electric street cars, furniture, and automobiles, the 1899 National Export Exposition could easily be mistaken for a simple trade fair. But such was not the case. Architects joined three pavilions "so as to form one complete structure, which at first view has the appearance of a great marble palace and conveys the impression of permanency." Adorned by heroic pediments devoted to themes of abundance, international commerce, and commercial development, the Main Building mirrored similar structures at world's fairs. Two additional buildings—one devoted to transportation, the other to displays of agriculture, vehicles, and furniture—made the indebtedness to the world's fair precedent even more apparent. The full extent to which Wilson depended on world's fair blueprints became manifest when he hired Edmund Felder, one of the individuals who had been responsible for the Midway Plaisance at the Chicago fair, to develop a similar entertainment strip for the 1899 exhibition. Felder's creation, the Gay Esplanade, was a resurrected Midway Plaisance. The Gay Esplanade included a Chinese Village, an Oriental Theater, an Old Plantation complete with "a party of Georgia Negroes, with songs, dances, etc.," an animal circus, and the Cuban midget show. So central were these shows to the exhibition that they lined either side of the avenue leading from the main entrance to the Main Building.[35]

Entertainment, however, was not the sole aim of the Commercial Museum any more than it was the primary purpose of the nation's international fairs. Just as world's fair managers saw themselves as educators and their expositions as "universities," so Wilson saw himself and his institution as performing a didactic function. From the beginning, Wilson emphasized the educational mission of the Commercial Museum. According to the museum's official historian, several hundred thousand school children visited the museum, and many others saw exhibits and heard presentations about displays that the museum sent to public schools around the region. Through its exhibits, daily operations, and educational mission, the Philadelphia Commercial Museum served as an institutional link with American fairs and perpetuated their ideological formulations. Until its slow death after World War I and transmogrification into the present-day Civic Center, the Philadelphia Commercial Museum helped translate imperial dreams into daily practice.[36]

To sum up, it would be a mistake to understand fairs as transitory spectacles that merely adorned the Gilded Age. True, America's world's fairs lasted, on average, about six months. But they wove their way into American life before, during, and after their months of operation. Before an exposition opened, state committees around the nation began the arduous task of accumulating material for display. This process, directed by state elites and covered extensively in newspapers, involved countless ordinary Americans who probably never traveled to a fair. As important as it is to remember that millions of Americans actually attended fairs (by 1916 aggregate visits totalled nearly one hundred million), many uncounted Americans contributed exhibits to the network of world's fairs that stretched across the country. Equally important, while it is true that numerous exhibits and staff-and-plaster buildings were demolished at the conclusion of fairs, other exhibits—anthropological and commercial—found permanent space in museums around the country. In the case of the Philadelphia Commercial Museum, an institution was constructed to enshrine permanently the gospel of imperial abundance on display at the Chicago fair and at subsequent turn-of-the-century expositions.

Amidst the turbulence that rocked America, world's fairs gave visible form and legitimacy to an emerging "culture of abundance." The world's fair, in Warren Susman's words, became "a key institution of a new culture based not like the older republican culture on principles of scarcity, limitation, and sacrifice, but on new principles of abundance, self-fulfillment, and unlimited possibilities."[37] In addition, fairs combined these new principles of abundance with new principles of empire, rooted in the racist vocabulary of social Darwinism and sanctioned by contemporary anthropologists. Tightly interwoven, the visions of materialism and imperialism at the fairs were threaded into the broader culture. By World War I, if not before, America had become a culture of imperial abundance.

To guard against slippage, especially in the face of growing isolationist sentiment after the war and mounting signs of class unrest manifest in the 1919 strikes that hit Seattle and Boston, leaders of American politics and business determined to continue the exposition tradition and adapt it to the changed circumstances of the postwar world. Even before America entered the war, civic leaders in Philadelphia, spearheaded by John Wanamaker, one of the driving forces behind that city's 1876 Centennial Exhibition, laid plans for a Sesquicentennial Exposition that would rouse patriotic fervor and "demonstrate to the nation and world the city's remarkable progress and achievements in the fifty years following the Centennial Exposition." As one contemporary described the deep anxiety that shaped their thinking: "European and Asiatic nations were embroiled in the greatest conflict of history. Armed forces of our own government were stationed on the border line of our sister republic, Mexico, ready to repel invasion by an insurgent leader of that country." However satisfied they were with their cultural achievements before the war, the organizers of these festivals of abundance and empire never regarded their success as anything more than partial. As they contemplated the postwar world, "prominent business and professional men" like Wanamaker never assumed that the public would automatically concur with the direction America's upper classes envisioned for the nation. Public support after the war would have to be won and the world's fair medium, given its immense prewar popularity and modular capacities for being reconstituted in new forms, remained a primary weapon of choice.[38]

While the uncertain state of international affairs prodded Philadelphia elites to recharge their exposition tradition, a massive race riot in the summer of 1919, followed by an economic downturn in 1921, gave Chicago's civic leaders pause for thought. Were Philadelphia's best and brightest contemplating a fair to celebrate the fiftieth anniversary of their 1876 Centennial Exhibition? Chicago should do no less. To offset the social unrest that gripped the city, Chicago elites in 1921 organized a "Pageant of Progress"—an event that served as the seedbed for planning the 1933–34 Century of Progress Exposition, a fair that would commemorate the fortieth anniversary of the 1893 World's Columbian Exposition.[39]

However motivated they were at the end of the First World War to rekindle the exposition tradition of the prewar years, nothing propelled the nation's governing elites to action faster than the 1929 stock market crash and ensuing collapse of the American economy. With the foundations of the culture of imperial abundance crumbling before their eyes, they mobilized a generation of experienced exposition hands, including Sol Bloom, the former impresario of the Midway Plaisance at the 1893 Chicago fair and one of the most powerful members of the U.S. House of Representatives between the world wars, to come to their aid in restoring the economic structure and popular faith in national progress. They also tapped a rich vein in the exhibition culture of the 1920s—the "fitter family" movement. Organized by leading eugenicists, "race betterment" displays proliferated at state and local fairs across the country and served as an important conduit between the racist formulations of America's turn-of-the century fairs and the popular culture of the interwar years. The intersection of the eugenics movement and the national exhibition culture, moreover, provided the backdrop for one of the most popular components of the New York World's Fair—the "typical American family" competition.

CHAPTER TWO

*"Fitter Families for Future Firesides": Eugenics
Exhibitions between the Wars*

Popular education is a necessary part of any program of scientific thought or research which touches in any way upon the vital phenomena of human existence. To use a pat expression
which has become almost trite, it must be made to "function in
the lives of people." This can come about only through the use
of disciples from among the people who will receive the bread of
science from the hands of research—Christ-men—and break it
again to their fellow creatures. Then again is the Word fulfilled
in that the baskets remain overflowing to the end. In the concrete instance of eugenics, the known facts of heredity must be
applied to human well-being and given to humanity in an effective and convincing way.
—Florence Brown Sherbon, *Eugenics,* 1928

None of these novelties [at the fair] was so stirring as the Eugenic Family, who had volunteered to give, for a mere forty dollars a day, an example of the benefits of healthful practices.
—Sinclair Lewis, *Arrowsmith,* 1924[1]

In the first third of the twentieth century, a group of scientists and
pseudo-scientists, with the help of best-selling books like Madison
Grant's *The Passing of the Great Race* (1916), captured American public attention, persuaded state legislatures to pass sterilization laws, and
convinced the U.S. Congress to extend racially-based immigration legislation that dated from 1882, when restrictions were placed on Chinese immigration. Why, despite the critique of eugenics mounted after
the First World War by anthropologists, geneticists, and literary intellectuals, were eugenicists so successful in appealing to the American
public?[2]

To comprehend this phenomenon—including the possibility that
eugenicist sentiment in American popular culture between the world
wars was so deep that it formed a reservoir of thought and feeling that
lasted well beyond the Second World War—it is important to understand how the eugenics message reached the American public. Printed
propaganda, consisting of pamphlets, periodicals, and books, may have

been an important mainstay of the movement, but eugenicists, like anthropologists at earlier fairs, also saw the exhibition medium as ideally suited to popularizing their race-betterment agenda. Beginning with the 1915 San Francisco Panama–Pacific International Exposition, American eugenicists became active in the nation's exhibition culture. After the war, they developed major displays in conjunction with international eugenics congresses held at the American Museum of Natural History in New York, and organized exhibits that became fixtures at state and county fairs around the country during the 1920s. When, despite the growing challenge by intellectuals, some of these displays spilled over into the century-of-progress expositions themselves, it became clear that builders of these fairs would share crucial presuppositions with pre–First World War exposition builders about the primacy of racial categories in determining citizenship in the world of tomorrow. Perhaps the best indication of this continuity occurred at the 1940 New York World's Fair where race-betterment ideas were articulated in an exhibit devoted to "typical American families." While not the sole component in the ideological scaffolding of the century-of-progress expositions, race betterment ideas did help shape the intellectual universe in which the world of tomorrow was mapped.[3]

The convergence of the American race betterment movement and the international exhibition movement was by no means fortuitous. If, as Daniel Kevles has argued, eugenicists tried to fashion the doctrine of race betterment into a secular faith, the international exhibition was the appropriate medium for them to utilize. From antiquity, fairs had been associated with religious festivities and had even acquired religious connotations (in German, the word for fair, *Messe,* signifies a mass). Not surprisingly, British eugenicists, as part of their drive to build a popular following and to secure anthropometric data, had established exhibits at British International Health Exhibitions as early as 1884. While nineteenth-century American developments in eugenics lagged behind those in Great Britain, American expertise in international exhibitions rapidly caught up with British precedent. By the turn of the century, and certainly by the second decade of the century, world's fairs were well established as one of the most effective vehicles for transmitting ideas of scientific racism from intellectual elites to millions of ordinary Americans.[4]

Exactly what made international exhibitions such effective media is by no means certain. Perhaps their influence derived from their overdetermined symbolism, from the intensity of their displays, and from the collective experience they provided masses of fairgoers. Or, perhaps expositions owed their influence to a broader cultural transformation—a transformation pinpointed by G. Brown Goode, Assistant Secretary of the Smithsonian Institution and renowned turn-of-the-century world's fair authority. As Goode observed:

In this busy, critical, and skeptical age each man is seeking to know all things, and life is too short for many words. The eye is used more and more, the ear less and less, and in the use of the eye, descriptive writing is set aside for pictures, and pictures in their turn are replaced by actual objects. In the schoolroom the diagram, the blackboard, and the object lesson, unknown thirty years ago, are universally employed. The public lecturer uses the stereopticon to reenforce his words, the editor illustrates his journals and magazines with engravings a hundred-fold more numerous and elaborate than his predecessor thought needful, and the merchant and manufacturer recommend their wares by means of vivid pictographs. The local fair of old has grown into the great exposition.

Because world's fairs provided "visible proof" in an age that prized "teaching by object lessons," exhibitions gained authority and were often regarded as "world's universities." [5]

The growing importance of world's fairs was no more lost on eugenicists than on anthropologists and advertisers. With world's fair enthusiasts in San Francisco confidently predicting that admissions to the 1915 Panama-Pacific extravaganza would total well over twenty million, delegates to the First National Conference on Race Betterment, held in Battle Creek, Michigan, in 1914, laid plans to hold their second annual meeting in conjunction with the San Francisco fair and to organize an exhibit at the fair that would drive home the need for urgent action to stop the supposed trend towards racial degeneracy. For exposition managers, a national conference devoted to eugenics dovetailed perfectly with their own plans to make America modern. As one exposition director told the delegates assembled at the San Francisco fair for the opening of the five-day conference: "Representing, as you do, a movement in race betterment, it seems to me that you represent the very spirit, the very ideal of this great Exposition that we have created here." In exchange for their support, exposition directors set aside the week of the conference as Race Betterment Week at the fair.[6]

The exposition directors' confidence was well-placed. Due largely to the efforts of John H. Kellogg, president of the Race Betterment Foundation, and David Starr Jordan, president of Stanford University, the Second National Conference on Race Betterment comprised nothing less than a presbytery of America's foremost racist thinkers. Officers of the conference included Judge Ben B. Lindsey, Yale economist Irving Fisher, Charles W. Eliot, Harvard University president-emeritus, conservationist Gifford Pinchot, U.S. Senator Robert L. Owen, and the director of the Carnegie Station for Experimental Evolution, Charles B. Davenport. Featured speakers included Kellogg, who emphasized the importance of establishing a eugenics registry to assure "obedience to biologic law" and thereby create "a real aristocracy made up of Apollos and Venuses and their fortunate progeny," and Jordan, who condemned the warring European powers for committing "race-suicide." Other participants addressed the need for social and personal hygiene, and discussed such issues as the principles of natural selection, and the treatment of the insane. But the high point of the meetings came during an exchange between plant breeder Luther Burbank and Kellogg—an exchange that followed Burbank's reading of a paper that had urged "*selection of the best individuals* for continuing the race." Kellogg pressed Burbank to clarify his ideas: "Is it possible, by the use of eugenics, and by the control of environment to create a new race of men?. . . . You think it is a biological possibility." Burbank replied: "Without question."[7]

Burbank's prediction captured immediate notice in the press and sparked the curiosity of fairgoers about the proceedings of the conference. What exposition-goers discovered was that the Second National Conference on Race Betterment involved much more than quasi academic proceedings. To the delight of fairgoers, eugenicists gave visible form to their race-betterment ideas by means of exhibits and pageants which at once instructed and titillated the popular imagination. In the context of the fair, eugenicists had become showmen.[8]

In fact, from the beginning of the fair, long before the Race Betterment Conference began, the Race Betterment Foundation had established a booth in the Palace of Education that quickly became one of the fair's most popular exhibits. The exhibit included charts, portraits of famous eugenicists, and vibrating chairs for weary sightseers. In addition to offering rest, these chairs played a special role in the exhibit; they convinced fairgoers of the need for reform. According to Frank Morton Todd, the fair's official historian, tired visitors who sat down for a moment in the vibrating chairs "usually looked resentful of the past and careless of the future, and as though they needed the good shaking they were getting." Unsuspecting—and seemingly uncaring—sightseers, in other words, were incorporated into an exhibit that, according to Todd, "was so admirably arranged that you didn't have to ask many questions; all you had to do was just to look, to see the necessity for its work." [9]

"Visible proof" for the eugenics creed abounded in the Race Betterment exhibit. Eugenicists, however, did not stop with artifactual displays. To conclude the conference, directors of the Race Betterment Foundation commissioned a "Morality Masque: A Dramatic Representation of the Great Truths for Which the National Conference on Race Betterment Stands." Ultimately entitled "Redemption: A Masque of Race Betterment," this pageant with its cast of over two hundred students from the University of California, Berkeley, thrilled an audience of five thousand in the Oakland Auditorium. Eugenicists were so pleased with its success that they made copies of the pageant available to social clubs across the nation. [10]

If the San Francisco fair marked the entry of American eugenicists into show business, they had every reason to be pleased with their debut. Just as the World's Columbian Exposition broadened popular awareness of anthropology, so the Panama–Pacific International Exposition had the effect of increasing popular knowledge of eugenics. Individual sessions at the five-day Race Betterment Conference attracted between 1,200 and 1,500 people. Total attendance amounted to nearly ten thousand. Associated Press and United Press news services provided coverage of each session and the Race Betterment Foundation estimated that nearly one million lines of newspaper publicity had been generated for eugenics as a result of participation in the exhibition. At the close of the fair, eugenicists noted with evident satisfaction "a growing interest on the part of the public in the subject of race betterment." [11]

The task of sustaining that momentum fell to Charles B. Davenport, director of the Station in Experimental Evolution at Cold Spring Harbor, New York and an "indefatigable organizer." With the help of a substantial endowment from Mary Harriman's railroad fortune, Davenport turned the Cold Spring Station into a center for advancing the cause of American eugenics. As he explained in a 1912 lecture to University of Minnesota students, eugenics entailed: "first, investigation; then, as knowledge grows, education. Finally, legislation based on sound public sentiment. For the carrying out of this program the public is quite ready and indeed waiting. It is seeking to be wisely led." As an opportunity for popularizing eugenics and for lending national legitimacy to the drive for race betterment, the Panama-Pacific fair fit snugly into Davenport's own agenda. But he set his sights higher. Since 1912, when he had served as a delegate to the First International Congress on Eugenics in London, Davenport had been struggling to persuade European eugenicists to agree to an international meeting in New York which would signal international recognition of and approval for American eugenics. When the outbreak of the First World War undercut tentative plans to hold such a meeting in New York in 1915, Davenport devoted his energy to making a success of the national conference in San Francisco. But he never abandoned his goal of organizing an international congress in New York that would equal, if not surpass, the 1912 London affair as a vehicle for legitimizing and popularizing eugenics. In 1919, his efforts were rewarded when the Permanent International Eugenics Committee reconvened and agreed to hold their second congress two years later in New York City.[12]

Plans for the Second International Congress of Eugenics unfolded in an atmosphere of crisis. From the perspective of eugenicists, the carnage of the war seemed to confirm their dire warnings about "race-suicide." On another level, increased immigration to the United States combined with increased labor radicalism made "race-degeneracy" seem an immediate threat to Anglo-Saxon purity and upper-class dominance of the American body politic. Concern for these issues led Davenport to join with several of America's foremost racist ideologues, including Madison Grant and Henry Fairfield Osborn, to found the Galton Society. Enthusiastic about eugenical reform and supportive of Davenport's efforts to hold an international eugenics congress in New York, Grant and Osborn decided to hold the congress at the American Museum of Natural History (AMNH). That decision was theirs to make—Osborn was president of the museum and Madison Grant served as treasurer—and followed logically from their own interest in making the museum a permanent monument to Anglo-Saxon supremacy. What better way to lend legitimacy to these efforts than to convene a veritable holy synod devoted to eugenics?[13]

Once the international committee agreed to hold the congress in New York, members of the Galton Society moved quickly to raise funds and arrange exhibits. A blue ribbon advisory committee was formed comprising such notables as future U.S. president Herbert Hoover, economist E. A. Ross, and psychologist G. Stanley Hall. Davenport's past contacts with Harriman again bore fruit as she contributed what amounted to one-third of the total cost of the congress. Never one to miss an opportunity for recognition, Davenport pressed the National Research Council (NRC) for an endorsement of the congress and in the process carved a niche for eugenics within the NRC's division of biology and agriculture. He also propelled his own staff into service: C. C. Little, director of research at Cold Spring Harbor, was selected secretary-general of the congress and Henry H. Laughlin, superintendent of the Cold Spring Station, was chosen to direct the exhibits committee.[14]

Laughlin's importance to the congress followed directly from his extensive involvement in popularizing eugenics. After his appointment to the Cold Spring Harbor staff in 1910, Laughlin had taken charge of training field investigators. In 1916, he became associate editor of *Eugenical News,* a position that allowed him to concentrate on education—he would have been comfortable with the term "propaganda"—and politics. He made it his special province to marshal public support for sterilization legislation and immigration restriction. In 1920, while the congress was in the planning stage, he took on a new responsibility by agreeing to serve as expert witness for the House Committee on Immigration. Immediately, Laughlin's role in the eugenics congress acquired newfound significance. If handled properly, the two aims of the congress—obtaining international scientific sanction for eugenics and educating the American public about its value—could be forged into a single weapon for influencing national policy. Exhibits that lent visible support to the racist philosophy of the delegates proved to be the key.[15]

When the congress opened on 21 September 1921, a standing-room-only crowd in the AMNH's Hall of Man listened to Osborn welcome the delegates with an ominous warning: "We are engaged in a serious struggle to maintain our historic republican institutions through barring the entrance of those who are unfit to share the duties and responsibilities of our well-founded government." The "melting pot" had failed, Osborn asserted, and had dangerously weakened the germ plasm of the nation. As a result, "the selection, preservation, and multiplication of the best heredity is a patriotic duty of first importance." Who constituted and what should happen to the "unfit"? Following a finely drawn line of imperialist reasoning, Osborn advocated segregation along racial lines:

> For the world's work, give me a pure-blooded Negro, a pure-blooded Mongol, a pure-blooded Slav, a pure-blooded Nordic, and ascertain through observation and experiment what each race is best fitted to accomplish in the world's economy. If the Negro fails in government, he may become a fine agriculturist or a fine mechanic. The Chinese and the Japanese have demonstrated in the history of their respective countries a range of ability in art, literature, and industry quite equal to our own in certain arts, and greatly superior to our own in other arts, like ceramics. Let each race consider its own problems and demonstrate its own fitness.

Major Leonard Darwin agreed wholeheartedly. The fourth son of the famed naturalist, Charles Darwin, and president of the Eugenics Education Society of Great Britain, Major Darwin was the keynote speaker at the New York congress. In his opening address, he extolled the "eugenic ideal" as "an ideal to be followed like a flag in battle." While Darwin prepared for war, another speaker, French eugenicist G. V. de LaPouge targeted the enemy: "A great movement has begun among the inferior races and classes, and this movement which has the air of being turned against the whites and against the rich, is turned against the superior intellectual element and against civilization itself." The battle lines were drawn: "The war of classes is indeed the war of races." Laughlin's task was to carry this message calling for eugenical reform to the public.[16]

With additional funding provided by Harriman and with administrative assistance from anthropologist Clark Wissler and AMNH curator Laurence V. Coleman, Laughlin obtained exhibits from 131 exhibitors that included "university professors, investigators in scientific institutions, physicians and field workers in institutions for the socially inadequate, statisticians and research departments of the great life insurance companies, scholars and authors of independent means, publishing houses, and state and federal government departments." Exhibits fell into two broad categories: anthropology and eugenics. The anthropology exhibits, located around the AMNH's Hall of Man where sessions of the congress took place, included portions of the museum's permanent collection as well as new material devoted to a "chronology of the world's culture" and to "the race problem of Hawaii." Exhibits pertaining specifically to eugenics were arranged in Forestry and Darwin Halls and consisted of:

mainly embryological and racial casts and models, photographs, pedigree charts and tables, biological family histories and collective biographies, graphical and historical charts on the character and analysis of population, material showing the principles of heredity in plants, animals and man, maps and analytical tables demonstrating racial vicissitudes, anthropometric instruments, apparatus for mental measurements, and books and scientific reprints on eugenical and genetical subjects.

Laughlin's overriding desire, as he explained in the prospectus, was "to make the exhibits of this Congress relatively few in number but striking in nature."[17]

Museum technicians, under the supervision of the committee on

*Exhibit of racial casts, Second International
Congress on Eugenics. From* Eugenics in Race
and State *(Baltimore: Williams & Wilkins
Co., 1923).*

exhibits, installed the eugenics materials in alcoves usually occupied by
forestry exhibits and in temporary glass cases placed along the central
corridor of Forestry Hall and in neighboring Darwin Hall. As they entered this sacristy of scientific racism, visitors encountered eighteen
booths that covered heredity, the family, "the factor of race," "applied
eugenics," and eugenical methods. If visitors followed the booths se-
quentially, they first found eugenics defined as "the science of the improvement of the human race by better breeding." Subsequent booths,
devoted to animal breeding and human heredity, urged visitors to perform "careful pedigree analysis" so as to "direct mate selection along
lines which will produce offspring of the most highly talented and fertile
nature." One booth devoted to "aristogenic families"—families like
those descended from the Mayflower "stock"—drew political conclusions for the uninitiated: "A democracy, in common with the science of
eugenics, recognizes the aristocracy of personal ability, physical, mental

and moral. A democratic nation, in order to live, must foster good blood and hereditary talent, just as assiduously as an undemocratic country fosters special privilege." Other booths introduced visitors to anthropometric devices, explained intelligence tests, and listed states that had legalized sterilization "for the feebleminded, insane, criminalistic and the like." Not the least important of these exhibits, were those contained in booths devoted to the "races of man" and to "human migration."[18]

Exhibits devoted to race centered on the notion that "humanity is composed of many races differing widely in physical, mental and moral qualities." Crucial evidence for this proposition came from A. H. Schultz, an embryologist at the Carnegie Institution, and Aleš Hrdlička, curator of physical anthropology in the United States Museum of Natural History. Schultz arranged fourteen plaster casts of "caucasian" and "negro" fetuses to "illustrate the chief points of difference in fetuses of the two races." Laughlin deemed Hrdlička's exhibit to be of even greater importance and put it in a separate alcove in Darwin Hall. Consisting of seven cases, Hrdlička's exhibit was devoted to making race a biological category. In one part of his exhibit he arranged a series of American Indian skulls to show "the persistence to this day of Neanderthaloid forms and other primitive features." In another part of his display, Hrdlička contrasted data from his study of "Old Americans"— white Americans whose maternal and paternal families had lived at least three generations in America—with data gathered by A. H. Estabrook on the "tribe of Ishmael," a group of alleged "degenerates" who, unlike old-stock Americans were "still mating like to like and reproducing unsocial offspring." Highly charged with apparent scientific authority, these exhibits left little doubt of the need for implementing eugenic reforms.[19]

The Second International Congress of Eugenics lasted a week and generated two volumes of published papers. Museum officials considered the conference "perhaps the most important scientific meeting ever held in the Museum." Its importance, however, far transcended the week-long meetings and publication of proceedings. As Leonard Darwin exulted at the close: "Eugenicists are sometimes tempted to overlook the fact that environments pass on their beneficial effects to posterity by a kind of heredity of their own, and hence we may be sure that the seed sown in New York will spring up in many distant cities without those concerned [aware] in the least from whence they have drawn many of their inspirations." As an "organizing process," the repercussions of the Second International Congress of Eugenics would be felt at least for the rest of the decade and, in the case of national immigration policy, until 1965.[20]

After the congress closed, eugenics exhibits remained open to the public for a month. No accurate attendance figures were kept, but museum officials estimated that between five thousand and ten thousand visitors saw the displays, with over eight hundred signing a register intended to record names of individuals interested in becoming involved in promoting eugenics. Throughout the duration of the exhibition, staff members from the Eugenics Record Office remained at the museum to explain exhibits. Davenport and Laughlin personally escorted biology teachers around the museum. A far more momentous event occurred when the exhibits were dismantled. Many displays were returned to exhibitors, but those that "pertained directly to immigration were installed on the walls of the [U.S. Congress's Committee on Immigration] in Washington for the use of the Committee in analyzing certain historical and new data in reference to immigration." In less than three months, Laughlin's exhibits, originally intended for popular education, became sources for shaping national policy as well. It may be overstating the case, but not by much, to claim that Laughlin converted a U.S. congressional committee into an plenary session of the eugenics congress.[21]

In addition to affecting national immigration legislation, the Second International Congress of Eugenics also confirmed eugenicists in their zeal to transmit the gospel of eugenics to a wider mass audience. Due largely to Irving Fisher's insistence on "continuous popular eugenic education as supplementary to the widely separated international congresses," Henry Fairfield Osborn created the Eugenics Committee of the United States of America and appointed Fisher as its chairman. Fisher obtained backing from financiers John D. Rockefeller and George Eastman which enabled him to organize a staff of eight paid workers. In 1924, the committee acquired the services of two dedicated volunteers, Mary T. Watts and Dr. Florence Brown Sherbon, who devoted great energy to making an essentially upper-class ideology acceptable to a broader audience.[22]

Watts and Sherbon had worked together for over a decade. They first collaborated at the 1911 Iowa State Fair where Watts, one of the directors of the Iowa Parent-Teacher Association, had organized a "Better Babies Contest" to emphasize the importance of children's health. Sherbon, a child welfare specialist, was one of the judges of the contest. Their work attracted national attention, including a one-sentence postcard from Charles Davenport that read: "You should give 50 percent to heredity before you begin to score a baby." Over the next several years, Watts and Sherbon perfected a plan for baby contests which they believed incorporated Davenport's advice. The idea they hit upon was a contest involving entire families.[23]

With the help of the manager of the 1920 Kansas Free Fair, who set aside a separate Eugenics Building for the exhibit, Watts and Sherbon organized the first "Fitter Families for Future Firesides Contest" and, in the guise of improving family health, brought the message of eugenic reform to rural America. As Sherbon explained it: "The object of the fitter family movement is the stimulation of a feeling of family and racial consciousness and responsibility." In the plain surroundings of the Eugenics Building and in plain language Sherbon and Watts transmitted the message about race betterment to an overwhelmingly rural audience. Sherbon, who devoted her time to involving public health officials in the proceedings, gave Watts full credit for the exhibit's success. "This movement," Sherbon told Irving Fisher, "would not have been possible, it would not even have originated when it did, if ever, had it not been for the indispensable link between science and the public provided by Mrs. Watts. She has the vision, and, as she is fond of saying, she 'speaks the vernacular.'" Equally important, Sherbon later wrote, "Mrs. Watts had the single-minded enthusiasm of a prophet and the self-confidence of a good salesman."[24]

Watts offered ample evidence of her vernacular skill and salesmanship. As she told Davenport: "I realize that we are not quite scientific in all we do at these fairs but we do succeed in making people think. 'One must lead a horse to water before he can be made to drink' and this is just a popular way of bringing him up to the trough." Or, as Watts explained her approach to the readers of *Survey:*

We work from the angle that health is something of which one should be proud. The horticulturist brings his best fruit and flowers to the fair, the agriculturist his best grain and the stockman his finest specimens of livestock; then why not give parents the opportunity to show their fine families of boys and girls and stimulate others to improve the quality of their offspring?

She then provided a vivid example of her explanatory method:

We use the words "Eugenics" as a sign over the door of the building at the Kansas Fair where we test human stock and it causes considerable discussion. When someone asks what it is all about, we say, "While the stock judges are testing the Holsteins, Jerseys, and White-

"Fitter Families for Future Firesides" exhibit.
Courtesy of the American Philosophical
Society.

faces in the stock pavilion, we are judging the Joneses, Smiths, and the Johnsons," and nearly every one replies: "I think it is about time people had a little of the attention that is given to animals."

Watts's equation of livestock with human stock was effective. "Her eager, tumultous utterances and piquant disregard of niceties of construction broke down all barriers of reserve," Sherbon wrote. In everyday language she made eugenics comprehensible.[25]

Plain language and the opportunity to ask questions about family health brought droves of visitors to the Eugenics Building—a vernacular structure that conformed perfectly to the simplicity of Watts's language. "We usually have a rough little building or floored tent," Watts wrote to Davenport in mid-decade, "with an equipment consisting of kitchen tables, folding chairs, granite wash basins, paper toweling etc. Often the desk is too long boards on trestles at the side of the waiting room where a half dozen children and as many adults besides visitors are taking up space and making a babel of sound." Once inside, fairgoers found staff members, including Cho-Cho the health clown, providing information about family health, encouraging visitors to examine their family histories, and explaining exhibits pertaining to eugenics. In the first four years of the exhibit, eugenics workers selected nearly one hundred persons as participants in the "Fitter Families" contest. Contestants, in turn, were examined by

> busy physicians working on hour schedules, a faithful psychologist who cannot possibly handle all the entries although he works every minute, two or three student nurses to assist the doctors, athletic directors from local YMCAs or YWCAs hurrying to cover all the entries in an hour afternoon and morning . . . and a couple of untrained women at the desk trying to fill in names on score cards and keep up the clerical end of this work while the one available historian tries to write a history in twenty minutes that requires two hours to handle properly.

The staff's interest in these affairs was intense. While planning exhibits, Watts and Sherbon maintained close contact with Davenport. The latter regarded the fairs as important for popularizing eugenics and as important sources for gathering statistics. Sherbon and Watts happily obliged and sent him scorecards detailing physical and psychological measurements of individuals and families.[26]

The process of herding families into examination rooms for purposes of gathering statistical data and Watts's comparison of the eugenics contest to a livestock exhibition was no laughing matter. From start to finish state authority suffused the proceedings. All the competing families received state board of health certificates. U.S. Senator Arthur Capper awarded medals bearing his name to individuals with superior scores, and the governor of Kansas presented a silver trophy to the winning family. Through the efforts of Watts and Sherbon, in short, a particular variant of scientific racism—eugenics—merged into the stream of local beliefs and values while simultaneously receiving legitimacy from and lending legitimacy to the authority of the state and national government.[27]

From their positions of authority on the national Eugenics Committee, Watts and Sherbon saw to it that this educational process continued at numerous state and county fairs around the nation. Sherbon supervised the preparation of scorecards, while Watts, until her sudden death in 1926, lectured at local Parent-Teacher Association meetings and service clubs. To ensure inclusion of eugenics exhibits in local fairs, Watts traveled to annual meetings of the International Association of Fairs and Expositions—meetings that served to coordinate the timing

Left to right: Florence Brown Sherbon, Mary Watts, C. C. Little(?). Courtesy of the American Philosophical Society.

A "Fitter Family." Courtesy of the American Philosophical Society.

of local fairs and the exchange of exhibits. At the 1924 convention, for instance, she noted the success of the "Fitter Family" contest of the previous year at state fairs in Kansas, Georgia, and Texas and emphasized that at each fair "the local committee in charge had the active cooperation of state schools, state boards of health, state hospitals and local scientists, specialists and physicians." Each of these groups, she implied, would lend legitimacy to the educational thrust of the fairs. She also stressed the value of eugenics exhibits for publicizing fairs: "articles telling of this new idea of pedigreeing human stock have appeared in the *Survey*, the *Dearborn Independent, Popular Science, Hygeia, Wallace's Farmer, The Farm Journal*, the *Iowa Homestead* and the *Insurance Field*." "This [exhibition] plan," Watts informed assembled fair managers, "has not only proved itself capable of spreading the gospel of eugenics but has had the further recommendation of being able to sell itself to newspapers and magazines because it has news value." Publicity for the fairs in turn meant a great deal of publicity for eugenics. For Watts, the effort required carried its own reward. As she wrote to Davenport: "All I dare to hope from our crude plan is the opening of a way for scientific facts to filter into the consciousness of the masses and then the people will save themselves." [28]

Under the leadership of Watts and Sherbon, the eugenics exhibition movement blossomed. "Fitter Families" competitions spread from Kansas, Texas, and Georgia to fairs in Michigan, Massachusetts, Arkansas, and Oklahoma. In 1926, Watts's committee sent an exhibit to the Philadelphia Sesquicentennial International Exposition. By mid-decade, Watts's committee had even arranged a mobile exhibit that could be transported by truck and "shown under canvas (a tent)" by local eugenics committees. Possibilities for eugenics reform seemed endless. As Sherbon exulted:

I see not only these very remarkable staffs which we are assembling for fair work, using these [scorecards] for competitive work at fairs, but I see scientific groups everywhere begin to use them, carefully, non-competitively, and at any and all convenient times and occasions. I can even conceive of an intelligent family taking this [scorecard] and seeking out an authoritative person to do each unit. . . . Eventually, I see this movement spread until it ought to contribute to the strengthening of the family as the organic racial and social unit.

At mid-decade, with eugenics exhibits carrying the ideology of "race betterment" into the home, eugenicists had every reason to exude confidence. Then, in December 1926, Mary Watts died and the eugenics

This light flash_____ v 15 seconds

Every 15 seconds $100 of your money goes for the care of persons with bad heredity such as the insane, feeble-minded, criminals & other defectives

Some people are born to be a burden on the rest.

This light flashes every 16 seconds

Every 16 seconds a person is born in the United States.

Fitter Families
CONTEST

EASTERN STATES EXPOSITION

This light flashes ___ ry 7½ minutes

Every 7½ minutes a high grade person is born in the United States, will will have ability to do creative work & be fit for leadership. About 4% of all Americans come within this class

Exhibition panel, "Fitter Families" display.
Courtesy of the American Philosophical
Society.

movement lost one of its most popular and effective voices. Voices of dissent among leading intellectuals, moreover, were on the increase.[29]

Ever since Franz Boas's 1916 condemnation of eugenics as "a dangerous sword that may turn its edge against those who rely on its strength," eugenicists had disputed anthropologists and geneticists who were in the process of creating a set of values based on the notion of cultural relativism and environmental determinism. As leading geneticists like Thomas Henry Morgan began distancing themselves from "race-betterment" ideas and as civil libertarians like Clarence Darrow and literary intellectuals like Sinclair Lewis increasingly questioned the moral and political credibility of eugenics, eugenicists redoubled their attempts to place a scientific patina on their product and win the hearts and minds of the populace. The assault by some intellectuals on the eugenics creed may have rendered eugenics a doctrine to be accepted on faith, but that did not necessarily dampen the enthusiasm of eugenicists or weaken support for "race-betterment" beliefs on the popular level.

In fact, to win additional support for their cause, eugenicists organized a Third International Congress on Eugenics and intensified their attempts to reach a national audience through the medium of exhibitions.[30]

The Third International Congress on Eugenics, held at the AMNH in 1932, was intended to mirror the 1921 affair. Once again, Davenport and Laughlin played major roles in organizing conference sessions that ran the gamut from endorsing Marcus Garvey's back-to-Africa movement to finding genetic causes for prostitution. If the small number of conferees—there were far fewer delegates to this depression-era congress than to its predecessor—disappointed congress sponsors, they could take satisfaction from the turnout for eugenics exhibits. Nearly 15,000 visitors, probably double the number that saw the 1921 displays, trooped through 267 displays covering 10,000 square feet of exhibit space. Although none of the displays traveled to the U.S. Congress, Laughlin could point with pride to the exhibit devoted to the "natural history of man" that AMNH curator William K. Gregory had specifically designed for the congress and as a permanent exhibit for the museum. At precisely some moment that eugenics was supposedly losing stature among some intellectuals, it was becoming the basis for a major exhibit in one of America's leading museums.[31]

Officials at other museums showed an interest in Laughlin's exhibits. After conducting Henry Field around the booths at the eugenics congress, Laughlin almost persuaded him to accept all of the exhibits for inclusion in the Chicago Field Museum's anthropology displays. When the museum's financial condition precluded purchasing the exhibits, Laughlin tried to convince Chicago's Century of Progress backers to include them in the 1933 fair. Again, financial considerations in the midst of the depression along with growing objections from scientists to "race-betterment" doctrines caused exposition officials to balk at Laughlin's plans. Nevertheless, he obtained an area among the genetics exhibits in the exposition's Hall of Science for a display devoted to eugenics. The exhibit was small, consisting of four panels, but that was sufficient for "establishing the fact that human characteristics are inherited in the same manner as are those of plants and animals." "That alone," the exhibit installer wrote Laughlin, "is a good step for our 'average' visitor." And visitors were impressed. As one fairgoer wrote Laughlin: "I pass the [Eugenics Records Office] exhibit twice daily and there are always a number of people studying the charts." Of greater consequence was the attention the exhibit received from Buffalo Museum of Natural History officials. In 1934, they expressed interest in

*"Typical American Families" selection
committee. Courtesy of the New York Public
Library, Astor, Lenox and Tilden
Foundations, Rare Books and Manuscripts
Division, New York World's Fair, Records
1939–40.*

incorporating the exhibit into their newly opened genetics display,
thereby institutionalizing the very message and ideology that geneticists
were increasingly condemning.[32]

Eugenicist principles also undergirded one of the most popular exhibits at the 1940 New York World's Fair—the "typical American family" display that was jointly underwritten by Ford Motor Company,
The Johns Manville Company, the Federal Housing Administration,
and world's fair authorities. World's fair officials dreamed up the "typical family" idea to help promote the fair. Through essay contests sponsored by local newspapers around the country, Americans were invited
to write essays explaining why they were typical. Winners, apparently
selected from all forty-eight states, received a free trip to the fair in a
new Ford automobile, and lived on the fairgrounds in houses built by
the Federal Housing Administration and sided with "Asbestos Cedargrain Siding Shingles" provided by The Johns Manville Company.[33]

*"Typical American Families," with Mayor
F. H. La Guardia (center by fence) and
Grover Whalen (behind La Guardia).
Courtesy of the New York Public Library,
Astor, Lenox and Tilden Foundations, Rare
Books and Manuscripts Division, New York
World's Fair, Records 1939–40.*

To help local civic leaders judge contest winners, world's fair authorities circulated a questionnaire that included "racial origin" as one of the categories to be considered. World's fair authorities also made clear that they hoped each family unit selected would "consist of parents and two children." The results were predictable. "Typical" American families were native-born white Americans. As the governor of Arkansas wrote the family selected to represent his state: "Your selection as the Typical Arkansas Family means that you typify the best that this nation can produce, for Arkansas, by virtue of its high percentage of native-born population, is the most American state in the union." [34]

The racist undertow of the New York fair also surfaced in the official poster designed for the exposition. As the theme of the 1940 fair shifted away from the futuristic tendencies of 1939 and emphasized the need for patriotism, a "typical American," Elmer, replaced the Trylon and Perisphere on the official poster. As historian Bonnie Yochelson made clear in a recent retrospective museum exhibition on the New York World's Fair, the emphasis on Elmer, along with a "hokey" cow-milking contest, reflected the degree to which world's fair authorities incorporated the traditions of county and state fairs—traditions that were suffused with principles of eugenics—to make their own futuristic designs appear less threatening. As Yochelson so aptly described the thinking of world's fair planners:

> Just as a seamless, streamlined form masked the complexities of a machine's inner workings, so the ideal of the "typical American" masked the complexities of American society. Despite its constant refrain of tolerance and freedom, the Fair proposed a future society that was homogeneous, exclusive, and harmonious by virtue of its shared heritage. There was no place for Americans who were poor, urban, non-white, or foreign-born.

Put another way, historian Warren Susman was certainly right to emphasize the centrality of the "average American" to world's fair planners. What needs to be stressed is that their vision of "average" or "typical" contained loads of ideological freight carried forward, in part, by the national experience with eugenics exhibits.[34]

To sum up, the eugenics movement figured prominently in the national exhibition culture of the interwar period and, while hardly the only influence on America's world's fairs, certainly made its presence felt. Through the exhibition work of eugenicists like Laughlin, Sherbon, and Watts—not to mention Cho-Cho the clown—the gospel of eugenics ceased to be the sole property of the upper class and became a subterranean stream in the broader culture that the century-of-progress expositions overlaid with their modernistic and modernizing designs. One of the decisive influences on these designs flowed from Europe, especially from the series of colonial expositions in Great Britain and on the continent that, in the context of growing isolationist sentiment in the United States, inspired century-of-progress organizers to incorporate "coloniale moderne" elements into their own visions for America's future.

PART TWO

The
Century-of-Progress
Expositions

CHAPTER THREE

Coloniale Moderne

Some mysterious historical law has managed for the past 60
years to make Universal Expositions coincide or immediately
follow serious political crisis. The 1878 Exposition opened only
a few months after the "Moral Order" upheaval and the election of the "363." The Exposition of 1889 blossomed in the
midst of the 'Boulangist' campaign. The Exposition of 1900 was
inaugurated at the very height of the Dreyfus "Affair." Three
years ago, it is true, France was shaken to her very foundations
by a serious political crisis.

—Leon Blum, *Paris 1937*[1]

Since 1883, when the Dutch held Europe's first international exhibition
devoted primarily to colonialism, the imperial powers had routinely
organized colonial expositions to build support for imperial policies at
home and in their colonies. After the First World War, in the wake of
mounting economic crises and attacks on imperialism by left-wing political parties, victorious European governments revitalized colonial
fairs as instruments for promoting national imperial policies. Of the
fifteen or so international fairs held outside the United States between
the world wars, roughly half were explicitly devoted to the preservation
and extension of empire, while several of the remaining fairs had massive colonial components.[2]

Put another way, it would be a mistake to overvalue the 1925 Paris
Exposition Internationale des Arts Décoratifs et Industriels Modernes
for shaping modernistic sensibilities. While important for understanding the popularization of a style that a later generation would call Art
Deco, the 1925 International Exposition of Decorative Arts was not
alone in shaping modernistic patterns of thoughts and feelings between
the wars. Colonial expositions, especially the 1931 Paris exposition,
which attracted one of largest attendances of any world's fair in the
period, played an equally decisive role. Designed to renew domestic
support for national imperial policies, these expositions helped give rise
to a defining, if often neglected, characteristic of modernity: the "coloniale moderne" sensibility.

Rooted in the exotic fascination with the "Other" cultivated at European fairs before the Great War, coloniale moderne—a conjuncture of modernistic architectural styles and representations of imperial policies that stressed the benefits of colonialism to colonizer and colonized alike—developed from the desire by European imperial authorities to decant the old wine of imperialism into new bottles bearing the modernistic designs of the interwar years. More specifically, the coloniale moderne practice—*habitus* may be a better expression—crystallized around the efforts by governments to make the modernistic dream worlds of mass consumption on view at fairs unthinkable apart from the maintenance and extension of empire. By making imperialism seem as fundamental to modernity as the architectural fantasies of Le Corbusier and Mies van der Rohe and the scientific discoveries of Albert Einstein and Niels Bohr, exposition authorities sought to convince their publics that imperialism provided the bedrock on which modern times and modern progress depended. Their example intersected with the drive by American business and political leaders to bring to fruition the vision of an American empire projected by America's Victorian-era fairs—a vision of empire that downplayed political and military domination, stressing instead the conviction that the productive capacities of American corporations could integrate the rest of the world, especially Latin America and the Far East, into the American orbit of consumerism.[3]

For American political authorities, the resumption of European colonial festivals of empire was a mixed blessing. On the one hand, given the high level of European wartime indebtedness to the United States and need for European governments to maintain control of their empires if they were ever to repay America's loans, Europe's colonial expositions could be tolerated. On the other hand, the cheerful resumption of these imperial pageants so soon after the war flew in the face of American rhetoric about the war having been fought about principles of self-determination. Layered into these concerns was another: the growth of isolationist sentiments among the American public during the 1920s.[4]

To counter the growing popularity of isolationism, America's resilient empire-builders, inspired by their European counterparts and by the example of America's own Victorian-era fairs, turned to the world's fair medium. The crucial moment came in 1930 when, for the first time in its history, the U.S. government agreed to an official representation at a European colonial fair and organized a major exhibit for the 1931 Paris Colonial and International Exposition that took the form of a prefabricated replica of George Washington's home at Mr. Vernon. Through this exhibit, filled with displays from America's overseas territories, the federal government reaffirmed its presence on the imperial stage and set in motion America's own variant of the imperial revival that was sweeping through the capital cities of major European colonial powers during the interwar years. By the close of the decade, America's imperial revival would break free from its eighteenth-century "colonial revival" casing and spring to life in the imperial fantasyland crafted on Treasure Island for the 1939–40 San Francisco Golden Gate International Exposition.

The resurgent tide of imperialism that crested in Paris and washed ashore in San Francisco began with two earlier expositions in France and England. Both the 1922 Marseilles Colonial Exposition and 1924–25 British Empire Exhibition at Wembley were conceived before the first guns of August 1914 were fired. Both represented continuing links in their respective nations' colonial exhibition traditions that in France dated to the 1866 Saigon Cochin China Exhibition and in England to the 1886 London Colonial and Indian Exhibition. Those fairs generated numerous progeny, including a cluster of imperial shows in turn-of-the-century London, and a major French colonial fair in Marseilles in 1906. The success of these expositions inspired imperial brokers in both countries to plan even greater colonial spectacles in the future.[5]

In 1910, plans were laid for an international colonial exposition in Paris. As one exposition enthusiast exclaimed: "Our empire overseas has expanded, its organization has improved, its wonderful resources have increased. It is convenient to take stock and establish an essential inventory to confront public opinion with facts and results. This is the work of an exhibition." When an acrimonious debate developed between politicians from Marseilles and Paris over the site of the fair, the government agreed to split the difference and sponsored an exposition of French colonies in Marseilles in 1916 and an international colonial exposition in Paris in 1920. So committed were political leaders from Marseilles to this plan that, within two days of the armistice ending the First World War, they began clamoring for permission to proceed with their exposition. After further negotiations with Paris officials, the government renewed its original commitment, awarding a French colonial fair to Marseilles in 1922 and an international colonial fair to Paris that, after several postponements, would open in 1931.[6]

Like their French counterparts, British Empire Exhibition enthusiasts began touting the desirability of a massive British colonial exhibition before the outbreak of the First World War and regarded the war as a momentary interruption in their plans. Shortly after war's end, the British Empire Club, with the active support of the Prince of Wales, revived the idea of a colonial fair and Prime Minister David Lloyd George threw the weight of the government behind the project that would culminate in the 1924–25 British Empire Exhibition at Wembley.[7]

The Marseilles and Wembley Expositions were cut of the same cloth. Conceding that Wembley was larger, lasted two years, and left behind a monumental stadium constructed to lure working-class football fans to the fair, what the *London Times* wrote of the British Empire festival could just as easily have been written about the smaller fair in Marseilles. "Impoverished by a great war fought in defense of our national ideals," the *Times* demanded, "where are we to turn for relief?" "Wembley supplies the answer," the newspaper informed its readers. "Within the compass of the Empire, collected there in miniature, we see ourselves to possess all the needs of our progressive civilization, and the necessary outlet for our own production." Colonies, rich in resources and dependent on finished goods, held the key to economic progress at home.[8]

To get this point across, exposition organizers in both countries, following the example set by previous fairs, set up extensive colonial representations. The Marseilles fair covered roughly five times the area of the colonial displays at the Paris 1900 Universal Exposition. Dominated by a towering model of Angkor Wat and multicolored pavilions representing French North Africa, the fair included thousands of "living exhibits" of French colonial subjects that turned the exposition park into a "veritable land of dreams."[9]

Not to be outdone by their imperial rivals, the British government organized an even larger colonial show covering 220 acres at Wembley. Inspired by American uses of cement, exposition authorities built many of the pavilions with concrete to demonstrate the permanence of empire. Edward Elgar composed the fair's official music; Rudyard Kipling named its streets; and Henry Cole, nephew and namesake of the prime mover behind the Crystal Palace Exhibition, took charge of the government's exhibits for the fair. Given these distinguished contributors, there was little doubt that the fair would pack a powerful punch. As the guidebook boasted:

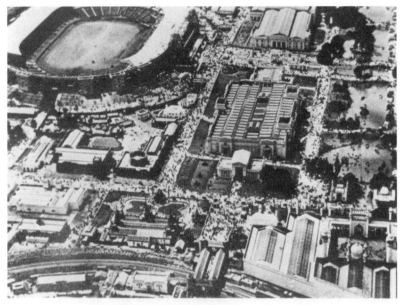

THE BRITISH EMPIRE EXHIBITION. From the Air.

British Empire Exhibition, aerial view.
Courtesy of California State University,
Fresno, Henry Madden Library, Department
of Special Collections.

The grounds at Wembley will reproduce in miniature the entire resources of the British Empire. There the visitor will be able to inspect
the empire from end to end. From Canada it is but a stone's throw
to Australia, from Australia a short step to India and the Far East,
from Hong Kong a few minutes' walk to New Zealand or Malaya.
In a single day he will be able to learn more geography than a year
of hard study would teach him. And he will be able to see in each
case the conditions of life in the country he is visiting. That is the
importance of the British Empire Exhibition. It is a stock-taking of
the whole resources of Empire.

The *Handbook of General Information* was more precise: "First, [the
exhibition] aims at taking stock of the resources of the Empire, and at
showing how those which are as yet undeveloped or only partially uti-
lized can be converted into wealth." Among the resources on display
were human beings, including, according to the official guide: "Malays

20, Burmans 30, Hong Kong Chinese 160, West Africans 60, Palestinians 3. In addition there are Indians, Singhalese, West Indians, and natives of British Guiana, who live outside the Exhibition, but attend their respective pavilions daily." To help visitors take stock of the empire, exhibition authorities sponsored a "Pageant of Empire" with fifteen thousand performers and hundreds if not thousands of animals, as well as a colonial boxing tournament and a host of popular amusements designed to call attention to the colonies.[10]

Just as important as imperial entertainment was the display of imperial science. Organized by the Royal Society, the display of "pure science" in the Government Building reflected, on one level, an effort by British scientists to restore popular confidence in the scientific enterprise after the devastating effects of science applied to military pursuits in the war. As one pamphlet explained: "Science, which has gone so far to destroy the world in a recent past, may do still more to recreate it in a near future." On another level, the point of the pavilion was to get across the message that science had a major role to play in the development of empire. "The truth is," the official guidebook explained, "before we can make use of the resources of Nature, we must know all about them." In the case of tropical disease, science was especially relevant to imperial control: "In the tropics *health is the foundation of successful trade*, a sick man is a poor organiser, a weak administrator, and a bad worker." For British scientists, the point of the exhibit was not simply that science could advance the cause of empire, but that imperialism could advance the cause of science and enhance the prestige of scientists, perhaps restoring both to prewar levels of respect and authority. It was exactly this kind of thinking, so manifest at Wembley and also recorded in the pages of *Science,* that fired the imaginations of American scientists who, as the next chapter explains, set out to construct an "empire of science" rooted in the wedding of American science to corporate capitalism.[11]

Much was made at the time of the British Empire Exhibition's financial failure (it ended with a deficit of nearly £2 million). But not everyone saw it in those terms. Despite the financial losses, one exhibition organizer declared: "I am absolutely convinced that it has been one of the greatest assets to the Empire as a whole that was ever contemplated." However much British literati like P. G. Wodehouse and Noel Coward ridiculed the affair, the government held to its course. For the rest of the interwar period, the British government, through its Board of Overseas Trade, displayed its colonies at foreign fairs and, amidst worsening economic conditions in the early 1930s, sponsored colonial fairs of its own in South Africa and Scotland. Because it also forced governments in France and Belgium to take notice and fire up their own colonial exhibition traditions, it is tempting to suggest that, far from being a failure, the British Empire Exhibition did for the colonial exhibition movement what the Crystal Palace Exhibition had done for the world's fair tradition as a whole. But that would overstate the case. The Wembley affair lacked precisely what the Crystal Palace possessed at its very core: a novel design form capable of capturing public attention. Like French imperial authorities at Marseilles, the British at Wembley had revitalized a national colonial exhibition tradition without making that tradition seem sufficiently modern to appeal to the mass public. What was needed were new architectural designs to sell national imperial designs. For imperial enthusiasts everywhere, the 1925 Paris Exposition could not have come at a more opportune time.[12]

Located in the center of Paris, the Exposition International des Arts Décoratifs et Industriels Modernes splashed the cultural landscape with dazzling "machine-age" architectural and artistic patterns that led to a fundamental re-ordering of modern life. While Le Courbusier's *Pavillon de l'esprit nouveau* and Konstantin Melnikov's Russian pavilion helped focus attention on the modernist architectural movement, artists and interior designers from the *grands magasins* put on public view a modernistic art style—later called Art Deco—in fashion, furniture, sculpture, glass, metal, ceramics, and bookbinding. Towering above it all was the Eiffel Tower, that, for this occasion, was draped with banks of two-hundred thousand lights that flashed a variety of images across the night skies of Paris, including the name of the French car manufacturer Citroën. A grand advertisement for the "modernistic" way of life, the fair was a self-proclaimed break from precedent. For French imperial authorities, this sensibility could not have been entirely comforting. A complete break with the past was, after all, just what anti-imperialists were demanding. The 1925 exposition, therefore, presented a special challenge for imperial propagandists. Not only were they up to it, they turned the exposition to their own purposes.[13]

For the 1925 exposition, French colonial authorities commissioned pavilions representing their African and Southeast Asian possessions as well as a building devoted to French colonial art. Within these structures, rich "productions of the crafts of yarn, wood, metal, lacquer, and of numerous samples of shell and ivory work" were spread before the eyes of fairgoers, hinting at the value of colonial natural resources for modern decorative arts. Lest anyone miss the point, colonial authorities stressed the forestry resources of its African colonies: "Priceless woods

I - PARIS — EXPOSITION DES ARTS DÉCORATIFS
PORTE d'HONNEUR (par Henry Favier et André Ventre, Architectes, réalisée par Edgard Brandt, maître ferronnier

Exposition des Arts Décoratifs, Paris, 1925.
Courtesy of California State University,
Fresno, Henry Madden Library, Department
of Special Collections.

grow in these forests covering an extension of thousands of kilometers . . . along with essences of lesser value which are used in joinery and carpentry." For those who still had doubts, the ministry invited tourists to look around the interior designs of the buildings where they could see "balustrades, stairs, glasscases," and study actual "artisans indigenes" on display, and learn about "the prospect of an artistic collaboration of the metropolis with the colonies." With designs as daring as L. F. Popova's stage sets or Jacques Lipchitz's sculpture, French imperial designers did their best to make the modernistic sensibility on view at the fair unthinkable apart from imperialism. Over the next six years, they redoubled their efforts to make the same point on a grander scale at the long-awaited Paris Colonial and International Exposition.[14]

While French imperial planners were hard at work on the period's penultimate colonial show, their Belgian counterparts joined the parade of governments organizing interwar colonial expositions. In 1930, the Belgian government opened two expositions to celebrate the centenary of national independence: the Exposition Internationale Coloniale, Maritime, et d'Art Flamand in Antwerp; and, the Exposition Internationale de la Grande Industrie, Science et Application d'Art Wallon in Liège. While the latter emphasized the industrial potential of Belgium, the former highlighted Belgium's imperial conquests in Africa and included impressive imperial shows by the French, British, Dutch, Italian, and Portuguese governments as well. Displays from the Belgian Congo concentrated in the Palais du Congo were supposed to be the centerpiece of the exposition, but the most visually striking displays were the electrically lit dioramas in the British Empire exhibit building and the modernistic designs of the Dutch, Italian, Norwegian, and Finnish national buildings. Together with the standard potpourri of fake habitat settings with colonized people on display, these splashes of modernistic architectural forms reinforced the overall message of European imperialists that modernism and colonialism were two sides of the same coin—a message that French exposition planners would transmit to more fairgoers than visited the 1889 Paris Exposition made famous by the Eiffel Tower.[15]

Long regarded by imperial planners as "the apotheosis of greater France," the 1931 Exposition Coloniale Internationale occupied over 200 acres of the Bois de Vincennes on the eastern edge of Paris and served as a stunning imperial fantasyland complete with transplanted vegetation and indigenous people on display in so-called native villages. The engine behind the fair was Louis-Hubert Lyautey, aptly described by anthropologist Paul Rabinow as an "aristocratic dandy, military man, and colonialist" renowned for his "pacification" of Morocco. No stranger to expositions, Lyautey had organized several colonial fairs in Morocco to promote his technocratic vision of a modern colony. As much as anything else, the fair was a testament to his life's work as an imperial visionary possessed of the conviction that the lessons of colonial administration could be applied to ordering the French body politic. Under Lyautey's supervision, leading French colonial architects did their best to fulfill his dream of representing an efficiently run, modern empire.[16]

By opening day, visitors could see hundreds of exhibits in the Algerian pavilion; clamber up the steps of a representation of Madagascar's royal palace; compare colonial economies in the modern Cité de L'Information building; drink exotic beverages in cafes while looking at "natives" everywhere on display; examine wild animals and birds in the ten-acre zoo; gawk at the gigantic mud huts finished in bright stucco; and bask in the glow of French imperial accomplishments in

"Round the World in One Day": official poster, Paris, 1931. Courtesy of the Smithsonian Institution, National Museum of American History, Warshaw Collection.

Indochina. The Indochina section was the exposition's largest drawing card. Inspired by the success of Angkor Wat at the 1922 Marseilles exposition, Paris exposition promoters constructed their own replica of Angkor Wat and surrounded it with twenty-five multicolored pavilions displaying material exhibits and indigenous people from Southeast Asia.[17]

Importantly, this striking representation of French imperial fantasies between the wars did not go unchallenged. On the eve of the 1931 fair, French anti-imperialists, probably inspired by Comintern's decision the preceding year to step up its anticolonial activities, organized a small counterexposition, the "Exposition anti-impérialiste," complete with photographs of colonial wars, biting satirical cartoons, and art from the colonies that had been banned at the official fairs. Monitored carefully by the Paris police and government intelligence units because of its Communist connections, this counterexposition, according to historian Charles-Robert Ageron, drew an attendance numbering about

Reproduction of Angkor Wat, Paris, 1931.
Courtesy of Nederlands Foto & Grafisch
Centrum, Spaarnestad Fotoarchief.

five thousand. Although this number was small in comparison with the millions who visited the show in Vincennes, the counterexposition movement was a thorn in the side of French imperial authorities that made the unexpected show of support from the United States all the more welcome.[18]

Of all the arresting sights at the 1931 fair, not many rivaled the American display. The exhibit stood out for two reasons. First, in an exposition suffused with overdetermined "native" habitats and modernistic architectural forms, the American pavilion took the form of a prefabricated Mr. Vernon stuffed with artifacts from George Washington's home and America's overseas possessions. Second, it was the first officially sanctioned U.S. exhibit at any European colonial exposition.

The American exhibit was born of a host of intersecting domestic and foreign policy concerns. Leading the charge for an officially sponsored exhibit in Paris were Chicago's Century of Progress Exposition supporters. They had good reason to suspect that, given the worsening international economic climate, unless the United States sent an official exhibit to Paris, the French government would refuse to send one to the 1933 fair. This contingency was especially clear to Charles G. Dawes, the American ambassador to England, who, along with his brother, Rufus Dawes, chairman of the Chicago exposition board, had provided substantial funds to underwrite the fair. Also, as Rufus Dawes made clear to his brother, the absence of an American colonial exhibit at the Paris fair would be a "disgrace" to the memory of William Howard Taft, one of the architects of America's turn-of-the-century imperial policy. The Dawes brothers had plenty of support in Congress, especially in the person of the powerful chairman of the House Committee on Foreign Affairs, Sol Bloom. A longtime world's fair promoter, Bloom had his own agenda. President Hoover had recently appointed him to a commission to plan for a nationwide celebration of the George Washington bicentennial. The commission had been singularly lethargic and Bloom, with his experience in show business, saw abundant opportunity to turn the U.S. exhibit in Paris into the firing pin for an international celebration of the Washington bicentennial. He needed to overcome reluctance in Congress to put America on display in the context of a show glorifying European imperialism. At this juncture, Ambassador Dawes and his counterpart in Paris, Walter Edge, persuaded French exposition authorities to change the name of their fair to the

International Colonial and *Overseas* Exposition, thus allowing Bloom and his supporters in Congress to plunge into the seas of deep denial about the avowedly imperial aims of the Paris exposition and gain the votes necessary to secure an appropriation for the American exhibit.[19]

The White House was never more than a step removed from the planning process. Hoover had never tried to hide his enthusiasm for world's fairs. He often recalled with great fondness the impact of a photograph of the Corliss Engine at the 1876 Philadelphia Exhibition on his own career and, during the planning stages of the 1915 Panama–Pacific International Exposition, had served as the special representative of San Francisco world's fair interests in England. In 1925, however, as secretary of commerce, Hoover had brought a great deal of embarrassment to the American arts community by his refusal to support an official U.S. exhibit at the 1925 Exposition des Arts Décoratifs with his infamous declaration that there was no modern art in the United States. Nudged by his high-ranking London ambassador and impressed by plans for the Mount Vernon exhibit, President Hoover saw in the Paris fair an opportunity to trumpet the value of America's own overseas dominions and to turn his earlier convictions about American architecture into a self-fulfilling prophecy. That Hoover also shared Bloom's enthusiasm for linking the Washington bicentennial with the American display in Paris became clear when he asked Bloom to head the Bicentennial Commission and selected another bicentennial commissioner, C. Bascom Slemp, to serve as the U.S. commissioner general for the Paris exposition.[20]

Like Lyautey, Slemp brought considerable energy and the weight of a privileged social position to bear on his responsibilities. Born in 1870 to a family active in Virginia politics, he became a lawyer, served in Congress, declined the offer of an ambassadorship to Peru, served as a member of the Republican National Committee, and, while working as President Coolidge's secretary, compiled notes that enabled him to write *The Mind of President Coolidge*. To assist with the enormous task of arranging exhibits, Slemp drew on the talents of Charles G. Burke, a real estate investor, former congressman from South Dakota, and, most recently, the commissioner of Indian affairs in Warren G. Harding's administration. Burke was the perfect choice. While lacking the aristocratic pretensions of Lyautey and Slemp, Burke, in his role as commisioner of Indian affairs, had been an imperialist at home, using the power of his office to degrade many Native American cultural practices. Burke, moreover, shared Slemp's vision of how America should be represented at the fair and shared his view of the American exhibit as a means for ordering modern life. What kind of order did these men envision? The answer lay in the "colonial revival" movement that had been building momentum during the 1920s.[21]

The "colonial revival" movement had several sources. In 1924, a resolution was introduced in Congress to commemorate the bicentennial of George Washington's birth and President Calvin Coolidge appointed a national commission to lay plans for the celebration. Two years later, organizers of the Philadelphia Sesquicentennial Exposition fabricated an eighteenth-century colonial street scene that proved one of the most popular attractions at the fair. Meanwhile, John D. Rockefeller decided to finance the restoration of colonial Williamsburg. As historian Warren Susman observed, this revival of interest in an idealized colonial American past was the result of deepening concern in American society about the loss of traditional values—integrity, character, liberty—once assumed to be at the core of American political culture. In addition, as Karal Ann Marling and William B. Rhoads have noted, the colonial revival reflected growing concerns about the impact of immigration on the future of the country and, in part, was intended to hasten the "Americanization" of the nation by shaping a public culture that would remind Americans of a heroic past that all "true" Americans shared. Through eighteenth-century tract houses, pseudo-colonial shopping streets, celebratory school pageants, and forests of nostalgic books and magazine articles, the colonial revival gained momentum during the interwar years and influenced the decision of New York World's Fair planners in 1940 to shift the public focus from the Trylon and Perisphere to James Earle Fraser's heroic statue of George Washington.[22]

Given the growing enthusiasm for the colonial revival among national elites and given Slemp's personal involvement with the George Washington bicentennial, it is hardly surprising that government exposition planners turned to the colonial revival for inspiration for the American pavilion at the 1931 Paris fair. After intensive consultation with French exposition officials, American diplomats in London and Paris as well as with the irrepressible Bloom and White House officials, Slemp and Burke determined that the official U.S. government pavilion at the fair would take the form of Mt. Vernon. As luck would have it, a Richmond, Virginia, architect, Charles K. Bryant, read a newspaper story about the government's plan to participate in the fair and reminded government officials that he had reproduced Mt. Vernon at the 1915 San Francisco fair for the Virginia State Building and still had the blueprints in his possession. Bryant, moreover, had a good working relationship with Sears, Roebuck and Company and was convinced that the company could prefabricate the structure for easy shipping and reassembly in Paris. With the exposition scheduled to open in less than a year, Slemp quickly investigated the feasibility of Bryant's idea. When Sears agreed to construct the Mt. Vernon replica at cost, the commission shifted into high gear. In less than six months, a replica of Washington's Potomac residence, the archetypal colonial revival building, would be transformed into a modern plantation and America's imperial resurgence would be underway.[23]

The "Mt. Vernon on the Seine" had several unusual features. For the main building, Anne Madison Washington, a descendant of George Washington and James Madison, persuaded the Grand Rapids Furniture Association to make exact copies of Mt. Vernon's furnishings. "These are not mere museum exhibits designed to give an impression of the originals," a government official insisted. "In these rooms the wall paper, the moldings on the ceiling, the lamp fixtures, the rugs, the paintings, the four-poster beds, and a multitude of minute details, have been faithfully reproduced, or are genuine articles of the colonial period." Gazing at Washington's private study, visitors were encouraged to let their imaginations soar: "There, at the round 'tambour desk' sits George Washington, studying, writing, planning perhaps one of his campaigns. He gets up and takes a book from one of the shelves in the wall, puts his finger on the globe in order to refresh his mind on some geographical point, he sits down at the desk again, and bends over his work." Pausing before Lafayette's portrait or standing outside the room where Lafayette stayed when he visited Mt. Vernon, visitors were invited to illuminate their dark corridors of memory with visions of Franco-American friendship and cooperation.[24]

Beyond the big house, the prefabricated colonial world of eighteenth-century America gave way to an equally graphic representation of American neocolonialism in the twentieth century. In annex buildings that bore an uncanny resemblance to Washington's slave quarters, the government arranged exhibits from its overseas territories—including the Philippine Islands, Puerto Rico, the Virgin Islands, Hawaii, and Alaska—as well as displays about colonial sanitation and hygiene and Native Americans. Initially, U.S. government planners wanted territorial governments to put indigenous people on display, but changed their minds as it became clear how costly this proposition would be and how much resentment lingered over "living exhibits" that had been organized for an earlier generation of American fairs, especially the 1904 St. Louis fair when over one thousand Filipinos had

EXPOSITION COLONIALE INTERNATIONALE — PARIS 1931

Charles K. Bryant, Arch.

U.S. pavilion, Paris, 1931. Courtesy of the
Smithsonian Institution, National Museum of
American History, Edward J. Orth World's
Fair Collection.

been put on display on a "Philippines Reservation." Instead of living exhibits, the government settled for static exhibits depicting the economic and cultural resources from its overseas possessions. In the Philippines annex, wax figures depicted Filipino "types." Photographs, charts, and dioramas portrayed "the rapid social, educational and sanitary development realized through the kindly tutorship of the United States." In another annex shared by Puerto Rico, the Virgin Islands, and Hawaii, recorded music together with photographs of "bronzed men riding surf boards" and "women dancers in hula skirts" suggested the possibilities of developing Hawaii into a recreational paradise for westerners, while the displays of the Virginia Islands (centering on bay rum and sugar) and Puerto Rico (emphasizing the production of cigars and lace work) gave the impression of exotic lands making progress under American guidance.[25]

Not all of the exhibits were static, however. To deepen the impression of contentment under American rule, the U.S. commissioners, on the recommendations of Vice-President Charles Curtis and Federal Bureau of Investigation Director J. Edgar Hoover, contracted with a private showman, Thomas O'Brien, to bring his twenty-three-member Indian band to perform as part of the American exhibit. Whether the U.S. commission took O'Brien up on his proposal to erect tepees behind the Alaskan exhibit to give "an Indian camp effect" is unclear. What is clear is that the Indian Band played at the official opening of the American exhibit and spent more than a month performing as part of the display. According to O'Brien, Slemp had offered unequivocal praise for his performers. "You have made my Exhibit," Slemp exclaimed to O'Brien. In many ways, Slemp was right. In an exposition crammed with French colonials on display, the Indian Band served as an important reminder that the United States was anything but a novice in strategies of imperial expansion and display.[26]

That point was driven home in a host of public ceremonies designed to illustrate the close relationship between American and French imperial outlooks. Shortly before the exposition officially opened, one of Lyautey's lieutenants, Marcel Olivier, gave a radio address broadcast to the United States inviting Americans to the fair. Quoting from remarks made by the French ambassador to the United States, Olivier stressed that the "Overseas Exposition is neither an exhibition of trophies nor a slave market. . . . It is not a question of enslaving or exploiting backward races, but to extend a friendly hand to them, so that they may rise toward a higher plane of life." Responding to Olivier's remarks, Burke lavished praise on Lyautey and emphasized that "the United States of America is privileged to be associated with him in this magnificent enterprise."[27]

Several weeks later, two thousand invited guests assembled on the landscaped lawn of the American exhibit awaiting the arrival of the day's speakers and visiting dignitaries, including Lyautey and General John J. Pershing. As the dignitaries moved toward their positions on the speakers' platform, the Indian Band, "in full tribal regalia, struck up the 'Marseillaise' to the beat of tom-toms." When the applause died down, one American speaker after another approached the microphone that would carry their remarks to forty radio stations in the United States and Europe. The representation of Mt. Vernon had been carefully chosen, Slemp explained, to stimulate memories of Franco-American cooperation during the American War of Independence. Ambassador Walter Edge was more explicit. As a former colony, he explained, America was excited to have the opportunity to demonstrate its "intelligent" policies for its overseas territories. America, he emphasized, was not a colonial power in the traditional sense, seeking to expand its political influence. Rather, he said, the Americans have established "overseas political relations on economic bases, and, consequently, while seeking to consolidate the security and influence of our people, have avoided recourse to political expansion." America, in sum, had developed a colonial policy appropriate to the modern age and, as Edge told his audience, was "proud to offer examples of our civilization migrating westward, while joining with France to celebrate this magnificent review of colonial progress." General Pershing was no less enthusiastic about the pageant of empire that spread before his eyes: "I cannot close my remarks without a word of tribute to the men who built and defended the French Colonial Empire, the greatness of which is now being commemorated in this Exposition, and which today constitutes one of the bulwarks of the country's strength and prosperity." [28]

If American speakers showed no hint of embarrassment at displaying enthusiasm for imperialism from the portico of a national shrine of American independence or in listening to John Philip Sousa's "March of the Legionnaires," composed especially for the U.S. exhibit at the exposition, French speakers similarly found no disjunction between France's historical actions on behalf of American political independence from England and their own profuse display of imperial control at the exposition. Indeed, French politicians seized the opportunity of the opening of the American exhibit to trace their own imperial fortunes to "the French explorers as they pushed their way westward through the Mississippi valley." "Since those days," Paul Raynaud, French minister of colonial affairs, informed his American guests, "your pioneers have started on their wonderful race to the West. They have carried out the gigantic work of colonizing the empty spaces of a continent. And now it is the privilege of Americans themselves to carry beyond the Pacific the blessing of civilization." Summing up, Raynaud asserted: "We believe that profit is not the ultimate goal of colonization, and that only by entering into the feelings of those who live beneath the shelter of our flags, can we blend the harmonies of civilization without striking a discordant note. And I know that in this sphere, your ideal is ours." Lyautey underscored these sentiments and mildly chastised the American delegation for apologizing for the modesty of America's representation. "But, Mr. Commissioner-General," Lyautey asked, "why do you speak of the modest participation of your country? First of all, you are here, and you desired to come, and your presence by itself is the most brilliant participation, by what it represents and affirms in total force. We know that you are masters of economic development, but you also insist no less on moral development." [29]

Lyautey's words were full of meaning. The "total force" of the American presence at Paris lent an important stamp of moral approval to French imperial efforts which the French government was only too happy to reciprocate by approving America's own coloniale moderne status. The official U.S. report on the opening of the American exhibit explained the significance of the ceremonies this way: "One would have to go back, perhaps, to General Pershing's visit to the tomb of Lafayette to find an event which so profoundly stirred, by the souvenirs it evoked, the friendly feelings towards each other of the French and American people." Put in somewhat different terms, the formalities of the opening ceremonies enabled both the French and American governments to reinvent their histories in ways that would further integrate the modern world system under the dominance of western imperial powers.[30]

It was precisely this process of imperial reinvention and consolidation that nearly caused the U.S. exhibit to backfire. As word got out that the American government was planning to put representations of their overseas possessions on display in a modern plantation setting as part of the largest colonial exposition ever organized, groups of "malcontents," as the U.S. government described them, especially in Puerto Rico and the Philippines, seized on the exhibit to unmask the fiction that the United States was not an imperial power. As the French consul to Puerto Rico described it, "American demands [for an exhibit] unleashed an anti-American movement of unusual violence." "We are not going to be dragged forth and exhibited like a degraded people which accepts the condition of inferiority fastened upon it," one San Juan newspaper editor insisted, "while calling for a campaign to resist any attempt to classify Porto Rico as a subject 'colony,' with a status like that of Senegal or the French Congo." As it became clear that the core of the Puerto Rican representation would be drawn from an exhibit originally developed for Atlantic City, opposition to the exhibit grew in the Puerto Rican House of Representatives, which passed a bill prohibiting the representation of Puerto Rico at the fair. American officials, however, simply ignored the measure.[31]

Amidst the worsening condition of the Philippine economy, U.S. War Department officials also had to fend off a resolution in the Philippine legislature opposing the $50,000 appropriation American officials had requested for Philippine representation in the Paris exhibit. Eugenio Perez of Pangasinan led the opposition charge, claiming that approval of the exhibit "will mean an acceptance by the Filipinos of a colonial form of government." The appropriation bill passed, but opposition to the exhibit grew with reports that the U.S. government would follow the precedent established at the 1904 fair and exhibit a group of Igorots—regarded as a "primitive" people—as part of its efforts to demonstrate the progress of the Filipino people under American tutelage. Protests were evidently sufficiently strong to force U.S. government officials to abandon plans to organize living groups of Filipinos as part of the display, but U.S. officials insisted on "native" Filipino demonstrators to describe the exhibit to visitors.[32]

As might be expected, the protests by Filipinos and Puerto Ricans were never acknowledged in the elaborate fiction—one is tempted to call it a modern plantation narrative—spun for visitors at the Mt. Vernon replica at the Paris fair. Rather, all signs of protest and opposition were erased and displaced by a fantasy extolling the positive advantages accruing to America's overseas possessions under American rule. The results, as a sampling of responses recorded in visitor registration books suggests, were impressive. "This pavilion is the most interesting of all the Exposition," one French fairgoer penned. "A precious gem set in the beautiful crown of the French show," wrote another. Visiting Americans were no less pleased. "I am glad we own them," one Connecticut resident declared about America's overseas territories. "Really wonderful," exclaimed another. After seeing the exhibit, another American, identifying herself only as Roxy, combined rapture with a new resolve, writing: "A thrill of a lifetime—a shrine, beloved by every American so wonderfully transplanted, that sent the thrills helter, skelter thru one— I am now resolved to learn the second and third verses of The Star Spangled Banner." The editor of the European edition of the *New York Herald* was equally enthusiastic: "Not only physically is our exhibit almost perfect in its conception, but morally it has been a tremendous success from what I hear on all sides."[33]

As revealing as these comments are, they do not do justice to the full impact of the imperial world enclosed by Mt. Vernon or of the exposition as a whole on American culture. Press reports and occasional radio broadcasts kept the American exhibit before the American public. So did a massive advertising campaign financed by French exposition authorities. In August 1930, Olivier wrote a confidential memo conveying his decision to spend $40,000 to advertise the fair through the George Harrison Phelps agency of Detroit. Phelps, Olivier noted, "possesses an enormous political influence and enormous technical and financial resources" and would use all the modern publicity techniques, including electric signs, printed media, and cinema to promote the exposition around America. Use them he did. During the exposition's run, Phelps's agency generated over eight million lines of publicity for the fair, especially for the American exhibit, that resulted in inquiries from over six hundred American cities for more information about the exposition.[34]

Of all the stories Phelps ran about the exposition, what particularly captured the fancy of American newspaper editors were releases about the impact of the exposition on the world of fashion. Long before the exposition opened to the public, Paris fashion designers and interior decorators saw the potential of converting Third World cultural forms on display at the fair into the fashion craze of 1931–32. As one designer put it: "I predict a profusion of colonial fabrics, of colonial themes, of colonial forms in hats, gowns, and decorations. The colonial influence will extend to necklaces, bracelets, combs and jewels." That prediction proved too cautious. With Paris fashion designers introducing clothes that were "colonial in feeling," an imperial contagion took hold that even led some Paris bar owners to refashion their establishments into tropical oases with desert motifs. As Paris fashions hit the United States, they became an immediate sensation. American fashion columns alerted readers to the latest creations: pajamas in Algerian colors, "coolie hats," "Arabian burnous interpreted as a lounging robe for beach wear," and "red accessions of African brilliance." By the time the exposition closed, the colonial "mode" had become the rage among America's smart set.[35]

In the course of bombarding the American public with stories about the latest fashion styles in Paris, Phelps did not ignore the American exhibit proper. To the contrary, he saw to it that stories circulated to newspapers around the country about the construction of Mt. Vernon, about comparisons between the Mt. Vernon replica and the reproduction of Angkor Wat, and about French plans to celebrate the Washington Bicentennial.[36]

Amidst this public relations blitzkrieg for the American exhibit at the Paris fair, Sol Bloom put the finishing touches on his plans for the Washington bicentennial. He capitalized on the reinvention of America's imperial tradition at the Paris fair and made the bicentennial seem like a natural outcropping of the exposition. Throughout 1932, under American pressure, governments around the world—including Germany under Hitler and Italy under Mussolini—dedicated statues and renamed streets in honor of Washington. Nowhere would these ceremonies leave a more pointed legacy than in Southeast Asia. For the occasion of the Washington bicentennial and as an expression of gratitude for American participation in the French colonial fair, French colonial officials, joined for the festivities by American actor Douglas Fairbanks, Jr., dedicated a monument to George Washington in downtown Saigon.[37]

The future course of U.S. involvement in Southeast Asia would underscore the fateful nature of the decision that the government made when it agreed to abandon precedent and participate in the 1931 Paris Colonial Exposition. In the long run, by strengthening relations with France and endorsing French imperial policy, the government's participation at the 1931 fair would help pave the way for American support of French efforts to retain its colonies in Southeast Asia in the 1940s and 1950s. In the short run, the results of the 1931 Paris fair were encoded in America's century-of-progress expositions.

For Chicago's 1933 world's fair promoters, the 1931 Paris fair was a revelation. Chicago's exposition executives made pilgrimages to fairs in Barcelona, Seville, Antwerp, Liège, and Stockholm, but none, with the possible exception of Antwerp's colonial fair, captured their fancy quite like the Paris fair. Over the course of the summer of 1931, a veritable parade of Chicago world's fair managers, including the exposition's architect-in-chief, Daniel H. Burnham, Jr., visited the Paris fair and prepared extensive reports. "In the succession of postwar expositions," one report concluded, "it may fairly be said that Vincennes represents the zenith of progress." [38] Burnham, whose father had designed the World's Columbian Exposition, called the Paris fair at the Bois de Vincennes "the greatest Exposition of all times." [39] So captivated were Chicago's world's fair managers by the colonial villages stocked with indigenous peoples that they urged similar exhibits be included in the Century of Progress Exposition. They especially encouraged their London Office to secure colonial exhibits for the fair. If this proved impossible for political or economic reasons, they recommended the inclusion of privately owned "native bazaars" that "should make Chicago as far in advance of Vincennes as Vincennes has been in advance of any other exhibition." [40] As Ambassador Dawes summed up in a letter to Lenox Lohr, the Chicago exposition's general manager, the "Colonial Exposition drew 30 million people, largely because of what might be termed exotic features." [41]

The likelihood that the Chicago fair would resemble its Paris predecessor became even greater when, at Ambassador Dawes's urging, the exposition corporation hired none other than Henry Cole to take charge of its European operations. Cole, who had been the guiding hand behind British exhibits at the British Empire Exposition and the recently concluded Antwerp fair, opened doors for visiting Century of Progress executives, introducing them to European exposition planners, and provided invaluable knowledge about the dioramas that been such

*Mayan Temple, Chicago, 1933. Courtesy of
the Hall of History Foundation.*

stunning successes at British exhibitions. Worsening economic conditions, coupled with Cole's declining health, threw a wrench in plans to secure official European colonial representations at the Chicago fair, but the exposition nevertheless incorporated exotic bazaars, an African village concession, a Native American village, and boasted a massive Mayan Temple that became the Century of Progress Exposition's answer to the Angkor Wat reproduction at the Paris colonial fair.

The African village concession revealed the imperialistic underbelly of the fair. The show, initially called the All-African Exhibit, was the brainchild of one of the directors of the Chicago fair and several African Americans in Chicago. Prominent anthropologists including Fay-Cooper Cole, M. J. Herskovits, and George Herzog endorsed the plan, convincing exposition authorities that the show "would be really a sort of complement to the exhibit in Anthropology which is being made by the Exposition and which centers around the life and culture of the American Indian." "The African Exhibit," the fair's director of exhibits emphasized, "would be really a sort of analogue for this exhibit based on Indian life in America."[42]

What kind of show did they envision? With the help of Owen Rowe O'Neil, son of a prominent South African politician, concessionaires proposed an African expedition that would net about twenty-five Africans for exhibition purposes. (He was, according to a press release, "speeded on his journey by the Chicago Adventurers' Club . . . at a Happy Landings dinner.") The show itself would include the Africans living in a jungle setting—complete with a "Congo River" capable of carrying exposition-goers in canoes "manned by dusky natives." "Other attractions," the press release announced, "include an oasis, a jungle bar, traders' and missionaries' huts, a Kano fur bazaar, an African Theater, a Dar Nuba Theater, a Plantation Cafe, a Capetown Road, a strand, a carnival and stands and pens of African jungle beasts." So audiences would get the full effect of being great white colonizers, plans for the show included a boardwalk high off the ground that encircled the entire concession "on which tourists may promenade, while they look down on the miniature African world below. At convenient intervals on the boardwalk there will be settees, parasol-protected tables and chairs." Despite the high costs, the fair's director of concessions declared: "The Exposition authorities are thoroughly convinced of the value of the proposed exhibit and are earnestly desirous of seeing it financed."[43]

Financing, however, together with the storm of controversy that the All-Africa Exhibit provoked among Chicago's African Americans, already sensitized to how they would be represented at the fair, made the show increasingly problematic for world's fair authorities. But the centrality of a colonial African village to the Century of Progress fair became evident when they awarded the intrepid showman Louis DuFour the "Darkest Africa" concession, which became one of the featured attractions along the exposition's midway.[44]

The 1933–34 Chicago fair, in short, was not simply a machine-age exposition. Embedded in its modernistic designs, was a "structure of feeling" that harmonized with the coloniale moderne thrust of contemporary European fairs. Chicago's example was so compelling and financially successful that it served as a model for the planners of future American fairs, especially the builders of San Francisco's Golden Gate International Exposition as they brought America's coloniale moderne movement to full flower on the West Coast of the United States.[45]

The dreams of empire that animated San Francisco's 1939 exposition builders were hardly new. Twenty-five years earlier, many of the same civic leaders had organized the Panama–Pacific International Exposition to celebrate the opening of the Panama Canal and to boost San Francisco's fortunes as the hub of the Pacific coast's growing commercial trade with Latin America and Asia. The years of work that went into the 1915 fair resulted in an imperial dream city, but the high aspirations of the exposition's builders were mitigated by the First World War and the ensuing decade of growing isolationist sentiment. When the depression hit, business leaders in Chicago joined forces with the federal government to build the Century of Progress Exposition to restore the faith of Americans in the strength of the American economic and political system. Civic leaders in San Francisco determined to follow suit and organize an exposition that would enclose the anticipated completion of two colossal engineering projects—the Golden Gate Bridge and the San Francisco–Oakland Bay Bridge—within a symbolic framework that would celebrate American westward expansionism and serve as an ideological bridge across the fault lines of the Great Depression. Specifically, they pinned their hopes for regenerating America, especially the floundering economies of the western American states, on the realization of "a Western Empire in every sense of the term"—an empire that would become synonymous with what a later generation of Americans would call the Pacific Rim.[46]

To help the public visualize "the Empire of the West," exposition directors—who included Leland Cutler, staunch Republican and head of the San Francisco Chamber of Commerce, and George Creel, equally staunch Democrat and former head of the U.S. government's propaganda and censorship office in the First World War—turned to a cadre of exposition specialists, including architects, former exposition managers, and leading intellectuals from Bay Area universities. Inspired by the exposition, they modernized the architectural form, updated the ideological message of the 1915 fair, and fixed the promise of economic recovery on the development of a consumer-based and leisure-oriented Pacific empire.

Their revamped dreams of empire began with a nostalgic and racist reinvention of the Pacific Rim's history. As one exposition official explained: "Since the Exposition was to be a Pageant of the Pacific, it was natural that the architects should select a structural style set by a race that ran a course and died, leaving remains of a forgotten people whose noble temples suggest a high civilization." If Mayan-moderne was the starting point for the architects, their vision quickly expanded to em-

Tower of the Sun and Elephant Towers, San Francisco, 1939. Courtesy of the Hall of History.

brace the broader trans-Pacific thrust of the fair. By opening day, Mayan-moderne had been joined by buildings designed in a mishmash of supposedly Asian styles that encircled the rocket-like Tower of the Sun and the heroic statue of "Pacifica" (which one commentator later likened to "an overgrown automobile radiator ornament.")[47]

However bizarre, the visual impact of the exposition's design was inescapable. Twin Mayan-cum-Cambodian Elephant Towers that seemed to derive from "both Oriental precedent and early skyscraper zoning studies" flanked the entrance to the Court of the Pacific. As they were transported from one end of Treasure Island to the other on ele-

86

phant trains, fairgoers could learn from the official guidebook that the "huge windowless exhibit palaces, 100 feet high, give the effect of an ancient walled city, and the interior courts with long rows of square pilasters are reminiscent of Angkor Wat." Exotic colors—aided by nighttime electrical illumination—gave added effect as exposition designers developed "an official palette . . . drawn from the coloring of the Pacific shores." "Sun of the Dawn yellow, Pagoda yellow . . . , Hawaiian emerald green, Ming jade green" and the like helped reinforce the exoticism of the exposition grounds, while heroic murals and statuary, with their narrative emphasis on a "peaceful procession of Trade and Commerce," reinforced the impression of the exposition's benign intent.[48]

To give substance to the architectural and artistic form of the fair, exposition managers organized thousands of exhibits that were intended to convince fairgoers that peace would follow from the creation of a trans-Pacific paradise superintended by American corporations joined by federal government agencies that attended to the welfare of American citizens. Organizing these exhibits was no small task, and exposition executives were fortunate to have in their employ Major O. J. F. Keatinge, a tried and true exposition hand. Keatinge was a British Board of Trade official who had, like Henry Cole, been involved in virtually every major world's fair since the British Empire Exposition at Wembley, where Keatinge had been in charge of imperial pageantry. His experience was indispensable to the thinking of San Francisco's exposition promoters, especially to their efforts to assume sponsorship of the Pacific Rim, an area of the world already carved into spheres of foreign colonial influence. The genius of Keatinge—and of Cutler, who travelled extensively in Asia to secure exhibits—was to persuade Pacific Rim countries and European colonial powers that it would be in their own self-interest to establish pavilions in the "Pacific Basin" area of the San Francisco fair.[49]

The measure of Keatinge's and Cutler's success was apparent on opening day. In addition to Hawaiian and Philippine Pavilions from America's Pacific empire, Australia, New Zealand, Japan, Johore, Java, the Netherlands East Indies, and French Indochina contributed buildings and exhibits that surrounded the theme-center of the Pacific Basin displays—the Pacific House. The significance of the arrangement was not lost on the French Consul General in San Francisco who informed his foreign minister about the growing alarm along the West Coast of the United States about Japanese expansion and that Californians, through the fair, were interested in showing support "for the work ac-

*Sioux chief Big Turnip and family, San
Francisco, with George Creel (standing left).
Courtesy of the Library of Congress, Prints
and Photographs Division.*

complished by the Netherlands in the Dutch East Indies and by France
in Indo China" in holding the line against Japanese advances in the
Pacific. In fact, the consul declared, the exhibit from Indochina, a duplicate of the structure erected at the 1931 Paris colonial fair, would go
a long way towards "maintaining the status quo and the equilibrium of
forces in the Pacific region" and towards building a "community of
interest" with the population of the American West.[50]

The foundation for constructing this community of imperial interests had already been laid by San Francisco's exposition builders in the
Pacific House and in the exhibit of Native Americans that formed part
of the federal government's display. In the Pacific House, organized by
the presidents of Stanford University and the University of California
at Berkeley along with Philip Youtz of the Brooklyn Museum, art made
the message clear. On the walls, above dioramas and exhibit cases, was

George Creel greeting
President Somoza, San
Francisco, 1939. Courtesy of
the Library of Congress,
Prints and Photographs
Division.

a series of mural maps by anthropologist and artist Miguel Covarrubias. Along with the murals depicting flora and fauna, house types, and
art forms was a color-coded, anthropological "people's map of the Pacific Area." Yellows and greens signified areas of the world with Asian
populations; ochres signified American Indian concentrations in the
western hemisphere; pink colors denoted areas peopled by Caucasians;
and various shades of purple and brown showed concentrations of Africans and African Americans. To heighten the effect, Covarrubias
added representative "types" to each land mass. While not unsympa-
thetic to nonwhites, Covarrubias's rendering of Pacific Rim history "in
terms of the culture of the different races around the Pacific," lent artistic and anthropological legitimacy to hierarchical modes of thought
that had been a mainstay of European and U.S. expansionism.[51]

Further buttressing the claims of San Francisco's exposition-makers
as legitimate imperial brokers were exhibits of Native and Latin Americans. At Creel's urging, the government building on Treasure Island
included nearly forty Native Americans, "living pages from history,"
who were at the exposition to demonstrate their superiority as artisans
producing for an international market. Heralded as a "spectacular announcement of the new Indian policy" developed by commissioner of
Indian affairs John Collier, the federal Indian exhibit seemed closer to

European, especially French, colonial exhibits that emphasized the ability of the colonized to pay for themselves, thereby giving them a measure of autonomy.[52]

The Pacific Basin ideal projected at the fair also envisioned Latin Americans as producers of "coffee, minerals, drugs, meats and crops" and Latin America "as one of the most important, if not the greatest, of the world markets for the products of the United States." By organizing Latin American pavilions, with their exhibits of natural resources and aboriginal artifacts, into a Latin American Court across from the Pacific Basin, exposition builders projected an image of Latin American nations as economically valuable producers of raw materials and colonial consumers of America's industrial surplus. For Latin Americans who might have had alternative visions about their future, exposition authorities had a ready response. Shortly after the fair opened, Nicaraguan dictator Anastasio Somoza visited the fair as an official guest of the U.S. government. Creel escorted Somoza around the fairgrounds, arranged for a nationwide radio broadcast from the exposition, and approved of the twenty-one gun salute for the dictator at the U.S. army installation. Somoza responded by making clear that he did "not share the fear which formerly at least was felt in Latin America against the imperialistic spirit of the Colossus of the North." Indeed, as one newspaper reported, Somoza "wants the United States to go to Nicaragua and do a little Colossusing." [53]

Exposition promoters never lost sight of the possibilities for directing seventeen million fairgoers toward experiences that would reaffirm the centrality of empire to the future development of the modern American west. The exposition's midway, or Gayway as it was called, was a case in point. "Thrill rides, exotic Pacific restaurants, show-world oddities . . . [the] talent of nearby Hollywood, supplementing the spectacular Pageant of the Pacific, will make the Amusement Zone the nucleus of the 'Finest Show on Earth,' as thrilling and merry a cavalcade of entertainment as ever captivated a show-going nation." According to another exposition publication, "the 1939 Midway will have all the glamor and romance of the Pacific Ocean to draw from: the South Seas, Latin-America, Lands of the Southern Cross, the Orient and Far East, and Arctic regions." Visitors were invited to take advantage of "Javanese and Oriental restaurants, complete with idol dancers, native foods and exotic decorations. . . ." The Gayway, in short, fulfilled the promise of the fair, namely that living the good life in the American West would be unthinkable apart from increased American involvement in Pacific affairs.[54]

90

At the very moment America's interwar imperial revival was reaching a climax on the West Coast, another facet of the coloniale moderne movement was reaching its zenith in New York City. With its emphasis on a world of tomorrow, where experts drawn from industry, government, and science solved social ills, the New York fair marked the culmination of a cultural offensive that began when some of America's foremost scientists saw in the 1933 Chicago Century of Progress Exposition an opportunity to implement an empire-building agenda of their own.

CHAPTER FOUR

The Empire of Science

> At a time when my responsibilities were not lightened by visible accomplishments, and when immediate funds for and recognition of our project were not available to uphold us, you put the stamp of sterling on our efforts. This gave to them an authority and value such as only the approval of a group as eminent as your own could have brought.
> —Rufus C. Dawes to Karl T. Compton,
> 23 July 1931

> Mr. Wallace: "You seen that thing that they have over at the Fair the Hall of Science?"
> —David Mamet, *The Water Engine,* 1977[1]

Vice reports contained in the records of the New York World's Fair Corporation offer an unlikely starting point for understanding the prescriptive function of science at American world's fairs in the 1930s. One letter from an indignant moral reformer to exposition officials, however, illustrates the lengths reached by scientists in their efforts to restore popular faith in science and industry through the world's fairs held during the depression. In his letter to the authorities, Bascom Johnson, director of the American Social Hygiene Association, castigated promoters of the fair for permitting nudity and complained about one exhibit in particular: "In the notable Preview of Progress, the scientific presentation in the General Motors Building at the New York World's Fair, a scientific experiment shows a dish floating in air with no visible means of support, and to make this doubly clear, the demonstrator passed a large ostrich fan under it calling the fan THE SYMBOL OF THE CHICAGO FAIR." "This," Johnson lamented, "shows how Sally Rand and her nude Fan Dance has permeated the warp and woof of the Nation." Sally Rand certainly left her mark on the 1930s. But at both the Chicago Century of Progress Exposition of 1933–34 and the New York World's Fair of 1939–40, some of America's leading scientists were also striving to influence the "warp and woof" of the country. They joined hands with corporate sponsors of the expositions and did a fan dance of their own.[2]

There was more to the fan dance of science than met the eye. It was part of the persistent effort by American scientists after World War I to popularize science, mold a "true" American culture with scientific values, and affirm the hegemony of the corporate state.[3] These efforts continued through the 1920s and intensified in the 1930s as scientists, confronted by a "revolt against science," joined corporate backers of the fairs in trying to pin popular hopes for national recovery on the positive results expected from the fusion of science and business.[4] Scientists participated in both expositions, but their role transcended that of exhibitor. They actually served as intellectual underwriters of the fairs, helping to design and implement the "century-of-progress" and "world-of-tomorrow" themes presented at the Chicago and New York fairs respectively. Such involvement represented nothing new for American scientists. For over thirty years scientists from the Smithsonian Institution had helped shape the colossal expositions that preceded World War I. But as the Smithsonian's golden years of institution building gave way to postwar inertia, exposition planners turned elsewhere for inspiration and dynamic planning.[5] They found it in the National Research Council (NRC).

Established in 1916 by Woodrow Wilson "to encourage the employment of scientific methods in strengthening the national defense," the NRC rapidly developed after the war into the primary agency for promoting cooperation among science, industry, and the military. By the mid-1920s the NRC stood at the epicenter of the military-industrial establishment, coordinating pure and applied scientific research in industrial as well as university laboratories. Despite its prestige, the NRC—an avowedly elite institution in a consumer democracy—represented something of a paradox. Not surprisingly, its leaders developed an interest in popular education. Through newspapers, radio, and especially through the Science Service, leaders of the NRC sought to restore public confidence in the scientific enterprise. Given its respected position as the "scientific arsenal" of the country, the NRC seemed the logical place for exposition planners to turn for expert guidance. Never shirkers, the leaders of the NRC joined the corporate battle to make America safe for democracy.[6]

The link between the fairs and the NRC was first forged in late 1927, when George Ellery Hale, an astrophysicist and the prime mover behind the creation of the NRC a decade earlier, met with Rufus Dawes, an oil baron and the president of the Chicago fair corporation, and suggested focusing the exposition on "the services of science to humanity during the past hundred years." In early 1928 Dawes dined with another NRC member, Michael I. Pupin, an electrical engineer at Columbia University, who applauded Hale's idea and intimated that the NRC might be persuaded to serve in an advisory capacity. That spring Dawes conferred with William A. Pusey, a fellow exposition trustee who had recently retired as head of the American Medical Association; Dawes confided his hope of enlisting the NRC "to mobilize the scientific intelligence of the country" on behalf of the fair. According to Dawes, the NRC embodied "the very thought we want to put into the fair, to wit: the advantages of a close alliance between men of science and men of capital." Pusey caught Dawes's enthusiasm, and in June 1928 he fired off a letter to Gano Dunn, outgoing chairman of the NRC. Dawes's plan, Pusey wrote, was "altogether sound" and represented an effort "to make the celebration an exposition of science and industrial development." Dunn, in turn, presented Dawes's idea for NRC involvement in the fair to members of the NRC executive board, who agreed to consider the matter over the summer.[7]

Meanwhile, Dawes and Pusey moved quickly. In July, they met informally with incoming NRC president George K. Burgess in Washington, D.C. Burgess was impressed by their ideas, and, as a result of their meeting, Dawes wrote to Burgess formally requesting NRC involvement in the Chicago fair "with a view to demonstrating the service of science to humanity, especially through modern industries." The fair, Dawes candidly explained, would have the effect of minimizing industrial competition while enhancing the value of corporate planning for American society. "We desire help," Dawes added, "not only to make an adequate statement of the philosophy of our exposition, but to have that statement endorsed by competent authorities." The possibility of shaping a philosophy for America's future also struck a responsive chord in the NRC executive council. When it reconvened in the fall, the council unanimously endorsed Dawes's request for NRC support.[8]

The value of NRC approval was obvious to Dawes, and he stressed its virtues to other corporate trustees of the Chicago fair. "It means," he informed them, "that the stamp of approval has been placed upon our plans by a thoroughly competent and authoritative organization . . . and indicates an opinion on their part of the possibility of accomplishing something of great value to the Nation." The NRC, Dawes assured the trustees, would not simply dwell on past scientific accomplishments. Rather, its members "are much more interested in suggesting the opportunity for further progress through the greater use of knowledge already gathered and by the better organization of the machinery for scientific research for the benefit of industry." Countering fears that the focus on science would unduly "interfere with the inclusion of all those features which, in the past, have proven to be attractive and valuable in connection with world's fairs," Dawes concluded: "On the contrary, it will tend to tie them together in a more coherent philosophy." [9]

Since the NRC had been charged with shaping that philosophy, Burgess moved quickly to organize scientists for the necessary planning sessions. He persuaded Frank B. Jewett, chief engineer and vice president of American Telephone and Telegraph, Co., to chair a preliminary advisory council that would determine the extent of NRC involvement in the fair. Jewett, in turn, mobilized six other salesmen-scientists to join him on the advisory council. Like Jewett, those joining him had distinguished themselves in research, education, administration, and public relations. Simon Flexner, a noted physician and pathologist, headed the Rockefeller Institute for Medical Research, and Max Mason, a mathematician and former president of the University of Chicago, served as director of the natural science division of the Rockefeller Foundation. Given the ease with which he moved between corporate and scientific circles, Gano Dunn, an engineer and vice president of a leading New York construction firm, was also a logical choice to serve on the committee, as was Vernon Kellogg, a biologist and an intimate of Herbert Hoover who provided the committee with valuable academic and political connections. Rounding out the group were two individuals who had helped shape the connection between the NRC and the fair in the first place—Michael Pupin and William Pusey. When he heard of these appointments, Dawes approved. "In the world of science," he observed, "the names of these men are something to conjure with." [10]

To satisfy their own curiosity about the nature of the exposition, Jewett and his council met with Dawes and several exposition managers in December 1928. According to Jewett, Dawes convinced the committee members that the exposition would "show the progress of science and its application to industries in the last one hundred years and make manifest to the public the recent important role of science in our national life." After the meeting, Jewett immediately endorsed NRC involvement in the fair and urged the NRC executive council to establish a much larger advisory committee, one representing the breadth of pure and applied sciences as practiced in the nation's universities and industries. [11]

Six months later, at the University Club in New York City, Jewett presided over that new advisory committee, now called the Science Advisory Committee (SAC) and funded entirely by the exposition corporation. Thirty-two eminent scientists and engineers formed the nucleus of this group, which also included representatives from the exposition company and various business concerns throughout the country. At their first convocation, Jewett explained that the committee's task was to formulate a philosophy for the fair, recommend necessary personnel to advise exposition managers, and, should disputes arise over specific exhibits, serve as a court of appeals. By March 1930, the SAC had created thirty-four subcommittees comprising over four hundred scientists and engineers. Over the course of nearly seventy meetings, many held in conjunction with annual professional conferences, these subcommittees produced hundreds of pages of recommendations about specific exhibits and generated ideas that Jewett and his fellow SAC members organized into an overall philosophy for the fair.[12]

The nature of this philosophy was fully articulated at the final SAC meeting. Summing up the accomplishments of the committee, Jewett noted that it had produced a "philosophy of showmanship for the contributions of science and their application" that would assume visible form in a Temple of Pure Science and surrounding exhibit halls devoted to applied and social sciences. The underlying purpose of this philosophy, he added, was to offer "a quiet unconscious schooling to the thoughtful people" who visited the fair. Visitors would "pass through the fair and go out of it, largely without any consciousness of having been educated," but they would "go out educated to the idea that science is at the root of most of the material things and many of the social things which make up modern life." That education, however, was more political than scientific, more ideological than philosophical. It centered on a deification of the scientific method and glorification of anticipated scientific solutions to social problems. Michael Pupin had already given it a name: "scientific idealism."[13]

Determining how to convey this idealism to fairgoers spun SAC members into surprising areas of discussion. Jewett suggested that "if this Temple of Science were the central core of this exposition, the very center of that Temple of Science should be some great allegorical figure produced by the greatest master mind that we could find for that purpose to depict the Spirit of Science." Pupin heartily endorsed Jewett's idea and recommended an allegorical presentation of "Science as a loving mother to whom man is listening." Another scientist, W. O. Hotchkiss, president of the Michigan College of Mining and Technology, advised caution, noting that this romantic vision was hardly in keeping with the modern design of the fair. What was needed, in Hotchkiss's view, was a "type of genius that could sketch in a few lines a broad comprehensive idea as a high-type cartoonist presents an idea with a few lines in the newspapers." Ultimately, scientific idealism found aesthetic expression in the murals placed in the science building and in the architecture of the building itself, though the SAC was concerned not with aesthetics per se but with subordinating art and architecture to the social implications of the philosophy it had crafted. As Jewett had earlier informed the SAC, philosophy came first. Then the architects could "proceed to put the skin around the core of the apple." [14]

The precise meaning of the cluster of ideas that formed the exposition's core science philosophy emerged in a letter Pupin sent to exposition trustees, in which he declared: "American science and American industries welded to each other by scientific idealism are the most powerful arm of our national defense." And national defense, in the aftermath of the stock market crash, meant shoring up public confidence in the future of the corporate state as much as protecting the state from external threat. Little wonder that scientists with corporate interests at heart took up the cause of the fair with the same zeal that exposition sponsors showed for science. [15]

To implement their philosophy, the SAC and exposition management moved in several directions. With SAC approval, the management, headed by Lenox Lohr, later president of the National Broadcasting Company, placed responsibility for the installation of scientific exhibits in the hands of scientists drawn from Chicago-area universities. Lohr organized a Division of Basic Sciences and put Henry Crew, a physicist at Northwestern University, in charge. From the moment he received Dawes's invitation to join the exposition management, Crew plunged enthusiastically into his work, though several SAC members expressed reservations about his commitment to showmanship. He consulted with architects, sculptors, artists, exhibit designers, fellow scientists, and showmen in the search for ideas and exhibits that would fill the planned Temple of Science. Recalling the legitimacy that the international scientific congresses organized by Hugo Munsterberg had bestowed upon the 1904 St. Louis fair, Crew arranged for the American Association for the Advancement of Science to hold its annual meeting—termed a "carnival of science" by one exposition publicity release—at the Chicago fair. He travelled with Century of Progress directors to Europe, where they visited science museums and fairs in Glasgow, Antwerp, Liège, and Paris. In Antwerp, Crew scribbled in his diary, the Chicago exposition executives "shot the chutes . . . , rode in the electric motor cars." "Great fun," he added. More to the point, Crew consulted with numerous European exhibition planners and met with such renowned researchers as Niels Bohr and Max Planck for advice on how to display complex theoretical ideas to the public. His inspiration, however, came less from the world of theoretical physics than from the example set by the British Foreign Office in demonstrating British imperial prowess at the Antwerp fair. After seeing the map of the British Empire, Crew confided to his diary: "Raised the question . . . of doing for the history of science—or, if you like, the Empire of Science, at the Chicago Fair—something similar to the horizontal panorama, illuminated by electric lamps from below." [16]

The SAC, having accomplished its primary mission by issuing a formal plan to exposition trustees, remained involved with the exposition for another year. From November 1930 through May 1931, the SAC produced thirty fifteen-minute nationwide radio broadcasts—required listening in many college science classes—that promoted scientific features at the fair and the gospel of scientific idealism generally. The executive secretary of the NRC, Maurice Holland, for instance, told radio listeners that "science is a modern Aladdin's lamp whose light illuminates the path of progress." In another broadcast, John Goetz, representing the National Industrial Conference Board, played down the threat of technological unemployment and stressed the centrality of science to social welfare. Were listeners worried about food and clothing shortages as the Great Depression worsened? F. W. Tanner, a biologist, promised relief through applying improved industrial bacteriology to food and linen production. The utopian thrust of these programs culminated in the remarks of F. K. Richtmeyer, dean of the Cornell University Graduate School. "Truly," he told the radio audience, "scientific research pays large dividends. There is no telling when a scientific Columbus is going to discover another America." Or as Goetz put it: "One must be entirely insensible to the achievements of the past to doubt that the future is bright with promise." Similar messages continued to reach the public even after the SAC ended its formal participation at the end of 1931, as the exposition's publicity department kept newspapers and magazines abreast of scientific exhibits planned for the fair.[17]

By opening day, the official guidebook to the fair had distilled the received scientific wisdom into a terse epigram: "Science Finds—

Industry Applies—Man Conforms." This message reverberated throughout the entire fair as numerous ceremonies, exhibits, and even the design of the buildings themselves made science, industry, and progress into a new holy trinity for the modern age. The fair actually opened with a scientific "miracle" dreamed up by exposition manager Lenox Lohr. To make the opening of the fair as dramatic as possible, Lohr arranged for observatories around the country to beam light from the star Arcturus to photoelectric cells that in turn produced electric impulses carried via Western Union lines to the exposition. Arcturus, or Job's star, was not just any star; it was chosen for symbolic reasons. The light received by the observatories had left Arcturus forty years earlier, at precisely the moment President Grover Cleveland had opened the 1893 World's Columbian Exposition.[18]

Just as science opened the fair by recalling the cultural authority of the past, so the language of scientific idealism suffused the architecture of the Century of Progress Exposition with a powerful cultural message. The fair, visitors were told, constituted a "huge experimental laboratory" in design and construction. Neoclassical forms of earlier expositions gave way to a modern and—in the case of the Administration Building, guarded by heroic statues depicting industry and science—even "ultramodern" aesthetic. "Windowless," the guidebook noted, "these buildings assure, by virtue of the advancement in the science of interior lighting, that on no day of the Fair, no matter how dark and gloomy, can visitors be deprived of the full measure of beauty in interiors and exhibits." Modern industrial design, visitors were led to believe, would "bring cheer and liveliness to workers in factories." Specific exhibits—including robots, working auto assembly lines, and the rocket-shaped cars of the Sky Ride—added weight to the message that science was modern man's salvation and that the scientist-engineer was priest, if not savior. The place of formal scientific worship, originally conceived as the Temple of Science, had by opening day become a place of study as well as a place of inspiration and had been christened the Hall of Science.[19]

The ceremonies held to dedicate the Hall of Science underscored the significance of science for the Century of Progress Exposition. Ceremonies began with a playing of the building's carillon, the beauty of which persuaded one visiting South African to have a duplicate built and installed in the Pretoria City Hall. At the striking of the last note, a choir of Chicago schoolchildren sang the "Prayer for America." Then Bernard J. Sheil, auxiliary bishop of Chicago, delivered an invocation which Dawes followed with a short speech lauding NRC support for the fair and praising the SAC report. Henry Crew spoke next and ex-

Hall of Science: opening day ceremonies,
Chicago, 1933. Courtesy of the University of
Illinois at Chicago, University Library, A
Century of Progress Records.

plained the purpose of the ceremonies: "We are here . . . to dedicate ourselves to the spirit of this report and to the original theme of the Fair." To dedicate the structure, Crew called Jewett to the podium.[20]

Jewett spoke at some length concerning the service of science to civilization and noted that any effort to prevent the growth of science would surely fail. "This would be so," Jewett explained, "even if many of the things of science did not themselves involve irresistible forces destined to bring about that widespread correlation of operation which we have come to designate as monopoly." Science, as the handmaiden of monopoly capitalism, could not be restrained. Given this dictum, his next proposition followed logically: "every new bit of scientific knowledge acquired is an addition to the strength of the social structure and not a revolutionary threat to the existing order." Public understanding of the "place and influence of scientific progress," therefore, was essential, for it would assure "continued support of the quest for new knowledge and new things" and "simplify the solutions of many problems." Public understanding of scientific progress would moreover, serve to stabilize the general political culture. Jewett left this last corollary unstated, but the finale to the dedication ceremonies left no doubt as to its presence in the minds of the Hall of Science designers. Just after Jewett concluded his speech by declaring that "this fair offers a unique opportunity for service," the choir sang "Ecce Sacerdos Magnus" and Dawes invited the audience to sing the "Star Spangled Banner." That evening, neon light illuminated the Hall of Science in red, white, and blue.[21]

For visitors to the Hall of Science, the value of science to American progress was everywhere on view. Immediately outside the U-shaped building, located on a prime nine-acre site just inside the main entrance to the grounds, stood a heroic fountain entitled *Science Advancing Mankind*. It depicted "the figures of a man and woman being advanced by Science—a powerful robot—with its hands at the backs of the two [human figures]." Once inside the building, visitors found two floors of exhibits devoted to mathematics, physics, chemistry, biology, geology, and medicine. The ground floor, which housed the medical exhibits, also displayed exhibits of "industrial applications of science."[22]

The separate guidebook issued for the Hall of Science recommended that tourists, before examining any of the exhibits, pause to study the central mural in the Great Hall. It depicted the tree of knowledge "[bearing] fruit in the shape of Applied Sciences which depend upon the roots—the Basic Sciences"—and set the stage for the scientific morality play that unfolded in the rest of the building. After sampling

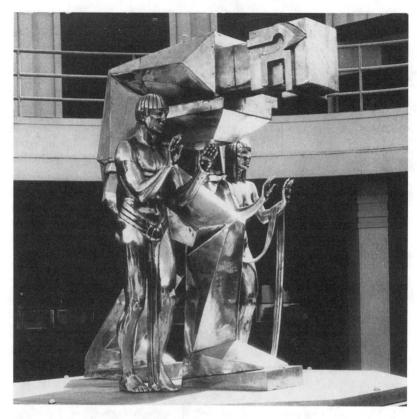

"Science Advancing Mankind," Chicago,
1933. Courtesy of the Smithsonian
Institution, National Museum of American
History, Edward J. Orth World's Fair
Collection.

the forbidden fruit, fairgoers were not expelled from paradise, but invited into a scientific Eden to discover for themselves that the "unity of
the basic sciences" rested on the experimental method, or "common
sense," and to realize that "there is nothing mysterious in science." Inside Eden, they were told, scientific grace was democratic, available to
anyone "willing to examine the facts and exert his intelligence to follow
the logic of the explanation." Numerous exhibits tested this conviction.[23]

"A Scientific Miracle," Chicago, 1933; Rufus Dawes (second from the left). Courtesy of the University of Illinois at Chicago, University Library, A Century of Progress Records.

After they had made their way around the periodic table of the elements that formed the base of an enormous revolving globe, fairgoers were encouraged to solve the "weekly paradox" in the mathematics division, thrill to the "romance of oil" (complete with a working model of an oil refinery), examine magnified microorganisms in the Microvarium, and understand the principles behind television as explained in the physics section. The building also housed a "theater of science" that amused spectators with pageants of scientific discovery and application, including an enormous model radio station. By the time visitors stood face to face with the six-foot-tall Transparent Man in the medical section, they saw themselves exposed before a powerful deity—the modern god of science.[24]

If nothing else, this shrine had been designed to instill in visitors a faith in the power of science. But what of the redemptive service of science so heralded first by G. E. Hale and then by Jewett in his dedicatory address? The more complete answer to the question lay across the lagoon from the Hall of Science in exhibits devoted to the social sciences and technology.

Buildings beyond the Hall of Science were planned with one fundamental goal in mind: to convince fairgoers that America had progressed and that scientists would continue to guarantee American progress into the future. Immediately across the lagoon stood the Hall of Social Science, where Fay-Cooper Cole, a University of Chicago anthropologist and NRC member, had, with the help of Howard M. Odum, a sociologist at the University of North Carolina, supervised exhibits showing how social science could resolve the problems caused by rapid industrial change and smooth the way to the future.[25] That social scientists' recommendations for the future followed directly from the route already taken in the recent past became evident in the displays that Cole directed. Harvard University anthropologists, for instance, installed a physical anthropology laboratory to measure visitors at the fair and enthusiastically proclaimed that they would lead the world to perfection. "So crowded was [the laboratory]," one fair official exclaimed, "that appointments often had to be made a day or two in advance." To give Americans an idea of the distance already traveled, Cole organized an exhibit of five living groups of Native Americans, put them under the direct charge of a local real estate speculator, and placed the resulting Indian Village adjacent to an exact replica of a Mayan Temple, between the concession avenue and the automobile manufacturing exhibits. The Indians were supposed to "live primitive existences as their ancestors did before them." An exposition publicity release summed up the intended effect: "The General Motors tower rises, a bright orange tribute to Modernism, over the wigwams and tepees and hogans of the oldest Americans, over the dances and feathers and beads in the Indian stadium. . . . 'What a distance we have come,' is the theme of the World's Fair, but nowhere does it come home so sharply to the visitor as when he attends the Indian ceremonials." Reminiscent of Frederic Ward Putnam's attempts to popularize anthropology at the World's Columbian Exposition, Cole's efforts added an important layer of affirmation to the definition of American progress laid down at the fair. Social science in the service of corporate visionaries, it seemed, could only perpetuate a racist morality by converting victims of American progress into sources of popular entertainment.[26]

Scientific exhibits at the Century of Progress Exposition stressed the theme of service to American civilization, but service in fact meant serving the needs of the modern corporation. Although scientists

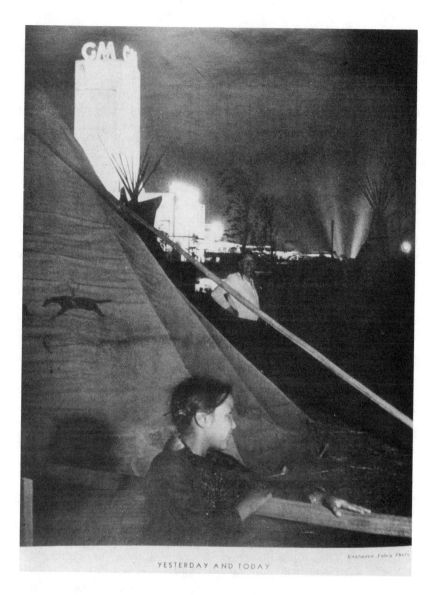

YESTERDAY AND TODAY

Progress, Chicago, 1933. From World's Fair
Weekly, *3 September 1933, p. 4. Courtesy of
the National Museum of American Art.*

preached social responsibility, a SAC memo had made clear as early as 1929 that responsibility centered on stabilizing the body politic. From the start, the science exhibits were intended to exemplify "the idea of scientific and industrial unity" and to inject "system" and "order" into the exposition and by extension, into American culture as a whole. The impact of the fair on 32 million visitors over the course of two years is difficult to assess, but Franklin Delano Roosevelt, for one, had no doubt about its value. He urged the continuation of the fair into 1934 and appointed several world's fair scientists to serve on his newly created Science Advisory Board. Indeed, as chapter 6 makes clear, the exposition medium became so central to the political culture of the New Deal that Roosevelt endorsed and participated in succeeding expositions in San Diego, Dallas, Cleveland, San Francisco, and New York. At each fair, promoters continued to extol the virtues of the scientific method, praise the unity of science and industry, and underscore the value of this combination for bringing the depression to an end. At the New York World's Fair, this formula became more than remedy for the depression; in the hands of several NRC scientists and corporate boosters, it became a prescription for utopia itself. As exposition president Grover Whalen declared: "By setting forth what has been beside what is, the fair of 1939 will predict, may even dictate, the shape of things to come."[27]

Planning for the New York World's Fair began in 1935, close on the heels of the Chicago celebration. From the start, New York World's Fair designers decided to recast the philosophy developed for the Century of Progress Exposition into a new mold that would make science seem even more integral to American culture. Instead of building a central shrine to house scientific displays, they decided to saturate the fair with the gospel of scientific idealism by highlighting the importance of industrial laboratories in exhibit buildings devoted to specific industries. So confident were exposition executives of their ability to organize science exhibits from their own industry-run laboratories that at first they saw no need to involve the larger scientific community in planning the fair. Their overconfidence, however, nearly backfired.[28]

Scientists quickly realized that their position in planning the New York World's Fair was a far cry from the full partnership that industrialists had granted them in 1933 when building the Chicago exposition. Scientists suddenly found themselves facing instead a corporate take-over of the cultural prerogatives that they had asserted at the earlier fair. As it became increasingly clear that science, but not necessarily scientists, would determine the shape of the 1939 fair, the outcry from the scientific community, already reeling from cutbacks in federal research money, reverberated throughout exposition headquarters in the Empire State Building. Speaking for many of his colleagues at Columbia University, the chemist Harold Urey expressed outrage that instead of allotting space for a science building, exposition designers provided space for the "meaningless symbol of a sphere." "The world of tomorrow," Urey wrote with specific reference to the planned Trylon and Perisphere, "will be built by ideas and not by meaningless symbols such as a sphere with a long shaft beside it." [29]

Confronted by this unexpected uproar, which threatened to undermine the scientific credibility of their undertaking, the exposition promoters moved to defuse criticism. They appointed Gerald Wendt, an acclaimed chemist and scientific popularizer, as Consultant on Science and empowered him to organize an Advisory Committee on Science (ACS) that would, in Whalen's words, "guide and strengthen and extend the plan for science." Once constituted, the ACS looked like a compact version of the earlier SAC in Chicago. Indeed, with the exception of Wendt, the NRC-based leadership of the SAC carried over largely intact. Frank Jewett, Gano Dunn, and Maurice Holland assumed important posts representing industry, engineering, and industrial research. Two additional SAC members joined Wendt's group of advisers: Karl Compton, president of the Massachusetts Institute of Technology (MIT), agreed to represent physics, and the never-modest Waldemar Kaempffert, science editor of the *New York Times*, agreed to represent the public. Rounding out the committee were a chemist, R. H. McKee; a botanist, Edmund W. Sinnot; a zoologist, Robert Chambers; an educator, Paul Mann; and a specialist in industrial exhibits, Charles Roth. Together they made the voice of science heard at the New York World's Fair. [30]

At the first ACS meeting in March 1938, exposition managers described their plans in detail and received assurance from the committee that their overall ideas for scientific exhibits were "excellent" and "very reassuring in view of the general impression that science will be ignored at the Fair." The main problem in the eyes of ACS members was the manner of presentation. As they understood the plans of exposition promoters, science exhibits "would be in horizontal layers" throughout the fair, and the ACS would have "to find a means for connecting these layers vertically, that is, for cutting through the various applications of science, to single out and connect with each other the pure science incorporated in them." The solution to this dilemma came directly from the Century of Progress Exposition. The ACS proposed establishing a separate building for science.[31]

As simple as it seemed, the proposal for a separate structure dedicated to science brought the already existing controversy with academic scientists to a head. Suspicious that a separate building might imply recognition of an independent function for scientists, exposition managers dragged their feet over this proposal and claimed they lacked the space. Kaempffert, however, would have none of that argument. He wrote an editorial in the New York Times calling attention to the area recently vacated by Nazi Germany and urged that it be set aside for a science hall. Science displays, he added, "should not be left to industrial companies alone, not because their primary and natural concern is the heightening of their prestige, but because they have not the requisite knowledge of the history of science, of the social effects of discovery and invention, of educational values and of the theatrical devices that can be legitimately employed to drive home the story of man's technical ascent." For Kaempffert, unlike the protesting professional scientists, this controversy had nothing to do with scientific expertise or with the control of science in corporate America. In his eyes, scientists simply made better historians, sociologists, and entertainers than did industrial designers.[32]

Whether exposition planners found Kaempffert's line of reasoning persuasive, it alerted them to the high level of distress in scientific circles over their plans. Rather than further alienate the scientific community, managers agreed to a compromise of sorts. They offered to convert a preexisting building—though not the German structure—into a hall for joint displays devoted to science and education. There was, however, a catch: the authorities refused to provide funds for exhibits. Since federal funding for science had reached its nadir, this decision left the ACS with three alternatives. They could operate without funds, or they could seek private funding for exhibits, or they could abandon their role in the fair altogether.[33]

For Wendt and his ACS colleagues there never was any question about which avenue to pursue. In June 1938, Wendt provided the committee with detailed and positive reports concerning the exposition promoters' plans for science at the fair and expressed his own willingness to seek funds from various foundations. Plans for scientific displays in industrial exhibit halls, he assured his colleagues, had already reached an advanced stage. Each major exhibit building—the so-called focal exhibits dedicated to Community Interests, Production and Distribution, Transportation, Communication, Foods and Nutrition—would "adequately cover the social consequences of science" and visitors would everywhere be struck "by the pervading influence of science" in the fair. Virtually all of the corporate exhibits, he continued, would include "striking science features" in their own halls of science, and Westinghouse had plans for a working laboratory for high school students. Even such noncommercial buildings as the Children's World planned "well-equipped demonstration rooms, workshops, and museums for the major branches of science." Given this situation, Wendt saw continued ACS involvement as essential:

If this is done we shall achieve a large social objective and may influence the course of American thinking for the next generation. Our goal—the full integration of science with society—is so high that success will be priceless. It is well worth the sacrifice of those specialized professional interests that have demanded a science building and have expected the World's Fair to engage in the active teaching of science. It is thus our intention to demonstrate in the Fair that scientists are not merely scientists, but are indispensable members of the social structure and the foundation of the world of tomorrow.[34]

As Wendt realized, sacrificing "specialized professional interests" was easier said than done. To head off criticism from that quarter, he took the important precautionary step of inviting Albert Einstein to serve as the nominal chairman of the ACS. Until opening day, Einstein played no discernible role in the fair—indeed he never attended a single ACS meeting. Yet, as the personification of pure science, Einstein's name affixed to the ACS roster had the effect of making the advisory committee's mission seem not only serious and authoritative, but objective and independent as well. As Wendt and his colleagues knew, however, their mission was fundamentally cultural, and its success depended upon developing a theme that would bring order to the diversity of science exhibits on the fairgrounds.[35]

The irony of the exposition, Wendt recognized, was that its promoters intended "to integrate science thoroughly with all phases of life, but the more successfully this integration is done, the more science will tend to disappear from the consciousness of the visitor." To rectify the paradox, Wendt proposed an exhibit in the Science and Education Building exemplifying "what should be the outstanding theme for all science, namely its dependence on research."

At this stage of history, it seems inadequate merely to show that applied science depends on pure science. Public education should be carried one step further, namely to a simple but convincing portrayal of what research is, i.e., the instinct of curiosity and creation, plus the "scientific method" of thinking and experimenting. A dramatic presentation of the scientific method would have repercussions far beyond the field of science itself, for science can show that the secret of its success is research and imply that research is therefore the key to the future of society.

To dramatize this theme, Wendt's committee worked closely for the next six months with the education committee, headed by Harry Woodburn Chase, chancellor of New York University. Most of Wendt's energy, however, went into writing a popular book explaining the importance of science at the fair.[36]

Science for the World of Tomorrow, published by W. W. Norton just in time for the opening of the fair, offers remarkable testimony to the guiding ideas that shaped the scientific presentation at the New York fair. It represents an even more remarkable summary of the efforts by scientists over the course of the depression to ground popular faith in America's future in the cardinal principles of scientific idealism—an ideology perhaps better termed scientific pragmatism. If, in Wendt's view, modern man was "struggling feebly to be the image of a distant deity," that was no reason to despair. Man had only to realize that his "outstanding achievement has been in the use of his intelligence to improve the environment of human life." "If we are similarly to add to the content of Life," he added, "visions of humanity will have to be still greater but will also have to be subject to the test of reality." Wendt's admonitions—applying intelligence to improve the environment, testing ideas against reality, and using the scientific method to improve society—constituted a statement of faith in the central tenets of scientific pragmatism. His wholehearted identification with pragmatic values shone through his proposed remedy to the chaos threatening to engulf humanity. "The detached study of human affairs," Wendt declared, "seems the only solution to the problems of humanity. It is for this reason that the age of science will not be here until science is an integral part of a valid American culture."[37]

Implementing a scientific utopia would be difficult, Wendt conceded, but not impossible. He provided a concrete example of what he had in mind by contrasting the plight of the housing industry with the triumph of the automobile industry. "The obstacles to change [in housing]," he wrote, "are great and involve many established interests, such as the enormous number of individual architects and of small contractors, the practices in the real estate and subdivision business, present housing regulations and the demands of labor organizations, the lack of large housing corporations and the failure to perceive that a house is a machine for living." This situation, he argued, represented "an ideal instance of a great social problem which could easily be solved by the methods which science has so successfully used in its struggle with nature. The problem is definite. The facts are known. The automobile industry has shown an example. The conclusions are inescapable." "What America needs most," Wendt announced, "is a Henry Ford for the American Home." In the hands of right-thinking, science-minded corporation executives, in short, the scientific method could become the means for creating a "true American culture." Science could become a way of life and utopia would be nigh. Evidence for this proposition abounded at the fair.[38]

Had starlight opened Chicago's fair? Wendt believed that the opening of the New York fair could be equally spectacular. At his suggestion, cosmic rays replaced Arcturus and Einstein threw the switch that illuminated the main buildings on opening night. Soon thereafter the amusement avenue opened with another compelling scientific demonstration. Current generated by an electric eel, wired for the occasion in the New York Zoological Society exhibit, ignited magnesium flares along the Great White Way. Indeed, the scientific message was so pervasive that it soon reached self-parody in one midway show, the Congress of Beauties, where Yvette Dare had trained a macaw named Einstein to remove her bra at the sound of tom-toms in the neighboring Seminole Village. Corporate exhibitors bent on paving the way to utopia also blended entertainment into their serious educational displays. Westinghouse, for instance, in addition to its high school laboratory, introduced fairgoers to Moto, the mechanical robot, while General Motors transported them on moving chairs through its Previews of Progress and Casino of Science. Countless murals, statues, and motion pictures also had science as their theme. Even the abstract Trylon and Perisphere were intended, in Whalen's words, to offer visitors "a glimpse of the community of the future—a future conditioned by science." But the footings of the ideological construct presented at the New York World's Fair rested firmly in the Science and Education Building.[39]

The Science and Education Building, Grover Whalen proclaimed at its dedication ceremonies, "constitutes the true focus of the New York World's Fair more definitely and accurately than any other exhibit in

*Science and Education Building, New York,
1939. Courtesy of the New York Public
Library, Astor, Lenox and Tilden
Foundations, Rare Books and Manuscripts
Division, New York World's Fair Records,
1939–40.*

the 1216+ acres of exhibits." The *Scientific Monthly* was equally blunt, informing prospective tourists that the building "answers the fundamental question as to what science really is and reveals the secret of its success. This is, of course, the 'scientific method.'" To reveal this secret, the ACS determined to dramatize the story of aviation in the wing of the building turned over to science. As visitors entered the structure, they stood in a rotunda dominated by an aluminum airplane supported by a pillar with fourteen medallions depicting the pure sciences that contributed to aviation. Around the rotunda were transparencies showing the contributions from the applied sciences. From the rotunda, visitors walked into the main hall of science, where seven glass transparencies illustrated the "scientific method of thought." Each depicted a scene from the history of scientific discovery, including astronomy, oceanography, and atomic research, and all were intended to demonstrate "the extent to which scientists go in securing reliable knowledge."

"The thesis"—and note that the panels had a thesis—"is the direct one that science is a method of achieving success by straight thinking." The intended effect, however, was expressly religious. As a publicity release explained: "Striking in design and rich in color, they might well serve as stained glass windows for a cathedral of science." In this sanctum sanctorum of scientific idealism, one message was clear: "Facts plus imagination, tested by experiment, yields a conclusion. Truth is accepted without fear. From the conclusion arises still new facts; and, in their train, new industries, new social conditions, new problems." [40]

But if truth lay in changes wrought by scientific discovery, how should human beings respond? To answer that question, scientists turned the show over to the committee on education. The committee included the university presidents Robert Gannon of Fordham and Edward Elliot of Purdue, social scientists Howard Odum and James T. Shotwell, and such noted educators as Lyman Bryson of the Teachers College of Columbia University. They had a one-word answer to the problem of social change—adjustment: "As science is the best use of the human intelligence to study and improve the environment of human living, so education is, broadly speaking, the effective adjustment of the individual to his environment." The education exhibit, consisting largely of panels and murals, "featured the responsibility of citizens in a democracy to keep pace with this changing world and the necessity for regarding education as a life-long process." Above all, the exhibit stressed that education "is not merely an institutional activity" and highlighted the value of the radio, motion picture, and theater for providing "extra-curricular" instruction to Americans. When seen in light of the scientific exhibits, the lesson of the Science and Education Building—and an overriding lesson of the exposition movement of the 1930s as a whole—was crystal clear. Through the scientific method, exposition designers hoped to adjust Americans to a political culture increasingly dominated by corporations.[41]

At both the Chicago and New York fairs, scientists sought to accomplish much more than the simple transmission of scientific information. They regarded the expositions as unsurpassed opportunities for embarking on a "cultural offensive" that would create a scientific culture with pragmatic values and thus provide Americans with faith in corporate leadership and in scientific expertise. Many scientists who participated in the fairs pursued another goal as well, namely, to teach Americans that scientific and technological progress toward a future perfect world required large corporations and that judgements about what constituted progress could be left to the scientists themselves or to their corporate sponsors. Although they left Americans ill-prepared to confront the complexities of the dawning nuclear age, scientists involved in the fairs did construct the intellectual scaffolding—the normative discourse—that served to perpetuate the corporation-run state into the postwar period.[42]

CHAPTER FIVE

Future Perfect

Then one rides around and is shown the America of 1960 as Mr. Norman Bel Geddes conceives it . . . and one realizes that this paradise of the motorist will have to be constructed not by private enterprise but by a public works administration. General Motors has spent a small fortune to convince the American public that if it wishes to enjoy the full benefit of private enterprise in motor manufacturing it will have to rebuild its cities and its highways by public enterprise.

—Walter Lippmann, describing Futurama,
New York Herald-Tribune, 6 June 1939

The public can be led to realize the difficulties that industry has overcome and the benefits which they have derived from it, to the end that public opinion can become one of industry's greatest assets in the years to come. Neither science nor industry could have accomplished what has been done for the betterment of living conditions without the mobilization of capital on a large scale, and its control by competent, responsible people.

—*A Century of Progress,* promotional
pamphlet, 1933[1]

The century-of-progress expositions trumpeted the scientific progress of the preceding century, hailed the arrival of the machine age, and, despite the wreckage of the American economy, promised the "dawn of a new day" that would culminate in a far better world of tomorrow if the American public would entrust the design of the future to the combination of powerful interests responsible for designing the fairs. For all of their utopian rhetoric, the century-of-progress expositions were ideological constructs designed to gain broad public support for "the mobilization of capital on a large scale." The century-of-progress fairs represented a powerful defense of corporate capitalism as a modernizing agency that would lead America out of the depression towards a bountiful future.[2]

Mobilizing capital on behalf of world's fairs made perfect sense in the context of the stock market crash. As Fred L. Black, a Ford Motor

Company executive responsible for overseeing the Ford exhibition buildings at the various fairs, recalled the decade: "There was a possibility of revolution." Corporate executives were not alone in their concerns. On the eve of the opening of the 1933–34 Century of Progress Exposition, one of President Roosevelt's political operatives informed the White House that Chicago was fraught with tension: "The city is experiencing parades of teachers and at times parades of communists and the unemployed." By mid-decade, a wave of industrial violence swept the country and any thought that politicians and business leaders could relax their vigilance vanished abruptly. The social and political strains of the decade crystallized in 1938 when the ten-mile-long preview parade of the New York World's Fair, complete with a motorcade with cars from every state of the union, was forced to obey traffic signals at the intersection of Thirteenth Street and Seventh Avenue in downtown Manhattan while one hundred thousand May Day paraders cut across its path. There were no reports of any disturbances, but the May Day parade highlighted what world's fair organizers already knew, namely that they could not automatically assume mass support for their vision of the world of tomorrow. Their preview parade was, in fact, part of what New York World's Fair president Grover Whalen described as "the job of 'selling the Fair.'" That job, in turn, was bound up with another—the task of selling Americans on the idea that the vision of the future projected at the fairs was worth pursuing.[3]

The idea of selling the future through world's fairs seized the imaginations of corporate executives who committed millions of dollars to underwriting the fairs and to mounting impressive exhibits at the expositions. Ford Motor Company alone spent between $13 million and $14 million on its exhibits. As Fred L. Black recalled: "The only criticism I ever received from [Edsel Ford] the entire time was when I tried to save some money." Other business leaders followed suit, spending extravagant sums to construct futuristic exhibition halls and hire industrial designers to stock them with process-oriented displays that would convince Americans to modernize by consuming the products of American industry and the visions of future abundance that accompanied them.[4]

Fundamental to this effort was an assault on remaining vestiges of values that were associated with what some historians have called a "culture of production." To hasten the dissolution of this older emphasis on restraint and inhibition, already under siege by world's fairs at the beginning of the century and by the steady barrage of advertising that saturated the country during the 1920s, world's fair builders in-

*Grover Whalen. Courtesy of
California State University,
Fresno, Henry Madden
Library, Department of
Special Collections.*

jected their fantasies of progress with equally heavy doses of technological utopianism and erotic stimulation. In pavilions like "Democracity"
and "Futurama" at the New York World's Fair, technology appeared
as a democratizing force that would simultaneously require a cadre of
experts to assure the rational operation of intersecting social, economic,
and political forces. As if to liberate these fantasies from their Victorian
moorings, exposition promoters gave increasing prominence to female
striptease performances on exposition midways that, by the end of the
decade, gave way to fully nude female performers in shows replete with
world-of-tomorrow themes. Condemned by vice crusaders and period-
ically raided by local police, these shows had the effect of increasing
exposition gate receipts and heightening the modernistic impression of
the fairs. By suffusing the world of tomorrow with highly charged male
sexual fantasies, the century-of-progress expositions not only recon-
firmed the status of women as objects of desire, but represented their
bodies as showcases that perfectly complemented displays of futuristic
consumer durables everywhere on exhibit at the fairs.[5]

Erotic stimulation might act as a solvent and liberate consumerist
fantasies about the future, but supercharging visions of future abun-

dance at the fairs with linked images of sexual and technological energy ran the risk of heightening popular anxieties about the direction of American society. To assuage those anxieties and to assure visitors that the welfare of the American people was uppermost in their minds, exposition masterminds turned to the federal government for assistance in developing exhibits that emphasized the concern of the world of tomorrow builders for its citizens.

Like so many of his predecessors, President Franklin D. Roosevelt understood the power of the expositions to frame public opinion. His own role in planning world's fairs dated to the 1915 San Francisco exposition when he served as the head of the U.S. government's national exposition commission. As president, he saw the fairs not only as opportunities to popularize specific New Deal programs, though federal exhibits certainly did just that, but as institutions for reinforcing the legitimacy and durability of the nation's political and economic institutions. In his complex pas de deux with the nation's business leaders, Roosevelt found in the expositions an opportunity, surpassed only by his radio addresses, for reaching the public with his message about the advantages that would accrue to the nation from cooperation between corporations and the government. The fairs put the New Deal on view, especially its promise of economic recovery and political stability that would follow from a commitment to rational planning by corporations and the federal government for the future. New Deal planners joined world's fair organizers in developing exhibits that held out the promise of a future perfect society—a promise that was wholly conditional on popular acceptance of the blueprints for the world of tomorrow laid down at the fairs.[6]

Obscene is not quite the right word, but the discrepancies between the wealth and power, not to mention the streamlined glamor, manifest in exposition buildings and the grim economic conditions of the depression can still jar the senses a full half century after the New York World's Fair closed its gates. The vast sums of money that went into these revelries of corporate capitalism underscored the differential impact of the depression on American social classes and highlighted the commitment of those atop America's economic pyramid to defusing the potentially explosive political situation that confronted them during the 1930s. As one Chicago world's fair executive declared: "In studying over the significance of this Exposition I have become convinced that we are offering one of the greatest opportunities for industries and in- vested capital to lay the ground for a more sympathetic attitude on the part of the public and for resisting foolish and radical legislation that has ever occurred." From the beginning, the century-of-progress expo- sitions were conceived as festivals of American corporate power that would put breathtaking amounts of surplus capital to work in the field of cultural production and ideological representation.[7]

The 1933–34 Century of Progress Exposition was one case in point. The idea for a fair to commemorate the 100th anniversary of the founding of Chicago originated with city civic leaders in the mid-1920s. After several false starts, two brothers, Charles and Rufus Dawes took charge of exposition planning and contributed materially to the narra- tive structure of the fair. Both men had made fortunes in oil and bank- ing. While Rufus had tended the family's corporate empire at home, Charles had turned his attention to politics, becoming Calvin Coolidge's vice president and Herbert Hoover's ambassador to En- gland. On the strength of the brothers' reputation, Congress, in Febru- ary 1929, endorsed the idea of holding a world's fair in Chicago, but made its support contingent on world's fair sponsors mustering $5 mil- lion to guarantee the financial solvency of the exposition organization. By November, despite the crash of financial markets the previous month, exposition authorities could boast that they had secured "$12,176,000 for the payment of the principal of an issue of Guaran- teed Gold Notes," adding that "[o]f the notes so authorized to be issued more than $5 million in principal amount has been subscribed for by responsible persons, firms and corporations. . . ." No trifling amount in the best of times, these millions of dollars were a king's ransom in the immediate context of October's Wall Street crash.[8]

Where did these moneys come from? British consular officials tried to provide their government with a clear answer. "General Dawes him- self was instrumental in raising the guarantee fund to a sum of ten million dollars, which he achieved in the middle of the panic on the New York exchange," one diplomat declared in amazement. Another British foreign service officer was more specific: "Big Business now gives its wholehearted support to the 'Century of Progress' as the scheme has been re-christened." The roster of guarantors that Dawes assembled read like a *Who's Who* of Chicago's power brokers. Among leading individual subscribers were three men, financier Julius Rosen- wald, Charles Dawes, and Rufus Dawes, who owned a third of the

*Lenox Lohr. Courtesy of the
University of Illinois at
Chicago, University Library,
Lenox R. Lohr Papers.*

notes between them. Major utilities, railroads, and oil companies, along with leading mercantile establishments guaranteed the remaining issues.[9]

Financing the fair was one thing; bringing it to life was another. To oversee their operation, Charles Dawes personally selected a young military engineer, Lenox Lohr, to serve as the fair's general manager.

Lohr, while not exactly a household name, was well known in the boardrooms of corporate America. After serving on the battlefields of Europe and teaching at West Point, Lohr edited *Military Engineer* and turned it into one of the leading engineering journals—one that counted a growing number of corporate executives among its subscribers. As editor, Lohr promoted the image of the engineer as a public servant and the corporation as an ideal organizational form. As he tried to build the stature of the journal and the Society of Military Engineers, the professional society that published it, Lohr became acquainted with General—then Vice President—Dawes and succeeded in helping the latter become president of the military engineering society. Dawes was so impressed by Lohr's right-thinking managerial prowess and fiscal talents that he decided to turn the general operation of his fair over to him. With Rufus serving as exposition president and Charles initially serving as the chair of the finance committee and subsequently as the power behind the throne through his contacts in foreign capitals and

120

Congress, the trajectory of the fair was set right at the outset. With its total construction and operation cost running close to $100 million, the fair would explode on the American scene in 1933 with the force of a supernova and establish Lohr as America's leading authority on world's fair management. It would also secure his reputation as an "engineer of mass education" and, after the fair's close, propel him to the presidency of the National Broadcasting Company and Chicago's Museum of Science and Industry.[10]

As civic and business leaders in Dallas, San Diego, Cleveland, San Francisco, and New York learned that the Chicago fair had employed 22,000 people during its months of construction, boosted Chicago retail sales by 19 percent, and returned a $160,000 profit to its investors, they determined to match, if not surpass, the triumphs of the Dawes brothers. They proceeded in much the same fashion as Chicago capitalists, turning to private and corporate sources of wealth to launch their exposition projects and calling in Lohr and members of his staff as consultants. In Dallas, control of the 1935 exposition fell to a "triumvirate" that included bankers Nathan Adams, Fred F. Florence, and Robert Lee Thornton, president of the Mercantile National Bank. In San Diego, banker Frank G. Belcher ran the show, while in Cleveland, W. T. Holiday, president of Standard Oil of Ohio, oversaw the operation of that city's century-of-progress exposition.[11]

Meanwhile, San Francisco's captains of finance and industry joined forces and selected insurance executive and Stanford University trustee Leland Cutler to direct their exposition enterprise. When Cutler learned that exposition sponsors would have to raise $760,000 within thirty days to secure federal support for their undertaking, he quickly assembled the exposition's directors. At a meeting of sixty directors in the boardroom at Standard Oil, the president of the giant oil corporation, who also served as the exposition's director of finance, asked each member of the board to contribute $15,000. The president of the Bank of America, A. P. Giannini, was more emphatic. He "stood up and said if the sixty present didn't give $900,000, he would give it all." After Giannini's spirited remarks, the directors agreed to the $15,000 amount and Cutler secured the federal moneys that enabled exposition sponsors to build a fair that would be as much a work of propaganda—a propagation of faith in corporate America—as a celebration of Bay Area bridge-building feats.[12]

Not to be outdone by their peers and rivals in other cities, New York World's Fair organizers mined sources of private and corporate wealth that only Manhattan could boast. Their success was such that the ever-exuberant Whalen could exclaim: "the money poured into the project is beyond the astronomical calculations of the wildest New Dealer. It is going to be a World's Fair to remember forever—or end World's fairs for all time, as you prefer." An early promotional pamphlet conveyed the same message with more specifics: "Preliminary activities have been financed through loans totaling approximately $725,000, negotiated with nineteen New York banks, some of which have officers or directors who are also officers or directors of the Fair Corporation." Indeed, as banker Harvey Gibson, head of the exposition's finance committee and president of the 1940 New York World's Fair, made clear to the affluent dinner guests assembled into a "fair court" at the Hotel Astor, the initial financing of the fair was provided by a "small group of men" who included the cream of New York's world of finance. Given the wealth and power of their primary underwriters, exposition organizers had little difficulty incorporating and receiving legislative authority to issue securities valued at $27,829,500. When the drive to sell securities stalled, New York banks again came to the rescue and purchased the outstanding issues, thus launching an enterprise that would cost some $40 million more than the Chicago fair.[13]

Powered by the captains of industry and finance and buttressed with the authority of leading scientists, all of the century-of-progress exposition organizers proceeded to cast their nets for exhibits and construction funds from major corporations. If the promise that the fairs would champion the cause of large concentrations of corporate capital was not sufficient enticement, exposition sponsors sweetened their offer to potential corporate exhibitors. To foster the image that the future would be guided by industrial cooperation, not cutthroat competition, sponsors of the Chicago fair broke with the precedent of earlier fairs and offered corporations free space to construct pavilions. That offer turned the trick. Corporate executives tumbled over each other in the rush to secure prime building sites. Contrasted with the nine corporations that set up displays at the 1893 exposition, twenty corporations built pavilions at the 1933 Chicago fair and, together with corporations that bought exhibit space within pavilions constructed by the fair, expended close to $33 million in the process. With the help of a growing cadre of "organization men" that included architects and industrial designers, the Chicago fair and each of its successors became theaters of operation for massive public relations campaigns to make the future seem unimaginable apart from the modernizing influence of American corporations.[14]

Their campaign to modernize America took form most immediately and visibly in exposition architecture, as some of the nation's leading architects crafted exposition structures that gave the appearance
of being "a regular knock-out of revolutionary protest against time-
honored architectural traditions." The modernistic results, while hardly
revolutionary, gave a distinctive feel and look to the modernizing process that unfolded at the fairs.[15]

This modernistic style, inspired by the European expositions discussed in chapter 3 and developed in the context of the search by corporate manufacturers for distinctive styles that would differentiate
largely similar products, debuted at the 1933 fair after a great deal of
debate by the architectural commission—a veritable supreme court of
distinguished building and landscape designers, including Harvey Wiley
Corbett, John A. Holabird, Raymond M. Hood, Paul Philippe Cret,
Ralph T. Walker, Arthur Brown, Jr., Edward H. Bennett, Daniel H.
Burnham, Jr., Hubert Burnham, Chevalieer Vitale, and Joseph Urban,
with exposition trustee Dr. Allen Diehl Albert serving as its secretary
and representative of the Dawes brothers. Albert insisted that the exposition's architecture break with neoclassicism and offer "proof of
courage and the spirit of progress." What that meant, according to
Lohr, was that buildings would be "designed to create an effect based
primarily on usefulness. New elements of construction, the products of
science and industry, would be the vehicles of achievement." The structures, in other words, would reflect what historian David Nye has aptly
termed the spirit of corporate modernism.[16]

The architects, trained for the most part in the American beaux-
arts tradition fostered by the World's Columbian Exposition, approached their assignment gingerly. One of the early designs for the
Administration Building, the first building to be completed on the exposition grounds, treated it as "an old fashioned steamboat" and failed
to impress Albert. The architects proceeded to consult with some of
their younger colleagues, especially Louis Skidmore, who catapulted to
the post of chief of design. Skidmore and some of his Chicago peers
suggested that the architecture of the fair frankly embrace a function-
alist, machine-age aesthetic and dress it in a blaze of colors. "The result," as Allen described it, was "the transformation of the Mississippi
steamboat into a modern office building of admirable practical utility."
From Allen's perspective, what was especially appealing about the
structure was the absence of windows and the necessity for artificial
lighting, in short, the possibility of creating a controlled environment
apart from natural limitations. "In its original nakedness," Allen ob-

served, the Administration Building "gave a definite shock to most observers." Other architects immediately caught the spirit, and windowless structures proliferated on the exposition grounds. As Corbett explained: "An exposition, being temporary in nature, theatrical in character and viewed by millions of people in the holiday spirit gives the designer his one chance of . . . creating a willingness on the part of the public to accept more rational and less stylized ideas." With their functional designs highlighted by brilliant red, blue, yellow, and white paints, the overall effect of the buildings became clear. For Allen, the "splendid symphonic crash of colors suggests the great moment in Wagner's *Rheingold* when Thor strikes the rock from which leaps the rainbow bridge spanning the Rhine." An architectural critic reached for a more contemporary metaphor to describe the buildings and suggested that the brilliantly colored structures of the fair amounted to nothing less than a billboard come to life. And, as numerous exhibits made clear, what that billboard advertised was a way of life governed by the admonition: "Modernize." [17]

At every turn, fairgoers were bombarded by pamphlets urging them to make use of the latest scientific research in industrial laboratories to modernize their kitchens, store fronts, and even their figures. The General Electric model kitchen held out the hope that the kitchen could be "as comfortable, efficient and time-saving as the modern office" if properly equipped with electrical appliances. Bearing the title "Freedom," the exhibit's souvenir pamphlet contrasted the drudgery of yesterday with the salvation provided by contemporary technology:

> Yesterday! The kitchen clock tolls away a woman's life. Toil worn hands, scarred by labor, monotonously dip into a greasy dishpan. . . . Today! A youthful hand that defies the years, touches a switch and a brilliant room is flooded with light. Clean, beautiful, efficient . . . every inch of this kitchen is arranged to save woman's steps. Magic electric servants work for her . . . she *directs* and they *do*. Her days are her own . . . her hours are free! World progress is marked and measured by man's success in lifting the burdens of daily life from his family, and there has been no greater achievement than that of vanquishing the dreary hours of household drudgery.

By modernizing their kitchens through technologies developed by engineers, the pamphlet continued, women could actually find time to entertain, not in the dining or living rooms, but in the kitchen itself: "Now days most informal home gatherings end in the kitchen! . . . It is the new guest room in the home." [18]

The task of modernizing America would not stop with the kitchen. In the "industrial and household arts" section of the fair, a group of thirteen houses conveyed the message that the American home would have to be transformed to lift the nation out of the depression. Highlighting the group were George Kerk's "House of Tomorrow," a steel and glass design complete with hanger for an airplane, and Howard Fisher's prototype for General Houses, Inc., a prefabricated dwelling that held out the promise of affordable housing to the masses. As historian Brian Horrigan describes the "dual image" projected by these designs: "Both had great potential appeal in depression-era America, the one offering escape into a voluptuous Hollywood future and the other promising industrial recovery and universal homeownership." In the hands of other designers, guided by exposition managers, these images were reworked into powerful formulas for modernizing the country.[19]

The Formica company, for instance, invested its product with layers of salvation potential. "Be Profit-Wise! Modernize!" its brochure intoned. From office walls to store fronts to countertops, the text declared, "Formica is helping those who have buildings to sell or to rent, to get a profit. It has eye appeal. People are drawn to it . . . It has the element of flash and appeal which frequently adds many times its cost to the rental or sale value of property." Furthermore, it "gives any room a very rich and handsome appearance—a real atmosphere of modernity and up-to-dateness." It "will make your place seem really modern," the pamphlet stressed.[20]

Other manufacturers highlighted similar themes. General Foods Corporation developed an exhibit "appropriately attuned to the modern spirit" and developed a veritable theater presentation for its food products. On a revolving stage mechanism, sixteen two-minute shows displayed a variety of goods. "As each of the shows is coming," a press release announced, "sliding aluminum doors close amid a splendor of changing colored lights focused on the front of the stages. At the same time, gigantic packages in full relief, towering ten feet above the stages, move in review until the beginning of the next series of shows. . . . For instance, when the Post Toasties performance is being enacted, the huge Post Toasties package stands directly above it." Product subordinated to process, quality to packaging, information to entertainment—the General Foods show perfectly captured the machine-age component of the modernizing strategy that unfolded at the Century of Progress Exposition and was evolving into a prescription for an American way of life.[21]

General Foods exhibit, Chicago, 1933.
Courtesy of Yale University Library,
Manuscripts and Archives.

A vital component of this modernizing strategy, consumer research as an aid to improving the public relations of corporations, came to light in the Bell Telephone exhibit where company officials, keen on promoting long-distance telephoning, made it possible for fairgoers to make souvenir long-distance telephone calls from the company's pavilion. There was a catch to these free calls, however. As the long-distance operator made clear in introducing the callers: "This is a souvenir call from the Bell System Exhibit at a Century of Progress; other people are listening. Go ahead, please." With up to fifty fairgoers and company researchers listening in on receivers, numerous callers telephoned friends and family around the country, giving phone company officials invaluable information about what people said in "social" long-distance conversations. "Simmered down," one company researcher concluded, "the cargo of this long-haul telephone traffic was comprised, in the main, of one single item—emotional thrill." Finding ways

126

to sustain that thrill became one of the chief concerns of phone company public relations experts who set up motion picture cameras
throughout their pavilion to monitor the movement of crowds around
particular exhibits. They also hired demonstrators with a "Ph.D. in
Showmanship" to make the public "telephone conscious" and studied
the "reception accorded [the displays] by the public" with alterations
"immediately made when it was believed an improvement in the
attention-attracting features could be effected or clearness added to the
explanations." For company officials, the exhibit proved a successful
experiment in "human nature and psychology" that did exactly what it
was supposed to, namely, "impress people with the influence of the
telephone upon the social order." [22]

At each of the smaller fairs that followed in the wake of the Dawes
brothers' triumph in Chicago, exhibition planners continued to ham-
mer home the message that modernizing America would hasten economic recovery and stabilize the social order. Each of the subsequent
fairs included variants on Chicago's modernistic architectural forms.
Dallas exposition officials received advice from Lenox Lohr and Louis
Skidmore and studied Daniel Burnham, Jr.'s report on the 1931 Paris
colonial fair before proceeding with their own eye-catching distillation
of coloniale moderne and machine-age forms centering around the
State of Texas Building, the towering Federal Building, the Esplanade
of States, and exhibition halls constructed by major corporations. In
San Diego, where exposition planners made use of many Spanish
colonial-style exhibition buildings constructed in Balboa Park for the
1915 fair and added new coloniale moderne structures designed in
pseudo-Mayan, Aztec, and Native American styles, they also included
corporate exhibition halls minted in the Chicago mold. Cleveland's
Great Lakes and International Exposition followed suit, becoming a
showplace of modernistic industrial architecture and industrial products dressed in the latest machine-age designs. No less carefully scored
than their Chicago predecessor, these regional fairs were intended to
keep Americans marching to the modernizing beat of an increasingly
public relations-conscious corporate America. By the close of the decade, the tempo increased and reached a crescendo-pitch in the New
York and San Francisco world's fairs—expositions that their promoters
believed would "work together as a major centrifugal force in getting
Americans to see America and buy more of its products." [23]

While the Golden Gate International Exposition confirmed American dominance over Latin America and idealized a community of interest with European imperial powers in the Pacific Basin, its promoters

Great Lakes and International Exposition,
Cleveland, 1937. Courtesy of the Hall of
History Foundation.

joined these visions of overseas empire with the machine-age promise
of economic abundance and leisure. Exhibits of automobiles, industrial
products, and foodstuffs overflowed from exhibit halls so as to suggest
that the "good life" would follow from popular acceptance of the blueprint for the Pacific Rim offered at the fair. To strengthen that argument, exposition planners included two closely related exhibition palaces, the Vacationland Palace and the Hall of the Western States.

Tower of the Sun, San Francisco, 1939. Courtesy of the Library of Congress, Prints and Photographs Division.

The Vacationland Palace, with its motto, "All Outdoors Brought Under One Roof," was the creation of America's transportation industries. The Southern Pacific Railroad built a scale-model railroad that wended its way through dioramas of western landscapes. Not to be outdone, Union Pacific developed an exhibit that advertised its newest resort, Sun Valley, Idaho. The intent of these exhibits was clear. As one official publication explained the purpose of Vacationland shows, they were designed to show "Recreation as the Heritage of the Machine Age."[24]

In the Hall of Western States, adjacent to the pavilions of the Pacific Basin area, eleven states echoed the theme of Vacationland and developed exhibits that hinged the promise of recreation to the development of extractive industries. California and Idaho exhibits emphasized "potential industrial areas and natural resources of the West," while other western states emulated Arizona's example of trying to put the image of the wild West to rest. "Wild West?" the official guidebook rhetorically asked. "No! Beautiful, scenic West."[25]

Another souvenir publication made clear the precise relationship between the pursuit of pleasure and industrialization of the American West:

This is adventure, and adventure is a product of leisure, just as leisure in America is a product of industry's efficiency. So adventure sets the pace for the Fair—leisure, travel, recreation, the yearned-for opportunity to gather into one beautiful setting the color of the Western World, not at work, but living, playing, roaming over its finest country. This makes industry important only as a contributor to Romance. This makes the Fair, instead of a factory manual, a saga of the West—a Pageant of the Pacific.

Here was a fantasy of paradise regained. Adventure, leisure, industry, bound together in a romance of empire, added up to a "new deal" for the American West—a place where, as San Francisco Mayor Angelo Rossi put it, citizen-tourists could realize the "dreamy enjoyment of mañana-land, spiced with American efficiency." [26]

The reasons for idealizing citizen-tourists were twofold. In the first place, tourists spent money and that bode well for struggling economies in the American West. As U.S. Commissioner George Creel declared in an address before San Francisco's prestigious Commonwealth Club: "And if the present $250,000,000 left in the West by vacationing tourists each year can also be doubled and tripled, it means a flooding prosperity that will reach into every corner of the eleven states." Exposition promoters certainly appreciated the economic value of tourism. At the same time, they also sensed what sociologist Dean MacCannell has described as the tourists' susceptibility to suggestion. According to MacCannell: "Although tourists adopt the rhetoric of adventure, they are never independent of a social arrangement wherein a host organizes the experiences of a sight-seeing guest." Exposition directors never lost sight of the possibilities for directing seventeen million sightseers towards experiences that would reaffirm the centrality of consumption, leisure, empire, and corporate leadership to the future development of the American West. [27]

Where San Francisco's corporate sponsors projected their vision of utopia in space, New York World's Fair authorities envisioned theirs in time. With the help of a cadre of industrial designers they took it upon themselves to engineer a fantasyland about a future perfect world that would develop under the benevolent guidance of corporations and social engineers. Calling themselves "founders" and regarding themselves as founding fathers, New York World's Fair authorities set out to gain mass approval for what, to borrow an apt phrase from political scientist Langdon Winner, was becoming a modernistic "sociotechnical constitution" for the nation. [28]

Among the framers of this constitution were several leading lights of the new industrial design profession. They were Walter Dorwin Teague, Henry Dreyfuss, and Norman Bel Geddes. Under the careful supervision of Robert Kohn, chair of the exposition's committee on theme and former president of the American Institute of Architects, and with the assistance of Stephen Voorhees, chair of the fair's architectural committee, industrial designers suffused the fair with a streamlined machine aesthetic that architects translated into structures that became the epitome of corporate architecture.[29]

The central axis of the fair ran along Constitution Mall between the exposition's theme center, concentrated in the modernistic abstractions of the Trylon and Perisphere, and the U.S. government's Federal Building. Between these structures stood James Earle Fraser's monumental statue of George Washington. Designers carefully placed the statue to create the impression that Washington was gazing at the Perisphere and Trylon, "his back on years of progress, his eyes on the future. The philosophical suggestion is that with 150 years of successful democratic government, founded by Washington and the men of his generation, behind the nation of today, America can face the World of Tomorrow, represented by the huge, modernistic and unorthodox structures of the Perisphere and Trylon, with the same cool assurance that the first president exhibits in his massive sculpture." As one world's fair publicist explained: "Perhaps to George Washington the Perisphere is a huge, crystal ball telling of the 'shape of things to come.' "[30]

Within the Perisphere, a vision of the future did take shape in the form of Dreyfuss's keynote exhibit, "Democracity." Termed by the official guidebook the "symbol of a perfectly integrated, futuristic metropolis pulsing with life and rhythm and music," Democracity perfectly expressed the obsession with order that gripped world's fair planners. As the guidebook described the exhibit:

Here is a city of a million people with a working population of 250,000, whose homes are located beyond the city-proper, in five satellite towns. . . . After you have gazed at the model for two minutes, dusk slowly shadows the scene. The light falls, and the celestial concave gleams with myriad stars. To the accompaniment of a symphonic poem, a chorus of a thousand voices reaches out of the heavens, and there at ten equi-distant points in the purple dome loom marching men—farmers stamped by their garb; mechanics, with their tools of trade. As the marchers approach they are seen to represent the various groups in modern society—all the elements which must work together to make possible the better life which would flourish in such a city as lies below. The symphony rises to diapa-

*Constitution Mall, New York, 1939. Courtesy
of Nederlands Foto & Grafisch Centrum,
Spaarnestad Fotoarchief.*

sonal volume, the figures assume mammoth size; the music subsides, the groups vanish behind slowly drifting clouds, and suddenly a blaze of polaroid light climaxes the show.

Accompanying the symphony was a chorus of voices singing the New York World's Fair theme song: "We're the rising tide coming from far and wide/Marching side by side on our way,/For a brave new world,/Tomorrow's world,/That we shall build today." Variously described as "inspiring," "breath taking," and "wonderful," Democracity, more than any other exhibit, bore witness to the corporatist nature of exposition planners' dreams for America's future.[31]

As pivotal as Democracity was to the overall theme of the fair, its popularity was overshadowed by another exhibit, Norman Bel Geddes's "Futurama" inside the General Motors building. Born in 1893, Bel Geddes gained renown as a stage designer, crafting "theatres for the age of the machine," including designs for several theaters and restaurants for the Century of Progress Exposition where he also served as a consultant on outdoor lighting. On the eve of the Chicago fair, he published *Horizons*—a treatise on the power of design to integrate American life into "a huge industrial organism." "We are entering an era," he declared, "which, notably, shall be characterized by *design* in four specific phases: Design in social structure to insure the organization of people, work, wealth, leisure. Design in machines that shall improve working conditions by eliminating drudgery. Design in all objects of daily use that shall make them economical, durable, convenient, congenial to every one. Design in the arts, painting, sculpture, music, literature, architecture, that shall inspire the new era." "As we progress," he concluded, "we will combine, which means we will work with the other person's interest in mind. To-morrow, we will recognize that in many respects progress and combination are synonymous." For the rest of the decade, Bel Geddes elaborated his vision of modernity—one that caught the attention of General Motors' top executives. In 1938 they hired him to bring their mutual vision of corporatism to life at the New York World's Fair.[32]

Bel Geddes's conception for an exhibit was elegant in its simplicity and premised on the conviction that the primary reason for lack of growth in the automobile industry was the absence of adequate highways. Building "super-highways," he argued, "would enormously increase motor car usage and sales." The problem was to convince the public that superhighways were indeed desirable. To get this idea across, Bel Geddes proposed an exhibit where fairgoers would find "thrills and entertainment and—in RESTFUL COMFORT." As visitors waited to get into the building, he explained to a rapt audience of G.M. executives, they would see others "being seated by uniformed attendants in comfortable, over-stuffed armchairs." As the chairs carried visitors through the exhibit, a lecture synchronized to the chairs would inform fairgoers about contemporary traffic problems and how a system of superhighways would solve them. G.M.'s top executives were so taken by his proposal that they signed Bel Geddes to a contract that awarded him $200,000 plus expenses to oversee the design of a multimillion dollar exhibit that would become the hit of the fair.[33]

Futurama focused visitors' attention on what a modernized America might look like in 1960. As visitors sat in chairs and listened to a

Assembling the Future, New York, 1939.
Courtesy of Nederlands Foto & Grafisch
Centrum, Spaarnestad Fotoarchief.

recording describing the wonders that awaited them in the future, they had the sensation of being on board a "low-flying airplane" that carried them over an American landscape transformed by a revolutionary superhighway system. This would be a world where problems of agricultural production had been solved by science and technology, where traffic congestion became a distant memory, and where the City of the Future allowed its inhabitants abundant fresh air and light. This was "a vision of what Americans, with their magnificent resources of men, money, materials and skills, can make of their country by 1960, if they will." As journalist Walter Lippmann made clear, this was also an ingenious piece of corporate advertising: "General Motors has spent a small fortune to convince the American public that if it wishes to enjoy the full benefit of private enterprise in motor manufacturing it will have to rebuild its cities and its highways by public enterprise." Futurama, in short, was more than an exercise in technological utopianism; it was an exercise in planning the future.[34]

Futurama drew rave responses from national elites. U.S. Senators Delwin W. Smith and Arthur Capper wrote to Bel Geddes to congratulate him on the exhibit. One of President Roosevelt's cousins told the designer: "To me, it is one of the most perfect things I have seen for a long time." Herbert Bayard Swope declared: "The General Motors Show is great. Congratulations." A visiting physician compared it "with a Shakespere play or a Rembrandt painting." The show was in such demand by people of wealth and influence that G.M. executives and Bel Geddes organized special showings for prominent individuals who refused to stand in line with the masses.[35]

The show, of course, was not primarily for the affluent. Nearly twenty-seven million people waited in line as long as two hours to see the exhibit. A satisfied Bel Geddes tried to put the impact of his creation in context: "This is more people than ever saw any motion picture, more people than attended all baseball games in the country those same two summers, and three-quarters of the total attendance of the New York World's Fair." Exactly how many of these visitors were persuaded by the show's message about the need for publicly financed superhighways is unknowable, but it certainly seems reasonable to suspect that after seeing Futurama many visitors would find it difficult, if not impossible, to imagine the future apart from Bel Geddes's representation of it.[36]

As important as it was, Futurama was not the totality of Bel Geddes's contribution to the ideological template of the New York World's Fair. At the same time he was feverishly working on Futurama, he was hard at work on a closely related modernizing fantasy that took form in a concession called the "Crystal Lassies," or "A Peep Show of Tomorrow." No less a design for the future than Futurama, the Crystal Lassies, along with other erotic shows, revealed just how much the "pursuit of happiness" in the future perfect world of the century-of-progress expositions depended upon eroticized fantasies of male power.[37]

When Bel Geddes proposed his strip-show concession, he was following a well-worn path. Since the 1893 World's Columbian Exposition, America's international expositions had included erotic shows along their midway avenues. These shows ranged from Fatima's notorious—by 1890 standards—belly dance at the 1893 fair to the Dream of Stella, a painting of an oversized seminude woman with a mechanically rotating stomach, at the 1915 San Francisco Fair. With the possible exception of Fatima's dancing, none of these shows gained the notoriety of Sally Rand's fan dance at the 1933 Century of Progress Exposition.[38]

Sally Rand, born Helen Gould Beck in 1904, began her career as a dancer in Kansas City. She followed her theatrical ambitions to Hollywood where she acquired her stage name from Cecil B. deMille, who purportedly drew inspiration from the title of a Rand McNally atlas in his office. Rand found work, though never stardom, in films. After the stock market crash, she made her way to Chicago and worked as a burlesque dancer in several speakeasys where she introduced her fan dance routine. As was the case for thousands of Chicagoans, the fair held out the promise of desperately needed income and Rand asked an acquaintance who held the beer concession at the Streets of Paris midway show to help her get a job as a dancer. Meanwhile, she was developing an acute awareness of power relations in Chicago that crystallized when she read a newspaper announcement about the Beaux Arts Ball at the Congress Hotel. "There were bread lines, and people were starving," she later recalled. "Yet, women in Chicago had the bad taste to have themselves photographed in gowns they were going to wear at the Ball. One was made of thousand-dollar bills. . . . It was in such bad taste." This display of conspicuous consumption made Rand so angry that she determined to crash the party and inscribe it with her own meaning. Drawing inspiration from Lady Godiva, she hired a white horse, and rode it seminude to the hotel. As she later told interviewer Studs Terkel: "It was like saying: How dare you have a dress of thousand-dollar bills when people are hungry?"[39]

When the Streets of Paris informed her that she would not get employment with the show, the rejection notice only confirmed her perceptions of social reality and strengthened her will to confront the hypocrisy of Chicago's upper classes. "The Streets of Paris was sponsored by the high and mighty of this town, the social set," she raged. "It was all French entertainment," she added indignantly. Acting on the suggestion of her friend with the beer concession, she made the decision to crash the show's preview performance which would feature Mrs. William Randolph Hearst "giving one of those milk fund dinners." Crash it she did. The night before the fair opened, with the preview party in full swing, Rand brought her Lady Godiva act to the fair. Because no motorized vehicles were allowed on the fairgrounds, she unloaded her horse onto a boat. The rest, as she later explained, became history: "At the yacht landing of The Streets of Paris there was a little Frenchman who spoke no English. He figured that a broad that arrives in a boat with a horse is *supposed* to be there. So he opened the gate. The master of ceremonies, poor soul, figured: God, here's a woman with a horse and nobody told me about it. . . . The fanfare sounded and the MC announced: Now, Lady Godiva will take her famous ride. Music played. Every photographer in the business, especially the Hearst ones, were there. Flashlights went off and the music played, and everybody was happy." The next day Sally Rand got the job and for the duration of the fair performed with ostrich feathers to Debussy's "Clair de Lune" and Chopin's Waltz in C-Sharp Minor. When asked why she became such a hit, she replied that she owed her success to her merchandising skills. No doubt that was partially true. But those skills involved her ability to subvert meaning through the manipulation of sexual fantasies. Those same fantasies, as corporate managers and world's fair organizers discovered, could also be redirected into powerful affirmations of the new modernizing order.[40]

Perhaps the best indicator of Sally Rand's importance to the Century of Progress Exposition was that the Streets of Paris turned a profit—some estimates put the figure as high as $500,000. That staggering sum made it inconceivable to think of holding a world's fair without women performers dancing nude. When Dallas exposition promoters learned, to their horror, that Amon Carter's rival Fort Worth Frontier Centennial Exposition had signed a contract for "Sally Rand's Dude Ranch," featuring the hit of the Chicago fair herself, they scrambled for a show that could compete. They settled for a "Streets of Paris" concession of their own featuring women who, according to one newspaper editor, "wore panties that would have a hard time hiding a vaccination scar." The dreams of San Diego exposition sponsors were wetter still. For their celebration of technological progress and future material abundance, San Diego exposition builders included Zoro's Nudist Gardens, which featured a performer dressed as a robot frolicking with nude women. When Sally Rand, after her successful engagement in Fort Worth, agreed to bring her rechristened "Nude Ranch" to San Francisco's Golden Gate International Exposition, rival exposition builders in New York might have gone limp were it not for the proposal brought to them by Futurama designer Norman Bel Geddes.[41]

What Bel Geddes had in mind was nothing less than a techno-porn extravaganza that would unfold within a gigantic stainless steel crystal set in a reflecting pool. Within the Crystal Gazing Palace, as he origi-

*Sally Rand, Streets of Paris exhibit, Chicago,
1933. Courtesy of Library of Congress,
Motion Pictures Division.*

*Sally Rand advertising
General Electric air
conditioner, Chicago, 1933.
Courtesy of Hall of History
Foundation.*

Nudists and robot in Zorro Gardens, San
Diego, 1935. Courtesy of San Diego
Historical Society, Ticor Collection.

nally called it in a playful parody of the 1851 Crystal Palace, an eleva-
tor would carry a seminude woman dancer to a platform surrounded
with mirrors that would give the illusion of multiplying her striptease
act several hundred times to spectators sitting in two tiers of chairs.
The effect would be "that of a ballet of several hundred girls dancing
with inhuman precision," an early draft of the ballyhoo explained.
"The mirrors not only serve to multiply the dancer but also to enable
the spectator to view her from all sides, from above, and from below,
simultaneously." This idea for a machine-age dance that made a woman's body seem infinitely replicable like the interchangeable parts on the
assembly line embodied what legal scholar Catherine A. MacKinnon in
her analysis of pornography would later call "technologically sophisticated traffic in women" that eroticizes the structure of male dominance
while "exploit[ing] women's sexual and economic inequality for
gain." [42]

Whose gain? The answer to that question goes a long way towards

Crystal Gazing Palace, New York, 1939.
Courtesy of the Smithsonian Institution,
National Museum of American History,
Edward J. Orth World's Fair Collection.

understanding the century-of-progress expositions as exercises in ideological construction and representation and as integral to the efforts by national elites to preserve dominant gender relations well into the future.

As his fantasy took shape, Bel Geddes knew he needed to raise a significant amount of capital to secure a concession contract from New York World's Fair authorities. In late 1938, the well-connected Bel Geddes approached "the C. Douglas Dillon crowd" with his idea. With Dillon as its "queen bee," this "crowd" represented a stratum of financial and political power that is rarely associated with underwriting striptease shows. But lawyers Frances Waite, Worthen Paxton, Benjamin L. Webster, and George Woods were convinced that the concession would reap enormous profits and agreed to become Bel Geddes's partners in incorporating the Crystal Gazing Palace, while a number of their associates, including some of New York's most prominent attorneys, joined together and invested nearly $75,000 in the show.[43]

What Bel Geddes's partners agreed to was spelled out in their official application for a concession from the fair: "Here is a glorified peep show, with the viewers standing in pairs looking through a slot into a brilliantly mirrored room where a seminude dancer, cavorting about on a stage, in the center of space, is reflected hundreds of times from dozens of angles—the effect being that of a ballet of several hundred girls working with the precision of the Rockettes." Little wonder a newspaper could report that several of Bel Geddes's unnamed friends "suggested he call his 'strip show in good taste' *Sexorama* to harmonize, one presumes, with his *Futurama*." [44]

Bel Geddes designed the show—a veritable "Peep Show of Tomorrow," according to one of its sponsors. He also hired the "girls," including Eve Arden, who had performed with Ziegfeld's Follies and would shortly get the lead role in "Our Miss Brooks." Ever the showman, Bel Geddes invited several hundred prominent New Yorkers to a debut cocktail party for his "prismatic contribution to the Amusement Section" and announced that the party would feature "Mary 'My Heart Belongs to Daddy' Martin" and the crystal lassies themselves. [45]

Once opened, the "Crystal Lassies," as it was renamed to avoid duplicating the name of another concession, became a major topic of discussion in the press and among moral reformers. In Goose Creek, Texas, the *News Tribune* repeated the barker's spiel for its readers: "Come on in; you'll like our show if you're not too bashful or the governor of Michigan. I see children in the crowd, so I can't describe further, and you'll have to use your imagination. You've all got imagination, ain't you?" The *Brooklyn Eagle* offered this teasing assessment: "The same showmanship which has made General Motors' Futurama the most popular exhibit at the Fair is responsible for the Crystal Lassies peepshow in which, by the use of mirrors, an undressed young woman, dancing on a glass butte, is multiplied and reflected until the spectator sees her about 800 times, which should be enough nudity for anyone's 15 cents." A correspondent for an Indiana newspaper agreed: "I should also add that with all the artistry the girls are among the nudest of the Fair's performers." Such accounts led Harry Bowlby, a minister from Brooklyn and a member of the Lord's Day Alliance, to "make it my business to make an investigation of some of the places in the Amusement Area which I had reason to believe were violating the laws of common decency and proving a menace to morals." In a letter to exposition authorities, he specifically complained about the Crystal Gazing Palace. "I saw a number of young women come on the stage with flowing robes," he reported, which the dancers proceeded to remove, exposing "on the front of the small trunks they wore over the most private part of their anatomy . . . the words in large letters AMUSE-MENT AREA."[46]

The centrality of nude women to Bel Geddes's design became clear when world's fair managers, under pressure from moral reformers and the police, issued a directive demanding that performers in the Crystal Lassies and other erotic shows wear bras and "net coverings." Rather than complying with the order, Bel Geddes quickly saw the publicity value of the directive and claimed the mantle of high art for his show. He posted a notice on the dressing room mirror that "told the girls that the wearing of brassieres was vulgarizing the show and that they should discard them." He similarly told them that the nets were "vulgar and obscene" and should be removed as well. By turning the rhetoric of morality back on his critics, Bel Geddes was able to buttress the modernizing appearance of his show and focus attention on its emancipatory effects from an era of Victorian sexual repression.[47]

Other concessionaires followed Bel Geddes's lead. At the Enchanted Forest concession, two policewomen reported, the barker stressed the artistic quality of the show, adding: "Of course many sins are committed in the name of art" and that there would be "No cover charge, only an uncover charge." At the Cuban Village, according to undercover police reports, the "man at the mike in making his bally invites patrons to see the 'Prohibited Cuban Dancers.'" Another inspector reported that the "girls in the Ice Show were absolutely nude except for a g-string." The ballyhoo for the Sun Worshippers concession caught the spirit of the shows and the reality behind their creation: "It's spicy, breezy, naughty, but—oh, so nice! The garden of unadorned, unashamed beauties . . . dancing and prancing about, dressed as Eve was dressed when she met Adam. . . . You can stay as long as you like and take pictures too. A beautiful man-made paradise."[48]

In their criticism of Bel Geddes's show, and the half-dozen or so other striptease shows, including the "Dream of Venus," "Living Magazine Covers," and "Extase," moral reformers and vice-squad officers missed the point in two ways. First, they misunderstood the significance of these shows for the efforts by world's fair promoters to equate entertainment with the "American way of life"—a phrase reiterated time and again at the fair. As one world's fair executive explained it, the amusement zone was "a symbol of the new appreciation of the American Way which has been stirred up by the tragic events abroad." "This is particularly true of the Amusement Area," he continued, "where the 'pursuit of happiness' attains its most literal and most down-to-earth

Ballyhoo for Midway Strip Show, New York,
1939. Courtesy of the Smithsonian
Institution, National Museum of American
History, Edward J. Orth World's Fair
Collection.

form of expression—in laughter and fun." Second, the problem with
the shows was not nudity per se, but the way the "harem illusion"
reproduced dominant power relations between men and women. One
newspaper captured the effects of the Crystal Lassies' production: "As
the spectator peers through the window, he has the 'illusion' of being
the only looker, for the 'one-way mirror' on the strip through which he
looks, prevents seeing anyone else on the circumference of the octa-
gon." In this private male fantasy world where so much depended on
the gaze and where women were presented as sexual commodities, a
crucial ideological building block of the modern world—and of the
world of tomorrow—was reproduced. Functioning less as a mirror
than a map, to borrow a phrase from MacKinnon, the Crystal Lassies,
like the other strip shows at the New York fair, indulged overwhelmingly male audiences in erotic fantasies of domination and acquisi-
tion—the very fantasies that comprised organizing principles of the
century-of-progress expositions themselves.[49]

The almost routine nature of these fantasies that targeted women's

*Living magazine covers,
New York 1939. Courtesy of
the Smithsonian Institution,
National Museum of
American History, Edward J.
Orth World's Fair
Collection.*

bodies as commodities to be purchased and as sites for "the pursuit of happiness" was evident in the fashion displays at the fairs. At the Chicago fair, for instance, the Formfit Company, makers of "foundation garments" that included "Thrill" brassieres and "Sleek" girdles, displayed a modernizing architecture for the female body that seemed to bear a close resemblance to the architecture of the fair. Advertising materials informed women, especially those who "are stout" with "superfluous weight," that "your excess flesh must be gently restrained into smooth, firm contours." [50]

Fantasies of streamlining women's bodies soared to greater heights at the New York fair where the World of Fashion was located directly across from the Trylon. As early as 1938, at a "World's Fair Night" extravaganza, the daughter of a local hair stylist "wore her hair shaped to resemble the trylon and perisphere." In no time at all, the "upswing" coiffure came into vogue and a "world of tomorrow" rage seized the imagination of fashion designers. Women's hats in the shape of the New York World's Fair theme center and dinner jackets with Trylon and Perisphere designs dotted the windows of Manhattan boutiques. "Architectural perfection in spun-rayon slack sets," was how one fashion design firm described its world's fair creations. World's fair officials went so far as to license a dress with block print designs of numerous world's fair buildings that stood side by side with Manhattan skyscrapers and assorted patriotic emblems.[51]

Industrial designers also got into the act. In response to an invitation from *Vogue* to design clothes for the "woman of tomorrow," Walter Dorwin Teague, Henry Dreyfuss, and Raymond Loewy, among other prominent designers of the fair, let their fantasies soar. Looking to the future, Teague predicted "near nudity" and designed a dress he believed would be appropriate—one that combined "Cellophane and an opaque 'Tecca' fabric." For his part, Dreyfuss constructed an ideal of woman-as-plaything. "Women will still want to be dolls at night," Dreyfuss declared, and designed, in his eyes, suitable clothing and attire—a dress with a "transparent net top" and a compact case in the form of a propeller fan. Under the heading "Donald Deskey Forsees a Great Emancipation," the famed designer of Radio City Music Hall forecast the triumph of streamlined bodies in America's future. "Bodies scientifically beautified. No underwear," he exulted. But what if women's bodies weren't trim enough for their designs? Loewy had a ready reply rooted in the "fitter family" movement of the previous decade: "eugenic selection may bring generations so aesthetically correct that such clothes will be in order." [52]

Determined to be in the advance guard of this "aesthetically correct" generation, fashion designer Alphonse Berge applied his fantasies to women's clothes on view in the World of Fashion. As he described a model wearing his "Beach mode of 1960" creation: "Beneath a transparent beach coat designed to repel the sun's rays, she wears a rayon acetate crepe bra with fluorescent spangles and abbreviated, cut-out bathing shorts of the same material." Or there was his "Queen Guinevere hostess gown," which he detailed with these remarks: "The full skirt is slit in front to reveal pantalettes beneath. Above the bodice is a broad metal collar set with electric bulbs, while on her head is set a transparent plastic turban, also set with bulbs." And, if that was not modernistic enough, he also displayed a "dancing dress of rayon crepe which reaches halfway to the knees and has a swallowtail back. A pliofilm jacket and 'centurion' helmet of the same material adds a 'Flash Gordon' motif to the costume." In the World of Fashion, techno-porn gave way to techno-fashion—with similar results, confirming historian Lois Banner's observation about women's place in American society during the interwar years: "Increased liberation had occurred, but only at the cost of the further commercialization of beauty." [53]

The world's fairs of the 1930s, especially the New York World's Fair, are often singled out for their presentation of new technological innovations to the American public. The fairs were certainly awash in new technologies appropriate to rebuilding consumerist fantasies. But the New York World's Fair, like its predecessors, also made clear that industrial designs went hand in hand with designs on women. At the century-of-progress expositions, body politics—the politics of women's bodies—framed the techno-social constitution mapped out for the world of tomorrow no less than fantasies of technological perfectionism. Put another way, Futurama and "Sexorama" were mirror images of each other and integral to the modernizing strategies of world's fair planners. With the help of New Deal government planners, the expositions' modernizing designs received a powerful stamp of political legitimacy and were incorporated into the political culture of the nation.

The dynamic interplay between the century-of-progress expositions and the Roosevelt administration has never been fully appreciated and should put to rest whatever remains of the myth of an irreconcilable rift between business interests and the New Deal. Had Roosevelt been interested in distancing his administration from corporate designs on America's future, he could easily have refused to endorse the participation of the federal government in the fairs. That decision would have had several immediate effects. First, it would have made it impossible for exposition promoters to secure the official participation of foreign governments in the fairs. Second, it would have made it highly unlikely that public works funds would have been used on behalf of the fairs, as, for instance, in San Francisco, where public works moneys were used to prepare the Treasure Island site for that city's fair. Refusal by the government to participate in the fairs would have saved millions of dollars in federal funds that were required for constructing U.S. government buildings, installing displays, and organizing military spectacles at each of the fairs. Had Roosevelt wanted to challenge corporate America, he could have done so in a grand symbolic gesture that would have distanced him from his immediate predecessor in office, Herbert Hoover.

Hoover, at the urging of Charles Dawes, had authorized government participation in the Chicago fair. In an earlier incarnation as secretary of commerce in the Coolidge administration, he had fought long and hard for federal funds for the Sesquicentennial Exposition. Indeed,

Hoover's early efforts on behalf of the Philadelphia fair were so appreciated by its sponsors that they offered him the presidency of their exposition corporation at a salary of $50,000 a year for five years. Conceivably, Roosevelt could have reminded the public of the utter financial failure of the Philadelphia fair and even gone so far as to suggest that its collapse was predictive of the more general economic collapse the nation had suffered under Hoover's leadership. It would not have required an extraordinary leap of imagination for Roosevelt to point to the financial failure of the Philadelphia exposition as a reason to cut funding for the Chicago fair and to refuse the offers from other aspiring exposition organizers for federal participation.[54]

As reasonable as these options may appear in retrospect, they were never seriously entertained by Roosevelt. Far from distancing his administration from the fairs or their corporate sponsors, Roosevelt embraced the exposition movement and joined its corporate sponsors to fashion the fairs into a political weapon that would sustain faith in American political institutions and build mass support for his New Deal policies. He deemed fairs so important for reaching a mass audience that he personally encouraged Chicago exposition authorities to reopen their 1933 fair in 1934. He made long journeys to Dallas, San Diego, and San Francisco to lend his personal endorsement to expositions held in those cities. And he gave the opening day speech at the New York World's Fair. Far from being ephemeral to the New Deal, the fairs served as a primary vehicle for giving the appearance of coherency to New Deal programs, for popularizing those programs, and for forging a partnership with corporate America for shaping the nation's future.[55]

The Roosevelt administration's New Deal vision for the nation rested on two basic convictions. First of all, New Deal planners were convinced that the depression had resulted from the inability of Americans to sustain the home market for agricultural and industrial goods. So they set out to build a sustained market for industry and agriculture and to establish a controlled business environment. To promote the latter goal, Roosevelt suspended many antitrust laws—an action that had the effect of encouraging the consolidation of American business. At the same time, he supported legislation that gave federal guarantees to unions to organize and bargain collectively. In other words, the Roosevelt administration sought to restore productivity through establishing a controlled business environment and to provide job security for workers that would enable them to purchase the output from the nation's factories and farms. Precisely because world's fairs encouraged

Luncheon for President Roosevelt at Treasure Island, San Francisco, 1938. Courtesy of the Library of Congress, Prints and Photographs Division.

consumer spending on travel, whetted appetites for new goods, and generally supported Roosevelt's efforts to rebuild national confidence, the century-of-progress expositions played an important role in the strategic thinking of the Roosevelt administration. As the president told the opening day throngs at the Golden Gate International Exposition: "I am quite open and unashamed in my liking for expositions." [56]

The symbiotic relationship between the century-of-progress expositions and the New Deal was clear to corporate planners and their government counterparts. As Frank G. Belcher, the president of the San Diego exposition, made clear, the San Diego fair was "principally occasioned by the tremendous construction programs now under way in the west, such as Boulder Dam, Metropolitan Water Aqueduct . . . and the Bonneville Dam projects in the northwest," all of which were intended to bring about "a tremendously increased potential population and further great development in the west." "This," he added, "may be

Dedication of Federal Building San Francisco, 1939. Courtesy of the Library of Congress, Prints and Photographs Division.

considered as the principal celebrative object of the Exposition, and, in brief, is symbolized in most of the theories and administrative efforts of President Roosevelt and the New Deal." On the administration's side, Roosevelt was absolutely explicit about his support for the corporate underwriters of fairs as evidenced by his enthusiastic telegram to New York World's Fair backers:

At this great Fair all the world may review what the United States has achieved in the 150 years since George Washington was first inaugurated as President of the United States; here millions of citizens

149

may visualize the national life which is to come. That it will be a memorable and historic Fair, that it will profoundly influence our national life for many years to come, and that success may attend every phase of its activities—these are the hopes of the people of the United States. All power to your sponsors.

Roosevelt's telling remarks concerning his support for New York World's Fair sponsors accented the depth of his commitment to utilizing the exposition medium to help Americans "visualize the national life which is to come" as well as his interest in complementing, not challenging, the modernizing visions of corporate America for the nation's future.[57]

The Roosevelt administration's fundamental interest in buttressing the blueprints laid down by corporate America came to light at the Chicago fair where the government exhibit unfolded in the monumental U.S. government building—a veritable government cathedral. With its three modernistic towers representing the three branches of the federal government, the building's exhibits recited a narrative of national progress designed to emphasize the temporary nature of the depression. Without a hint of irony, the keynote label in the Department of Agriculture section read: "Science has conquered the fear of famine and has created abundance, and now we must learn to live with abundance." Abundance, it seemed, carried a stiff price tag, but one that was well worth the cost. For those concerned about the ability of the government to use force should the occasion arise, the government constructed at the center of the fairgrounds a military encampment of over 400 troops, more than half of whom required "venereal prophylatic treatments" during their assignment to the fair. A Chicago journalist captured the intended effect of the federal exhibit in an article that was subsequently incorporated into the official government report on the fair. "The [federal] exhibition is a great patriotic service," James Bennett wrote. "It makes better Americans. I don't mean blatant 'hundred percenters,' but Americans who will be humbler, I should think, when here they view in epitome their mighty inheritance and come, please God, into the reverent consciousness that a people's possession of great riches carries with it a great obligation." "Consider thine inheritance," he reminded his readers, "and be thankful that thy lot is cast in such a land." An official exposition publication was less prosaic, but equally emphatic: "Your Uncle Sam Thinks of Everything."[58]

The only federal exhibit that sounded a slightly discordant note at the Chicago fair was the U.S. Labor Department's display. At the center of the exhibit, according to the official description, were "bronze figures of a working man and his family traveling on a spiral track around a modernized glass pyramid." As they made their ascent toward the apex of the pyramid, they passed panels that told the history of American industrialization. Just before reaching the top, a panel summed up the recent past: "The Machine displaces men. Labor's buying power drops. Production decreases. Wage cuts and unemployment destroy [living] standards." All was not lost, however. As they rounded the last turn of this modernized version of Nathaniel Hawthorne's story about the celestial railway "the upper part of the pyramid burst into flame color and revealed on the glass the goals of the future toward which the working man and his family are striving." Those goals included: "workers' participation in determining wage and employment policies; earnings adequate for living, saving, and leisure; regular employment, and economic security; health and education, and home life." This heavenly city, the exhibit promised, was just around the corner. But the explicit criticism leveled at the machine and at the nation's industrialists evidently proved offensive and led government planners to develop a labor exhibit for the next fair that fully embraced the machine aesthetic.[59]

For its display at the 1936 Texas Centennial Exposition, the Department of Labor raised the "question of whether men and machines are 'rivals or allies.'" The answer was apparent from the focal point of the display, a talking robot, that introduced itself with this disarming greeting: "How do you do, friends?" "It is true," the robot admitted, "that I, the machine, have taken the places of hand workers in some employments. . . . But in spite of that evidence, I am and can be a real benefactor to mankind. In almost every case where I appeared in industry, I actually created more jobs and provided more employment for men and women. . . . You see here examples of what I have done in providing quicker means of travel and communication, in protecting lives through automatic devices, and how I am making life easier and better for man, who is my master." Captions for illustrations around the robot reinforced the message, emphasizing that "while many men have been displaced by machines and labor-saving devices, such unemployment is usually not permanent." Another caption made this point: "labor-saving devices, machines, and mass production make possible lower costs, more sales, wider use of products." Of course, another label noted, "jobs and workers are never balanced" which was why "certain definite steps, among them unemployment insurance, public-works planning, and coordination of production are needed to lighten the load of recurring unemployment." Reforms were necessary,

*Department of Labor robot. Courtesy of the
Library of Congress, Prints and Photographs
Division.*

the exhibit stressed, but the structural dependence of the economy on
instruments of mass production and on the vast concentrations of capital that units of mass production required was absolutely sound and,
if the robot's uninterruptable message was any indication, beyond question.[60]

If one aim of the federal exhibits was to assure Americans of the
fundamental soundness of the economy, an equally important mission
was to build confidence in the ability of the government to meet the
social crisis brought on by the depression. The theme, central to all of
the government exhibits at the century-of-progress expositions, came
into sharp relief at the New York World's Fair. As Theodore Hayes, the
executive assistant to the U.S. commissioner to the fair, put it: "I saw
in this Fair a precious opportunity to revitalize, to new heights, the
fundamental faith in America of millions of Americans by selling and
reselling the achievements of Government." "From such a standpoint,"

he argued, "I believe that the United States Government exhibit will draw meaning from, and give meaning to, all the rest of the Fair." As the displays took form, they emulated the division of the fair itself and were compartmentalized into thematic zones that showed how different agencies of the government were cooperating to address particular problems ranging from food and shelter to education and conservation. As Hayes explained the narrative structure of the exhibition, it would involve "romance of high order" and tell the heroic story of the government's efforts to advance the American people's "struggle for the realization of all their hopes for physical existence over unforeseeable conditions, over want and hostile frontiers, tyranny from abroad, slavery at home, political inequality, social and cultural impediments and economic chaos." To reinforce the story of the government's victories over adversity, government planners lined their exhibit hall with mural decorations—"a mass of modernistic daubs in vivid colors," according to one government official, "infused with reverence for the nation's figures and institutions." And to highlight the government's determination to secure the national welfare, planners commissioned heroic sculptural groupings bearing the titles of the building's thematic zones. Modernistic in style, functional in content, the exhibit heralded the arrival of a welfare state perfectly tailored to sustaining the visions of corporate America.[61]

The extent to which Roosevelt was willing to go in accommodating the future perfect society projected by the century-of-progress expositions became evident in his personal appearances at the Chicago, Dallas, San Diego, San Francisco, and New York fairs. He gave open-air speeches to thousands of onlookers, while radio networks beamed his remarks to nationwide audiences. He exuded confidence, praised the visions of exposition authorities, and through the force of his own presence cemented the alliance between the modern welfare state and the modernizing and patriarchal visions of the corporate underwriters of the fairs. His deep involvement with the fairs underscored their fundamental significance for American culture as powerful vehicles of ideological accommodation and renewal. His presence, intended to restore confidence in American political institutions, also lent legitimacy to the new sociotechnical constitution that exposition authorities were framing for American society.[62]

The extent to which Roosevelt was immersed in world-of-tomorrow visions projected at the fairs and the extent to which those visions became central to American political culture became clear in his famous "Four Freedoms" speech, delivered in January 1941. In that speech, perhaps unconsciously, he evoked memories of key images that, at the suggestion of Arthur Sulzberger, publisher of the *New York Times,* had figured prominently in the symbolic universe of the New York World's Fair. For that fair, sculptor Leo Friedlander had designed thirty-foot sculptural representations of freedom of press, religion, assembly, and speech for Constitution Mall—representations that were also featured in a memorable fireworks show before the fair opened. As an exposition publicity release described the pyrotechnical display: "The set piece, depicting the Trylon and Perisphere, rose to a height of 70 feet—one-tenth the size of the original—and was surrounded by fifty floating Trylons and numerous fountains and lights, while the symbols of Democracy consisted of representations of the *Four Freedoms* sculptures of the Fair." When Roosevelt's speechwriters artfully reworked the fair's four freedoms into freedom of expression and worship and freedom from fear and want, they bore witness to the subtle influence of the fair's political symbols on the imagination of the nation's leading political figures.[63]

As Roosevelt's commitment to the century-of-progress expositions makes clear, America's world's fair builders certainly were successful in gaining endorsements from and even influencing leading political figures. But how successful were the masterminds of the fair in gaining popular approval for their visions of a new world order? Did century-of-progress exposition authorities win the hearts and minds of the American public? These were questions that Market Analysts, Inc., a public opinion research firm, never asked fairgoers in the course of interviewing several thousand New York World's Fair-goers during the late 1939 and 1940 exposition seasons. But the questions this market research firm did ask and the answers they received can, if used cautiously, help secure our footing on that slipperiest of popular culture's talus slopes: assessing audience responses.

By the time the 1940 version of the New York World's Fair closed, Market Analysts, Inc., which had been originally hired by the research division of the exposition in late 1939 to gather data to demonstrate the high purchasing power potential of world's fair visitors in the hopes of offsetting press criticism of a lower-than-expected attendance, had concluded that the attendance at the fair had been overwhelmingly middle class and that "a 'quality brand' of Americans visited the New York World's Fair." According to their surveys, one in six visitors was a professional, while one in fourteen owned or managed a business. Eighty percent had attended high school and fully half had attended college. Four percent of the visitors were unskilled workers and only two percent admitted to being unemployed. More married than unmarried people attended the fair and most fell between the ages of twenty and forty-five. More men than women attended the exposition—the ratio was 6:4. And sixty-one percent told interviewers that they owned cars. Especially impressive, according to one report, were the number of yachts docked at the fair: "During the 1939 season over 2,500 yachts, ranging from 25 feet to 120 feet, used the mooring and docking facilities of the Boat Basin." When asked for reactions to specific exhibits, fairgoers in both years selected the General Motors, General Electric, and Ford exhibits as their favorites. Very few—nine of nearly one hundred and thirty individuals interviewed for one poll—complained about the immorality of shows along the midway, while many more complained about the intrusiveness of the barkers. When pressed for more general reactions to the fair, survey gatherers were frustrated by the replies: "Here again we ran into the difficulty of getting people to crystallize their thoughts in the midst of so varied and confusing a spectacle." But there were, in the eyes of this marketing research organization, positive indications that the exposition had taken hold in the minds of those who attended the fair. Particularly significant were results showing that "companies with outstanding exhibits at the world's fair rated on average 15% higher with the public" than companies without good exhibits. Equally compelling was data showing that "[h]alf the people interviewed in August 1940 have been to the fair two to seven times—49% against 46% last [year]. It is notable that one-eighth of the people this year have been eight times and more." The high number of return visits, the research firm concluded, "indicates a high degree of approval." [64]

If the Market Analysts' reports are reliable, the New York World's Fair certainly buttressed middle-class support for the visions of the future projected by the century-of-progress expositions. But what about the responses of subordinate groups in American society? Perhaps because so many relatively affluent middle-class Americans seemed to approve the new order envisioned at the century-of-progress expositions—a new order designed to preserve, not reform, asymmetrical power relations in American society—visions of the world of tomorrow promulgated at the fairs did not go unchallenged. To counter the modernizing designs of the world's fair organizers, which included a heavy dose of machine-age racism, African Americans tried to force issues of economic justice and racial equality into the futuristic blueprints of world's fair planners. In so doing, African Americans charted a course for the future that provided an alternative route to the direc-

155

tions offered by world's fair authorities. The actions of African Americans, moreover, serve as an excellent case study in audience response, indicating how one group in American society was anything but passive in its response to the fairs and how the intentions of the exposition organizers to use the fairs as formal instruments of racial control were imperfectly realized.

CHAPTER SIX
African Americans in the World of Tomorrow

In the "World of Tomorrow," it seems that Negroes will be, for the most part, either pickets or soldiers.

—*Amsterdam News*, 6 May 1939[1]

For white Americans, at least, the century-of-progress expositions provided a welcome diversion from experience with depression-era "hard times" and promised abundance in a world of tomorrow that would be better than the world of today. For African Americans, the future forecast by white exposition authorities seemed less reassuring. As it became increasingly obvious that America's international fairs organized in the 1920s and 1930s were cast out of the same racist mold as their Victorian antecedents and continued to lend legitimacy to prevailing white supremacist values and practices, African Americans responded by developing strategies for converting these utopias of the status quo into engines for change.[2]

Recognizing the historical fact that America's world's fairs had always been battlegrounds for control of the future, African Americans tried to redirect the vision of the future projected by century-of-progress exposition authorities along lines of social justice and economic equality.[3] In addition to deeply rooted white supremacist attitudes in the culture at large, what complicated their efforts to pose an alternative to the corporate-run, white supremacist world of tomorrow on display at the fairs was that the class structure of the African-American community was changing. Traditionally, many African Americans had allied politically with upper-class white Republicans in the North or upper-echelon Bourbon Democrats in the South who shared, often discreetly, Republican ideological predilections. For African Americans, this alliance with the Republican party had translated into an anti-organized labor stance and, in international sympathies, a commitment to the Anglo-American status quo. After the First World War, this alliance began to crumble as the Harlem Renaissance and rumors of world revolution radicalized a number of African-American intellectuals. Poet Langston Hughes, for instance, underwent his own version of the "lost generation" syndrome and returned to America writing poems like "Ballad to Lenin." Historian and sociologist W. E. B. DuBois began moving to Marxism. Meanwhile, a growing number of African Americans who had joined the industrial work force in northern cities during the First World War were organizing into the militant Congress of Industrial Organizations. Growing class divisions found their reflection in politics. In Chicago, Oscar DePriest, the first African-American congressman since 1901 elected from the North and part of the Republican machine, was replaced by an African American running as a Democrat. In Harlem, African Americans began electing radicals to serve on the city council. These class divisions among African Americans—and consequent shifts in political alignment that included the massive electoral swing in the 1930s of African Americans from the Republican to Democratic parties—found expression in struggles among African Americans over their representation at the expositions.[4]

These struggles came to light at the 1926 Philadelphia Sesquicentennial Exposition, when labor organizer and socialist A. Philip Randolph gave an opening-day address. They continued through the 1940 Chicago Negro World Exposition, sponsored by the Roosevelt administration to control the growing militancy of African Americans in the 1930s. As battlegrounds for African Americans' ongoing war of position within dominant white society, the fairs reflected in microcosm the shifting political and class alignments of the period.

Shortly after the First World War, when Philadelphia's business and political leaders began developing plans for an exposition to celebrate the anniversary of the American Revolution, African Americans renewed their struggle for recognition from white fair sponsors. There were ample reasons for African Americans to be interested in the fair. Under the best of circumstances, the Sesquicentennial Exposition, or Sesqui, would have loomed large as an important occasion to remind white Americans of African-American contributions to American history, especially to the War for Independence and, most recently, to the allied victory in World War I. In addition to these incentives, another, more ominous, reason compelled African Americans to take notice of the fair. In 1925, fast on the heels of its massive parade through the streets of the nation's capital, the Ku Klux Klan announced plans to organize a national meeting at the Sesquicentennial that would culminate with a ritualistic burning of a gigantic cross on a float moored in the exposition's lake. When exposition officials approved the Klan's program, the Sesqui acquired new and dangerous significance.[5]

To combat the presence of the Klan, Philadelphia's African Americans joined forces with Jews and Catholics to persuade civic officials, especially Mayor W. Freeland Kendrick, who was also on the exposition's board of directors, to change their minds. Meanwhile, African-American civic leaders stepped up the pressure on exposition officials to give increased visibility to exhibits organized by African Americans. Exposition authorities dragged their feet until, with only eight months remaining before the scheduled opening, and with the outcry over Klan activities growing, Sesqui officials relented. They organized a Committee on Negro Affairs and appointed prominent African-American Republican leader and bank president John C. Asbury as its head. At an early meeting between African-American committee members and Sesqui officials held at the Union Baptist Church, Asbury's committee requested $25,000 to organize African-American exhibits and asked that an African-American speaker be invited to address the opening-day audience. The Sesqui's director-general, David C. Collier, ignored the request for an opening-day speaker and informed Asbury that, given the uncertain financial picture of the exposition company, no lump sum could be provided for African-American exhibits.[6]

If the absence of funds for African-American exhibits and the threat of a major Klan celebration as part of the national commemoration of the American War for Independence were not a sufficient indication, two other developments underscored the racist core of exposition planning. First, African Americans seeking employment in the construction of the fair encountered blatant discrimination. "I saw scores and scores of whites busily engaged in preparations, but not one black face," declared Nahum Brascher, editor of the Associated Negro Press. Second, there was the hypocrisy surrounding the organization of the Dempsey-Tunney fight at the fair. Initially, African Americans had proposed that a world championship fight between Jack Dempsey and African-American heavyweight champion Harry Wills be staged as part of the fair, but exposition officials and local white clergy had opposed the idea, arguing that this fight "would desecrate the stadium and detract from the sacredness of the Sesqui Centennial." When, several months later, the exposition directors had a change of heart and agreed to sponsor a fight between two whites, Jack Dempsey and Gene Tunney, the African-American press exploded with rage. City and fair officials, the *Philadelphia Tribune* exclaimed, simply wanted to be able to crown a white champion. In the context of growing frustration over the treatment of African Americans by exposition authorities, the *Tribune* hammered at the two-facedness of exposition officials and bemoaned the declining fate of African-American exhibits as members of the Negro Committee debated how to react to their treatment at the fair. In the early months of 1926, with funds still not appropriated for African-American exhibits, the *Tribune* editorialized that African Americans should "fight for proper recognition" and angrily condemned the use of public funds for purposes of securing exhibits from whites only.[7]

As the exposition's opening approached, Asbury continued to rely on his personal influence with the exposition's directors and secured minimal funds to cover the costs of transporting a handful of exhibits from African-American colleges to the Sesqui where they were arranged in the Palace of Agriculture, next to national and state exhibits organized by Japan, Denmark, and California. This modest accomplishment hardly satisfied exposition critics. "There is something wrong with this whole Sesqui-Centennial business," the *Philadelphia Tribune* observed in an editorial. "There has been much quibbling and 'craw-fishing.' The colored participation has been side-tracked, switched off and discouraged. Apparently colored people didn't know what they wanted and the white folk were determined upon a policy of discrimination." The editor would have been even more incensed had he known that five days before the editorial appeared, A. L. Sutton, the exposition's director of exhibits and a Klan sympathizer, had told the organizer of Ku Klux Klan festivities at the fair that special days had been set aside for their activities.[8]

By mid-May, it seemed as if African-American participation in the Sesqui would be minimal at best and disastrous at worst. But on 22 May, one week before opening day, Mayor Kendrick penned a startling invitation: "I have the honor to invite you to be the Orator for the Negro Race of the World at the opening exercises of the Sesqui-Centennial Exposition on Monday, May 31, 1926." He addressed the letter to the 34-year-old A. Philip Randolph, socialist editor of *The Messenger* and organizer of the Brotherhood of Sleeping Car Porters.[9]

Kendrick's invitation came as a complete surprise. Not since 1895, when Booker T. Washington delivered his "Atlanta Compromise" speech, had an African American been invited to deliver an opening-day address to a world's fair audience. And while Kendrick had been described by Asbury as supportive of African-American exhibits at the Sesqui, the mayor's actions, especially his reluctance to pressure fair officials for more funds, had often belied his words. More puzzling was Kendrick's decision to invite an African-American socialist labor organizer to share the opening day podium with Secretary of State Frank Kellogg and Secretary of Commerce Herbert Hoover. Philadelphia, moreover, was not exactly known in 1926 as a hotbed of union activity and African-American Philadelphians were relatively conservative. So, why, when "representative colored citizens of Philadelphia" asked Kendrick to invite Randolph, did Kendrick agree, instead of following the lead of Atlanta's exposition organizers three decades earlier, and inviting a conservative speaker from an African-American industrial college?

Unfortunately, the historical record is mute. Perhaps Kendrick was responding to pressure from community leaders about the involvement of the Klan in the fair and saw Randolph's presence as a way to defuse the rising chorus of protest. (Public protest, in fact, together with reports from his police department that serious riots would occur if the Klan marched, persuaded Kendrick, in June, to deny the Klan a parade permit—an action that had the effect of nullifying the Klan's efforts to convene at the fair). Whatever the reasons for Kendrick's actions, Randolph's unannounced presence on the speaker's platform proved even more startling once Herbert Hoover completed his address and Kendrick introduced Randolph to the radio audience and to the 60,000 fairgoers in attendance at the opening ceremonies.[10]

Randolph, following on the heels of addresses by prominent government officials and stalwart conservatives, pulled no punches. He began by outlining "three great outstanding problems" in the modern world: "The problem of peace between nations, the problem of peace between races and the problem of peace between labor and capital." After detailing the contributions of African Americans to building the United States, he condemned the "fallacy of Gobineau, Madison Grant and Lothrop Stoddard, the high priests of the Nordic Creed, whose racial hierarchy is implicit with social dangers, since it postulates the existence of inferior races." And, while a supporter of the Ku Klux Klan, probably Sutton, was slipping a hastily scrawled note to Kendrick urging the mayor to stop Randolph from speaking, Randolph proceeded to condemn the economic organization of modern American society. "But who are the chief victims of the misuse of economic power by the powerful corporations?" Randolph asked. "The answer is the plain people, those who work for a living"—a group that included a disproportionate number of African Americans. As Randolph put it:

161

Opening day ceremonies, Philadelphia, 1926.
Courtesy of the City Archives of Philadelphia.

"To allow any man to work and produce and deny him the benefits and protection of the society he makes possible is an inexcusable form of exploitation." [11]

To solve these problems, Randolph set out an agenda calling for "economic democracy," "collective bargaining," and "political equality." In fact, Randolph explained, African Americans would no longer be content with second-class status in American society. "In American social relations, the Negro insists upon equality, upon being recognized as the social equals of any man regardless of color, which [will] result in the abolition of disfranchisement, segregation and the abolition of the Jim Crow car." Then, Randolph concluded his half-hour address by recalling Booker T. Washington's speech at Atlanta. Whereas Washington had promised whites that "in all things that are purely social, we can be as separate as the fingers, yet one as the hand in all things essential to mutual progress," Randolph countered: "In the modern world, no people can live beside another and remain as separate as the fingers." "Mutual understanding," he added, "which can only come with the meeting of minds, is a condition of world progress." [12]

The overwhelmingly white audience was completely unprepared for Randolph's eloquent lessons in American history and his demand for civil rights. His name had not been listed in the opening-day program. Not until Kendrick introduced him did the audience have any idea that he would be speaking. His speech, moreover, according to the *Philadelphia Inquirer,* "was the longest of the ceremonies and at times his hearers manifested signs of impatience by handclapping, but upon the whole he was accorded close attention and received generous applause." Another white newspaper, *The Ledger and North American,* recorded that Randolph "was impressive in his earnestness." What these newspapers failed to record was the content of the speech itself. And whereas the white press reprinted copies of speeches by other opening-day speakers, Randolph's speech was only reproduced in the African-American press and in Randolph's *Messenger.* The censorship of the speech was, in fact, so pervasive that no mention was made of Randolph's presence, much less of his address, when Sesqui authorities published their official history of the fair. After all, Randolph had issued a manifesto for radical change, not a compromise for preserving the status quo. [13]

The African-American press was also uneasy. A few newspapers reproduced Randolph's speech, but rarely expressed editorial opinions about its content. The *Pittsburgh Courier* was an exception in its praise for Randolph's courage in presenting the "New Negro philosophy." The *Philadelphia Tribune* headlined the speech: "Booker T. Washington's Theory That In Theory Things Purely Social, White And Colored People Can Be As Separate As the Fingers Is Ridiculous." But that newspaper offered little commentary. It would seem that Randolph's "scholarly and at times impassioned" declaration of independence from Booker T. Washington proved as unsettling for conservative African-American leaders as for whites. After all, Randolph had tried to dismantle the scaffolding of the Atlanta compromise and replace it with a platform grounded in the language of class struggle and immediate equality.[14]

As Philadelphia's African-American community took stock of the Sesqui, they were left with decidedly mixed impressions. On the positive side, in marked contrast to the refusal by Centennial Exposition officials fifty years earlier to include African-American exhibits, Sesqui authorities had approved a small, but visible display devoted to African-American progress. And Randolph's prominent presence as an opening-day speaker certainly contrasted with the treatment Centennial officials had accorded Frederick Douglass when they had refused his request to deliver an opening day speech in 1876. Furthermore, if the struggle with the Klan at the Sesqui recalled the horrors of the Reconstruction years after the Civil War, Philadelphia's African-American community could take pride in its contributions to defeating plans by the Klan to use the Sesqui to fan the flames of racial hatred.[15]

Despite these accomplishments, there had been many frustrations. As if to lend weight to Randolph's assessment of the conditions that were crippling the fight for African-American progress, the practice of racial discrimination continued unabated during the exposition's months of operation and the exposition's accommodationist Negro Committee self-destructed midway through the fair over the quality of African-American exhibits. African Americans, moreover, had to endure the "Joke of the Century," as they dubbed the Dempsey-Tunney fight. And, Kendrick's decision to ban the Ku Klux Klan notwithstanding, the controversy had served as a stern reminder of the proximity of white hatred and violence.

At the conclusion of the fair, the *Tribune* tried to put the exposition experience in perspective:

Hopes ran high. Expectations were great. It is seriously questioned that the colored people used the "Sesqui" to the best possible advantage. In some quarters it is believed that the hopes were blasted and the expectations were never realized. Then there are some who say that the colored people made a comparatively good record. . . . [W]hether or not the colored people received their rightful proportion of benefits will be discussed in barber shops long after the busy mechanics have wrecked the last building.[16]

No doubt the fair was discussed in barber shops, churches, and political gatherings as African Americans pondered the changes that had taken place in their lives since the First World War. For the rest of the interwar years, as world's fairs mushroomed around the country, African Americans increasingly wrestled among themselves over strategies about the use of the exposition medium as a vehicle for bringing about a future free from the degrading practices of segregation and discrimination.

When Chicago's business leaders announced plans for a grand fair on a scale with the 1893 spectacle, that city's leading African-American politicians, business figures, and clergy determined to improve on the Philadelphia experience and direct the fair toward a positive vision of race relations in the nation's future. Shortly after learning about the exposition planned for 1933, a delegation of African-American civic leaders met exposition president Rufus C. Dawes and came away from their meeting convinced that Dawes would welcome African-American exhibits and support demands to ban discrimination in employment and in the treatment of African-American visitors. Led by Claude Barnett, editor of the *Defender,* one of the nation's leading African-American newspapers, African-American community leaders endorsed and actively cooperated with fair officials in promoting the fair. Believing he had secured a commitment from exposition authorities for substantial African-American representation, Barnett waxed euphoric about the Century of Progress Exposition. The *Defender* urged local African-American residents to help beautify the city in preparation for the fair and encouraged African Americans from around the country to visit the exposition. Cooperation with fair authorities did not stop there. As part of his advertising campaign on behalf of the fair, Barnett went so far as to organize and publicize a contest to find the most beautiful African-American woman in the country and to reward her with a free trip to the fair.[17]

As the exposition took form, however, Barnett's own world's fair correspondents came to the conclusion that the editor's wholehearted endorsement of the fair had been misplaced. From the moment construction of the fair began there were warning signs that Barnett's confidence in the exposition authorities had been excessive. During the leaden days of the depression, the Century of Progress Exposition provided thousands of jobs in construction. Then, once the exposition opened, it employed thousands in sales and service. For African-American Chicagoans, however, jobs at the exposition were virtually nonexistent. Few, if any, African Americans were employed during the building of the fair. And during the two years of its operation the number of African Americans employed on the fairgrounds was dismally low. A reporter for Barnett's *Defender,* disillusioned by developments at the fair, summed up the sense of frustration among African Americans:

There was a great shout in the land when it became known that a Race entrepreneur, Sam Hunter, had been given the washroom concessions. Everyone thought that was a good sign—that this was only a beginning. But the sad story ended with this being the beginning and the end of Race employment at the first installment of the fair.

This was no exaggeration. In 1933, only seventy-five African Americans found employment at the Century of Progress Exposition; in 1934, following the strenuous protests of the African-American community, the numbers increased to about three hundred. But with the exception of Rufus Dawes's private secretary, a handful of women who worked as maids in the model home exhibits, a smattering of African-American policemen, and African-American demonstrators in the Ford Motor Company exhibit and in the DuSable cabin, the overwhelming majority of African-American employees worked as toilet cleaners. To assure racial purity, exposition guides were actually measured at the fair's anthropometric laboratory which determined that "[n]early seventy-five per cent had that 'baby pink' complexion and skin . . ." and that the "predominantly Nordic" guides "just missed being pure specimens of the type by some slight mixture." [18]

There were additional grounds for resentment. If Dawes had guaranteed significant African-American representation in the fair, the few exhibits in evidence at the fair belied his claim. African-American universities sent industrial education displays; the National Urban League organized an exhibit in the Hall of Social Science that depicted African-American migration from the South to northern urban areas; and fair authorities installed a replica of the cabin constructed in 1779 by Jean Baptiste Point DuSable, a black Frenchman and Chicago's first settler. But overshadowing these exhibits emphasizing black contributions to national development were exhibits that "re-presented" racist beliefs and framed the outright discriminatory practices directed toward African Americans on the exposition grounds. [19]

From the moment the fair opened in 1933, African Americans were degraded at every turn. Several restaurants refused to serve them. White roller-chair pushers refused to push African-American patrons around the exposition grounds. "We have many southern boys here earning their way through school," declared one concessionaire, "and we don't

A "Century of Progress"? Chicago, 1933.
Courtesy of the Smithsonian Institution
Archives.

want to force them out of a livelihood because certain things are against their customs." Soft drink concessionaires provided beverages in glasses for whites, but gave African Americans refreshments in paper cups. Racial stereotyping even entered into common parlance about one of the most popular exhibits at the fair—the Sky Ride. "For some reason," the *Defender* reported, "the Sky Ride has taken on a 'Race' complexion. The two steel towers are named Amos 'n' Andy and the cars are named Ruby Taylor, Lightnin', Brother Crawford, Battle Axe, Madame Queen, and so on." Equally offensive was the "Africana" concession on the Midway. For ten cents, fairgoers received three chances to throw a ball through a slot that would tumble ten African Americans sitting on a plank into a tank of water.[20]

No less disgusting was the Darkest Africa concession, owned and operated by long-time showman Louis Dufour. Dufour presented an extraordinary show with the help of Bob Lucas, an African-American showman renowned for his antics with a troupe of Ubangis who had traveled extensively in the United States a few years earlier, and a Captain Callahan, who allegedly had been sexually mutilated by Africans while exploring the Congo River. The concession was constructed to

167

move visitors through various huts featuring dancing acts until they found themselves standing in front of Captain Callahan's hut. The barker lured crowds in with the following spiel:

Ladies and gentlemen, on the inside of this enclosure you will see and hear Captain Callahan, that brave and durable man who was so horribly tortured by a ferocious group of savages in the Cameroons, who were about to fling his ravished body into a steaming pot of boiling water, after a sadist beast had decapitated his penis and testicles. Please, please, just stop to think—what a terrible, despicable crime! . . . Now, please listen very carefully: everyone is invited to come in, this being the understanding—that the captain will be on an elevated stage. He will remove his robe. And after you see with your own eyes that the captain is absolutely devoid of sexual glands as I am now stating—then and only then, will you be expected to pay fifty cents to the cashiers as you pass out through the turnstiles.

When the Century of Progress Exposition resumed in 1934, one *Defender* correspondent could wonder in print if there had been a century of progress in human relations.[21]

As African-American newspapers increasingly exposed the overt racism at the fair, another set of issues came to the fore in Chicago's African-American community. Several African-American political leaders, headed by Chandler Owen, one of A. Philip Randolph's associates, persuaded exposition managers to set aside 12 August 1933 as "Negro Day" at the fair. Owen and his supporters, including Barnett, helped organize a "monster parade," a "Miss Bronze America beauty contest," and a historical pageant to commemorate African-American achievements since emancipation. As "Negro Day" approached, African-American Chicagoans divided into competing camps that reflected the strains brought on by shifting class relations and echoed the debates heard forty years earlier when Frederick Douglass and Ida Wells had disagreed about the appropriate response to a "Negro Day" at the World's Columbian Exposition. Oscar DePriest, an African-American U.S. congressman from Chicago, fearing political competition from Owen, sent a circular to the African-American press and to churches condemning "Negro Day" as a "racket" and pillorying the sponsors of the event for organizing what DePriest termed a "Negro Day Outside of the Fair." In fact, DePriest observed, the events planned for the special day were all being held away from the fairgrounds. DePriest's criticisms registered. Despite reports that the "Negro Day" celebration had widespread support in the African-American community, all but a few thousand African Americans—estimates of the crowd that participated

"Darkest Africa," Chicago, 1933. Courtesy of the Library of Congress, Motion Pictures Division.

in the day's events ranged from 7,000 to 20,000—stayed away from the festivities that were held at Soldier's Field. The *Defender* was forced to concede: " 'Negro Day' at Fair Flops." [22]

While the debate over "Negro Day" raged, the Chicago chapter of the NAACP unfolded a different political strategy for redressing the exposition's racist policies. By the summer of 1933, amidst increasing reports of discrimination on the fairgrounds, the NAACP determined that the recurrent instances of discrimination at the fair constituted a conspiracy to deprive African Americans of their rights and announced plans to file damage suits against the concessionaires and against the exposition corporation. Although they made little headway in trying to persuade the state attorney general to convene a grand jury investigation and secure an injunction against the fair and its concessionaires, local branch officials explained that "the theory of the branch is that it will apprise everybody that the branch is willing to take extreme measures for the protection of civil rights of Negroes." [23]

In 1933, the "extreme measures" announced by the NAACP had little effect. As the fair headed toward conclusion, exposition officials,

169

believing that the judicial system would not take complaints from the African-American community seriously, refused to modify discriminatory practices. The management's complacency ended abruptly when, at President Roosevelt's urging, Century of Progress officials decided to reopen the fair for another year and found themselves in the awkward position of needing support in the Illinois legislature from a handful of African-American representatives to reauthorize the private Century of Progress corporation to continue to use public land for the 1934 fair.[24]

At the special session of the legislature called in March 1934 to reauthorize the exposition corporation's use of public land, three African-American legislators threatened to delay passage of the exposition bill unless the legislature enacted a law prohibiting discrimination on the fairgrounds. With the reopening of the fair scheduled for May and with evidence of the fair's positive economic impact on Chicago's sagging economy staring them in the face, white legislators perceived the folly of lengthy debate. By a nearly unanimous vote in both houses of the legislature, legislators decreed that the world's fair "shall extend to all persons the full and equal enjoyment of the accommodations, advantages, facilities and privileges of said World's Fair, subject only to the conditions and limitations established by law and applicable alike to all citizens." Equally striking were the penalties and provisions for enforcement. Anyone found in violation of the law would be charged by the state attorney general with "operating a public nuisance" and, in the event the attorney general failed to act, the law provided that "any judge of the circuit or Superior court shall have jurisdiction to appoint a special Attorney General to prosecute said cause upon the sworn petition in writing of the aggrieved person." [25]

Much against the wishes of the exposition's managers and concessionaires and to the surprise of conservative African Americans in the community, the Century of Progress Exposition had become a laboratory for civil rights resistance. Emboldened by the legislative response to actions instigated by the NAACP, the African-American press began to demand that the law be enforced. The *Defender* recorded violations of the law and admonished African Americans to report instances of discrimination to the appropriate law enforcement officers. For the most part, African-American complaints were addressed by exposition officials and offending concessionaires were told to correct their practices.[26]

These developments had potentially far-reaching implications. For the first time in the history of America's world's fairs, a group of African Americans and their white supporters had succeeded in turning a medium that historically had been a primary bulwark of white supremacy, into a forum for challenging dominant racist values and practices. But, as the Chicago fair wound towards conclusion, a series of questions immediately arose. Could the momentum gained by the NAACP in Chicago be sustained? How would whites respond to the wedge and pivot inserted under the racist scaffolding at the Chicago fair? And, not the least nettling question: could African Americans reach a consensus about how to proceed in their efforts to redirect the future of race relations in the country?

At the close of the 1934 fair, it was already clear that partial answers to these questions were emerging in Texas, where African Americans and whites were locked in a struggle—one that would spill into state and national politics—over how to represent America's past, present, and future.

Plans for holding an exposition to celebrate the centennial of Texas's independence from Mexico dated back to the 1920s, but gained added urgency as civic leaders around the state, fastened in the grip of the depression, increasingly appreciated the economic benefits that would accrue to the city winning legislative approval as the exposition site. As the battle royal between city elites took shape in the early 1930s, an African-American business teacher at Booker T. Washington High School and head of the Dallas Negro Chamber of Commerce, A. Maceo Smith, joined forces with an African-American architect and industrial arts teacher from Houston, John L. Blount, to develop a strategy for securing funds from the state legislature for African-American exhibits at the centennial fair. They decided to support the exposition bid by white business interests in Dallas in exchange for the exposition promoters' promise to support a state appropriation for African-American exhibits as part of the general appropriation bill for the exposition. One week before the 1934 Chicago fair closed, the Dallas exposition contingent, including Smith and Blount, presented their case to the legislature. Smith's appeal for funds, like the appeal of Booker T. Washington to the U.S. Congress fifty years earlier on behalf of exposition planners from Atlanta, was heralded as "epoch-making." Smith's eloquence so impressed legislators that they allowed him to continue well beyond the allotted time and legislators generally agreed that his was the most persuasive of any presentation. Yet, despite Smith's impassioned appeal for funds, the 1934 legislature deadlocked over rival proposals from Dallas and San Antonio and adjourned without taking action on the state appropriation for the fair.[27]

When the Dallas contingent returned home, the remarkable coalition of African Americans and whites remained intact briefly as both groups tried to impress the legislature with the financial solvency of Dallas and supported passage of a $3 million Dallas bond issue to make municipal improvements necessary for the fair. What undermined this alliance of African Americans and white civic leaders was an election held to fill a vacancy in the Texas House of Representatives. When the seat unexpectedly opened and nearly seventy candidates declared interest, leaders of Dallas's African-American community decided that since the white vote would divide, an African-American candidate would stand an excellent chance of willing sufficient votes from African Americans to secure the seat. White politicos from around the state agreed with this assessment and made clear to Dallas civic leaders, white and African American, that should an African-American candidate win the election, the legislature would certainly deny Dallas's bid to host the exposition. As Smith later told historian Kenneth B. Ragsdale, white authorities told African Americans "to get the nigger out of the race . . . their condition was that if we pulled him out, they would assure us that we'd get our money to put on this Negro exhibit." Dallas African Americans refused to make a deal and paid dearly for their decision. When the African-American candidate, attorney A. S. Wells, lost the election, white exposition promoters retaliated by refusing to raise the issue of African-American exhibits with the 1935 legislature.[28]

Had it not been for Smith's leadership and the determination of African Americans around the state to take part in the centennial celebration, the matter of African-American representation at the Texas Centennial Exposition might have died at that moment. But, prior to these election shenanigans, Smith and Blount had set up local committees around the state to organize exhibits, and those committees were adamant about continuing the drive to secure African-American representation in the centennial fair. In the aftermath of the election debacle, Smith had no illusions about securing support from the state legislature. But he did realize the possibilities of appealing to the economic self-interest of white exposition authorities. Employing data gathered under his direction for the Dallas Negro Chamber of Commerce, Smith convinced exposition directors, increasingly anxious about their ability to raise sufficient moneys to make the fair successful, that African-American Texans would visit the fair and spend their dollars in Dallas, provided that the fair included African-American exhibits. White exposition officials remained skeptical, but Smith made them an offer they could hardly refuse. Smith offered the aid of his supporters in helping exposition officials sell exposition bonds, provided that some of the proceeds from bond sales be used to underwrite African-American exhibits. Furthermore, Smith wrung a concession from exposition organizers that, in exchange for this assistance in promoting bond sales, exposition authorities would make African-American exhibits part of their request to the United States Congress for federal funds to help underwrite the fair.[29]

Smith's gamble—and it was an enormous gamble given the general poverty of African Americans in Texas—failed. When even the few African Americans wealthy enough to purchase bonds refused to do so because of the high speculative risk involved, African Americans around the state became "frantic and panicky" about their prospects for representation at the fair and about possible repercussions to follow from whites who might feel betrayed.[30]

Against this backdrop of dashed hopes, Smith played his last card. When the congressional appropriation for the fair was announced, and it was clear that no provision for African-American participation had been made, Smith acted swiftly. With the exposition only a year away and African Americans sorely distressed by their apparent exclusion from centennial activities, Smith realized he would have to circumvent white exposition directors to be effective. He wrote a letter to Eugene Kinckle Jones asking Jones to intercede with cabinet-level administrators in the Roosevelt administration to set aside a portion of funds earmarked for federal displays at the fair for purposes of underwriting the costs of a Negro Building.[31]

Bold as this request was, Smith knew that Jones was well-positioned to lend assistance. Longtime executive director of the National Urban League, Jones had recently been appointed Advisor on Negro Affairs to Secretary of Commerce Daniel Roper. Jones, moreover, had long supported the organization of African-American exhibits at fairs as a stimulus for African-American commerce and industrial development. Now that he was part of the Roosevelt administration's "black brain trust," a small group of influential African-American leaders located primarily in the Commerce Department, Jones's role was to "explain to Negroes the various governmental sources to which they could turn to for aid" and to augment the general strategy of New Deal planners to encourage Americans, black and white, to spend more on more consumer items to help regenerate the American economy. For Jones and other members of the black brain trust, the idea of a Negro

Building at an exposition in Texas seemed a tangible goal and one well worth pursuing, if only to get across the conviction later expressed by Charles E. Hall, a specialist in "Negro statistics," that: "The Negro dreams of an opportunity to take a place in the sun of American opportunities rather than of the wreckage of our institutions." Smith had conveyed similar sentiments in a letter to W. B. Yeager, executive secretary to the United States commission to the fair. After explaining that African-American participation in the fair would remind Americans of the contributions African Americans had made to the nation's progress, Smith declared that participation in the fair "promises new life, new activity, inspiration, and a season of recreation which breeds loyalty and patriotism that generates interracial amity and good will, by encouraging the spiritual, intellectual, and economic ambition of a much neglected race." Smith had been even more emphatic on the issue of African-American participation in his original letter to Jones. Should the federal government fail to provide funds for the exhibit, Smith forecast that "the hopes and heart throbs of the Texas Negro citizens will be dissapated [sic] to a point that will increase the antagonism of these people toward the white man's sense of justice and fair play." Put another way, the choice confronting federal officials was funding an African-American exhibit that might help build a new political alliance between whites and African Americans in the Democratic party or exacerbating racial conflict.[32]

There was little resistance in the federal government to Jones's proposal for a Negro Building. New Deal planners, at the insistence of Eleanor Roosevelt, were becoming more concerned about the plight of African Americans and were increasingly aware of the momentous electoral shift that would occur if African-American voters shifted their allegiance from the Republican to the Democratic party. Funding a Negro Building that would be separate from the main Federal Building would have the double effect of projecting a positive image of the government interested in the welfare of African Americans while simultaneously convincing white Southerners of the government's commitment to maintaining the separate-but-equal doctrine. Furthermore, arguments about the potential to increase African-American consumer spending through the exposition were not lost on New Deal administrators. If these arguments were true about the Negro Building becoming an attraction that would restore the confidence of African-American consumers in the economy, then it made no sense to deny the request for an exhibition hall devoted to African-American displays.[33]

In the course of prevailing upon other cabinet heads to designate

$100,000 of the total $3 million federal exposition budget for the development of the Hall of Negro Life at the Dallas fair, Roper added another reason to support the exhibit. In late 1935 or early 1936, when Roper established within the federal government's own exposition commission a Negro Advisory Committee, with Eugene Kinckle Jones as chair, he made absolutely certain that the committee understood his thinking:

> I am interested not only from the standpoint of the development of the Negro, but also from the standpoint of his attitude toward the Government. One of the most commendable things, it seems to me, of your race is the fact that you always have been patriotic and always supported the American form of government. *It is not at all unlikely that there will come a time in the history of the country when the question of support of our nation's ideals will become a great and disturbing factor* [my emphasis]. This is not speaking politically, but it is very important that those divisions of our population which believe in this form of government should be kept in close touch with it and should understand its objectives and its purposes, because we will pass through periods of efforts to destroy or to supplant this form of government.

For Roper, the exhibition was an unsurpassed opportunity to ensure the loyalty of African Americans should the country go to war or—what surely seemed more likely in 1936—should the violent strikes sweeping the country threaten American institutions.[34]

Whatever Jones thought of Roper's reasons for supporting the exhibit, one point was clear: the efforts begun at the Sesquicentennial Exposition by A. Philip Randolph and continued by the NAACP at the Century of Progress Exposition to convert world's fairs into arenas for promoting social change had been derailed. When Jones selected Jesse O. Thomas, a longtime National Urban League associate and former student of Booker T. Washington, to manage the exhibit, the ideological footings of the Negro Building were set firmly in the tradition of economic accommodation and political compromise developed by Washington in the last century.[35]

In his dedicatory speech for the official opening of the Hall of Negro Life, Eugene Kinckle Jones rehearsed the rhetoric of the pre–First World War alliance between African Americans and white elites. Highlighting his own indebtedness to Washington's accommodationist philosophy, Jones asserted that the "enlightened self-interest [of whites] might yet be the firmest basis for approaching a solution to our most baffling social problems." And in sharp contrast to Randolph's emphasis on collective action by African Americans ten years earlier at the Sesquicentennial, Jones framed the problem of improving race relations in the classic language of "uplift." "Can the Negro be elevated?" Jones asked. "The Negro has proved beyond the shadow of a doubt that he can absorb and appropriate the best of American traditions and culture. Can white America rise to her own high ideals of democracy and accord to all within her borders the opportunity to appropriate the best in our national life as far as their abilities will permit?" The Negro Advisory Committee had long since joined Jones and fallen into line. According to Thomas, while the committee was "fundamentally opposed to discrimination or segregation based upon accident of birth, anywhere, or by anybody," it never "construed that it is the function of Negro participation in the Texas Centennial to completely change the social pattern of [the South]." If nothing else, these comments underscored the commitment by Jones's committee to seizing the opportunity afforded by the fair for reestablishing the commitment by African Americans to the principles of compromise and accommodation enunciated by Booker T. Washington at the Atlanta exposition forty years earlier. Like the "Atlanta Compromise," the "Dallas Compromise" provoked a storm of controversy.[36]

Despite his Washingtonian sentiments—Thomas, in fact, had been one of Washington's favorite students—white exposition officials took little solace from his accommodationist remarks. From the moment they learned of the federal government's decision to organize a federal African-American exhibition hall, fair managers adopted obstructionist tactics. As soon as word of the government-sponsored Hall of Negro Life reached Dallas, exposition officials determined at all costs to avoid having their fair transformed into a social experiment station. They refused to allow John Blount—the African-American architect who first proposed the idea of a Negro Building for the fair—to design the structure, arguing that this would require a new round of architectural bids which would violate contractual agreements with George Dahl, the exposition's architect-in-chief. They also decided to surround the building with shrubs which would segregate it from other exhibit halls. To subvert the undertaking further, fair managers left it up to a white contractor to choose the building's interior colors. When the contractor determined "that Negroes liked loud colors" and painted the interior of the building in garish reds and greens, African-American committee members had to protest to the federal commission to pressure the exposition management to repaint the walls in shades of blue and buff.[37]

To African Americans around Texas, it seemed patently clear that an iron curtain of racism was descending at the fair and several African-American newspaper editors took Thomas to task for acquiescing too readily to discriminatory practices on the fairgrounds. What made matters worse for the African Americans who originally had organized local committees to secure African-American representation in the Dallas fair was a sense that they had been bypassed by the government committee.[38]

Responding to criticism from African-American communities around the state turned into a formidable task for Thomas. He pointed to his appointment of A. Maceo Smith, the prime mover behind the African-American exhibit, as his assistant manager. Thomas also called attention to the strong letters he had written to fair managers protesting "For Whites Only" signs above lavatories on the fairgrounds and to his success in getting fair managers to remove the "Colored" signs from washrooms in the Hall of Negro Life, making that building perhaps the only public building in the South without segregated washroom facilities. Furthermore, Thomas was proud of his role in persuading the owner of sightseeing buses on the fairgrounds to provide seating, albeit segregated, for African-American fairgoers—a notable accomplishment since, when the fair first opened, the concessionaire had refused to transport any African Americans. In defense of his actions in bypassing local committees, Thomas reminded critics of the lack of time available to the government committee for organizing the exhibit. Indeed, the government had made federal funds available only in March, three months before the building was scheduled to open. Whether this delay was, as one critic put it, "an intentional flunk out" on the part of federal authorities was unclear, but it left Thomas's committee little time to work with local groups across the state.[39]

Given the shortage of time, the obstinacy of white fair managers, and the "squawking," as Thomas described it, from segments of the African-American community, the achievement of the Negro Advisory Committee was impressive. Despite its late start, the one-story, L-shaped Hall of Negro Life, with its nearly 14,000 square feet of floor space and 9,000 square feet of wall space for exhibits, was the first exhibition building to be completed at the fair. Situated midway between the General Motors Building and the Museum of Fine Arts, the building was located along the exposition's main thoroughfare and attracted more than four hundred thousand fairgoers, 60 percent of whom were white. As tour buses transported visitors around the fairgrounds, conductors barked: "To your right, you see General Motors' Exhibit; right across, is the old Globe Theatre and English Village, and just in between, the Hall of Negro Life." Fairgoers who actually entered the main lobby of the building received a pamphlet authored by W. E. B. DuBois on the contributions by African Americans to Texas and to the United States and a brochure describing the art on display in the building, including four murals on lobby walls by renowned artist Aaron Douglas. The murals depicted the history of the African American from "the time of his transportation from Africa to his present period of progress." Right below the murals were names of noted African Americans: Charles Young, Richard Allen, Benjamin Banneker, Wright Cuney, Daniel Williams, Paul Lawrence Dunbar, Harriet Tubman, Sojourner Truth, Booker T. Washington, Crispus Attucks, and Frederick Douglass. Beyond the foyer, thousands of exhibits from thirty-two states were organized into six categories: "education, fine arts, health, agriculture, mechanic arts and business" with portions of each exhibit area devoted to several federal agencies and their work on behalf of African Americans. Federal exhibitors included the Department of Education, the Resettlement Administration, the Public Health Service, the Works Progress Administration, and the National Youth Administration, with the latter two agencies supplying sixty persons to serve as guides to the exhibits. On their tours of the building, visitors learned about the development of African-American universities, witnessed an exhibit devoted to African-American musical and artistic accomplishments, received a copy of an African-American newspaper from the African-American newspaper exhibit organized by Chicago *Defender* editor Claude Barnett, learned about the variety of African-American churches, discovered the existence of federal loans for African-American farmers, learned about Civilian Conservation Corps camps for African Americans, found out about African-American inventors, and received information about African-American attorneys who had argued cases before the Supreme Court.[40]

White responses to the exhibits generally reflected prevalent racist convictions. Shortly after the Hall of Negro Life opened, Thomas reported that because so many white visitors refused to believe that an African-American artist had painted the Douglas murals, it was necessary to provide a label, "These murals were painted by Aaron Douglas, a Negro artist of New York City." Earline Carson, the librarian for the exhibit, told one reporter for the American Negro Press the story of a white woman from Corsicana who "advanced a few feet into the hall and was standing as one transfixed looking all about her. All of a sudden she exclaimed, and talking out loud to herself, 'no, no niggers did not do this.'" "I could see her still shaking her head as she later slowly

*Hall of Negro Life, Dallas, 1936. Courtesy of
the Dallas Historical Society, Texas
Centennial Collection.*

passed around the corner down the hall," the librarian remembered. Other reactions ranged from ignorance—"Will Booker T. Washington be in today?" or "Ain't you got no minstrels?"—to astonishment—"You mean to tell me darkies did this? Well I'm surprised. I did not know they had that much patience." According to Carson, the exhibit was well worth the effort: "I have been thrilled every moment of the time I have been on this job, because it gave such a wonderful opportunity to expose how little white people know about Negroes, their culture and advancement in science and art."[41]

Reactions from African-American visitors were tempered by their difficulties in securing accommodations in Dallas and by the discrimination they encountered on the exposition grounds. Thomas's efforts to force all midway concessionaires, including those with nude fan dancers, to open their shows to African Americans came to naught. And the treatment African Americans received on the exposition's opening day was anything but positive as "the only parts given to the Negro race in the mammoth parade were parts depicting all negroes as cotton pickers and other menial positions." White newspapers, moreover, seldom passed an opportunity to stereotype African Americans. In advance of

179

the fair's opening, the *Dallas Morning News* headlined an article: "History of Negro From Jungles to Now: Centennial to be Turned Over to Darkies Juneteenth." After the fair opened, the newspaper continued to pour ridicule from its pages. The coverage of the fair's celebration of the emancipation of slaves in Texas—the so-called Juneteenth celebration—was blatantly racist. "Joining in with the city negroes," the newspaper reported, "were thousands of dusky country merrymakers who had left catfish streams and left fiddle-faced mules to munch contentedly in idleness, farm work forgotten, to celebrate Emancipation Day." Fortunately, the reporter assured readers, the midway had been cleared of strip shows in advance of the "rolling eyes and flashing white teeth [that] dominated exhibit halls."[42]

These circumstances, coupled with the controversy in the African-American press about the elitist direction of the federal exhibit, gave African Americans good reason to be skeptical of both the fair and the Hall of Negro Life. Some African-American newspapers encouraged African Americans to boycott the exposition. But the presence of a federal exhibition building devoted to the achievements of African Americans together with Thomas's success in mitigating some discriminatory practices at the fair along with the presence of a growing number of African-American entertainers, including Cab Calloway, Duke Ellington, and a number of African-American actors who performed in Orson Welles's production of *Macbeth,* had the effect of increasing the number of African-American tourists. While the attendance at the dedication ceremonies for the Hall of Negro Life was a disappointing 7,000, Negro Education Day drew over 60,000 fairgoers, with half that number visiting the Hall of Negro Life. Equally compelling were the figures from the exposition's Finance Department. According to the exposition's chief financial officer: "The Negro day cash figure will be beaten only by the high July 4th receipts." Spending at the fair on Negro Education Day, in fact, almost doubled the spending of a few days earlier when a mostly white crowd of nearly 59,000 visited the exposition.[43]

By the close of the exposition, Thomas had reason to be pleased with his accomplishments. In the Hall of Negro Life, blacks and whites had mixed together, sharing an integrated lobby and restrooms. Equally noteworthy, in Thomas's eyes, were the lessons that the exhibit provided for whites "who had never seen Negroes function in an official capacity before. . . ." And there was the matter of consumer spending. Gate and concession receipts demonstrated convincingly that A. Maceo Smith, in his early negotiations with white exposition officials, had been right to suggest that African Americans would make good consumers. But, as Smith and Thomas soon rediscovered, admission to the world of tomorrow required more than good spending habits. The ticket to affluence in the world of tomorrow had to be held in hands of the right color.[44]

Given what he believed was his success in restoring the alliance between upper-class whites and African Americans, no one was more shocked than Jesse O. Thomas to learn that the Hall of Negro Life would not be continued when the exposition reopened in 1937 as the Pan-American Exposition and that the Hall of Negro Life would actually be torn down. When news of this decision was announced in early January 1937, the Negro Advisory Committee along with the African-American press blistered the exposition management and succeeded in persuading the White House to launch an investigation under the auspices of Texas Senator Morris Sheppard. Sheppard's report found no fault with the white management. According to his findings, African Americans "did not make as much use of the Hall of Negro Life as they should have." Furthermore, the report stated, the new exposition needed the space occupied by the Hall of Negro Life for a building devoted to Latin American exhibits. Finally, there simply were not sufficient federal funds to carry the exhibit through the next exposition season.[45]

Thomas had a different explanation. The argument for more exhibit space was clearly bogus since the Hall of Negro Life was the only building demolished after the 1936 fair. And Thomas had been assured of the availability of federal funds for the 1937 season. He put the blame squarely on the "anti-social attitude" of members of the United States fair commission, especially of W. B. Yeager, the commission's executive secretary. Yeager, a Texan by birth who had close ties to Dallas exposition officials, had routinely obstructed the Negro Advisory Committee since its inception. When Yeager noticed a slackening of interest in the African-American exhibits on the part of white United States exposition commissioners, he determined that Dallas exposition authorities would encounter little opposition from the Roosevelt administration if they decided the Hall of Negro Life would not be in keeping with the Pan-American theme of the 1937 fair. Without consulting its Negro Advisory Committee, the United States exposition commission acceded to the request from the Dallas exposition corporation to discontinue the exhibit. In the twinkling of an eye, the most impressive exhibit hitherto assembled of African-American contributions to the nation's development ceased to exist. African Americans were left with the empty promise that exposition authorities would continue to "do everything to encourage them in their cultural pursuits." [46] Thomas tried to find a silver lining in this episode. "When an impartial analysis is made of all that has transpired in connection with this Centennial and a trial balance is reached," Thomas concluded, "it may indicate that this elimination of Negro participation was adequately compensated for in the opportunity it gave Negroes in Texas to teach the white citizens of that state an important lesson." "Never again during the life of the white people of this generation in the State of Texas," Thomas rationalized, "will they undertake any program of a community or statewide character which in the very nature of the case involves the interest and welfare of the colored people, without first enlisting the intelligent and understanding cooperation of Negro leadership." [47]

Thomas had reason for concern about the traditional alliance between upper-class whites and African Americans. At the close of the 1936 fair, A. Maceo Smith, the person most responsible for laying the groundwork for the Hall of Negro Life and Thomas's assistant manager at the fair, showed his displeasure with the traditional politics of accommodation. Smith turned his considerable organizational skills to establishing NAACP chapters throughout the state.[48]

Like its more famous Atlanta antecedent, the "Dallas Compromise," whereby African Americans received a separate exhibit hall in exchange for tacit support of the Roosevelt administration and for an explicit show of consumer spending at the fair, necessitated choices dictated by expediency and resulted in consequences—like the demolition of the Hall of Negro Life—over which African Americans had no control. The Hall of Negro Life, lineal descendent of similar structures at southern fairs before the First World War, and set in the midst of a festival of abundance at a time of enormous economic strain, was perfectly compatible with the politics of segregation and discrimination.[49] But not all African Americans were content with the result of negotiations over the Dallas fair. As they looked ahead to the 1939 New York World's Fair, they jettisoned the model of accommodation practiced in Dallas and returned to the example set by A. Philip Randolph in Philadelphia and by the NAACP in Chicago. Having seen a blueprint unfold at Dallas that guaranteed segregation in American society, many African Americans determined to nullify the effects of the Dallas Compromise and to redouble efforts already underway in Harlem to recast the model for the future being erected in Flushing Meadows for the fast-approaching 1939 New York World's Fair.

Given African Americans' cumulative experience with exclusion, discrimination, and segregation at preceding fairs, Harlem's renaissance-minded leaders were under no illusions about the difficulties they would encounter at the New York World's Fair. Their concerns deepened when Grover Whalen, former police commissioner, became head of the world's fair commission. His predilections became crystal clear during his trip to Mussolini's Italy to secure Italian representation at the fair. In Rome, he routinely exchanged fascist salutes with police and military officers, before actually striking a deal with Mussolini for an official Italian exhibit. With Whalen at the helm, African Americans were anything but sanguine about the "dawn of a new day" world's fair authorities were promising.[50]

The NAACP prepared for battle. While the fair was in the early planning stages, Walter White, executive secretary of the NAACP, and his assistant secretary, Roy Wilkins, took a tough stand. They demanded that the district attorney enforce state civil rights laws and informed exposition authorities of their plans to provide legal assistance to persons discriminated against at the fair. Furthermore, they put pressure on exposition organizers to avoid the disgraceful employment practices of earlier expositions—patterns that were also in evidence in the "lily white" employment policy at the contemporaneous San Francisco fair. Their appeals fell on deaf ears, however. In 1937, African-American employment at the fairgrounds stood at twenty out of a work force of several hundred. When an African-American information clerk was fired for alleged insubordination to his white superiors, the NAACP requested that exposition managers purge their corporation of discriminatory practices.[51]

The response of exposition officials was revealing. One of Whalen's assistants categorically denied every charge made by the NAACP, declaring that the clerk had been fired because he had repeatedly threatened his superiors. As for broader complaints about discrimination in construction work, exposition authorities replied in equally blunt terms. Construction on the fairgrounds was the responsibility of private contractors, not exposition officials. In short, the management asserted, "there is absolutely no discrimination as to race, color or creed." Over the next two years, this pattern of accusation and denial would become as much a part of the world's fair as the Trylon and Perisphere. "What we have," wrote one NAACP official, "is enough to document not

183

voluminously, but sufficiently, a regime of persistent prejudice and discrimination in employment relations on the basis of colored-ness, accompanied by persistent professions of 'no discrimination.' The discrimination is of the usual type. The unusual feature is the insistence that there is none." [52]

As with earlier fairs, repeated complaints, vehement denunciations of world's fair practices in the African-American press, and an occasional meeting between African-American leaders and world's fair officials had limited effect. By April 1939, intervention by Mayor Fiorello La Guardia, concerned about the damaging political effect of anti-fair "propaganda" emanating from African-American churches, increased the number of African Americans employed by the exposition corporation to 392 out of a total work force of 6,335, with an additional 268 African Americans employed by concessionaires. African-American leaders welcomed the increase in employment at the fair, but were quick to point out that over two-thirds of African-American employees worked as sanitary attendants or porters. [53]

The other demand by the NAACP that African Americans be included in exposition planning sessions was turned aside. Following in the footsteps of earlier exposition managers, New York World's Fair authorities established a Negro Advisory Committee and took the unusual step of organizing an Interracial Advisory Committee, but Whalen refused to attend the meetings and left his lieutenant, Robert Kohn, to inform the latter group that their province was restricted to thematic matters only and did not include the subject of race relations. The Interracial Advisory Committee informed Whalen that, in the wake of Kohn's declaration, their efforts would be futile. Before the fair opened, both committees ceased to function. [54]

Despite the underemployment of African Americans, differential wages for blacks and whites in the same jobs, and separate cafeteria tables for blacks and whites, exposition managers steadfastly held to their claim that discrimination did not exist at the fair. Directors pointed to fairground performances by black entertainers, notably singer Marian Anderson, who earlier that spring had given her famous concert at the Lincoln Memorial after being refused the use of Constitution Hall by the Daughters of the American Revolution. A defiant Kohn, speaking to an African-American college fraternity, noted the large number of complaints by other ethnic and religious groups about their treatment at the fair. "It seems to me," the exposition designer told fraternity members, "that this is sufficient evidence that we favored no group, since all complained, but that we must have fairly carried out our intent of choosing on merit, suitability and experience of applicants."[55]

Kohn's reasoning typified the thinking of exposition management and, coupled with the actual practices at the Flushing Meadow site, led a group of militant African-American political and religious leaders to adopt a new tactic: picketing. As early as 1937, A. Philip Randolph had suggested that African Americans establish picket lines at the recently completed Empire State Building where the headquarters of the fair corporation were located. In 1938, with the situation worsening at the fair, African-American minister Adam Clayton Powell, along with other prominent African-American political and religious leaders, renewed Randolph's threat. Just before the fair opened in May, Powell's group organized pickets at the entrance to the Empire State Building and threatened to call out ten thousand pickets to block the entrances to the fair on opening day. Nearly five hundred pickets did demonstrate outside the fair while President Roosevelt delivered his opening day address. They held their ground despite efforts by the Secret Service and New York police to remove them. To make clear that they blamed exposition authorities, not the president, and to avoid embarrassing the latter by making him cross their picket line, protesters, according to historians Elliott Rudwick and August Meier, lowered their signs when Roosevelt's motorcade left the fairgrounds.[56]

With their cultural authority under visible and prolonged assault by African Americans and with the tremors of war increasingly felt on the fairgrounds (the Czechoslovakian pavilion remained partially built and the Polish and French exhibits were draped in black because of the German invasion), exposition managers found themselves confronting the very situation that Secretary of Commerce Roper had warned about at mid-decade: the need to secure the support of African Americans for American institutions in the event of war. When the fair reopened in 1940 under the banner of "peace and freedom," exposition designers, now under the direction of banker Harvey Gibson, modified their techno-scientific utopia of planned bigotry and stressed instead the theme of America's cultural pluralism as a way of unifying the country as the world plunged headlong into war.[57]

The pivotal moment in the transition between the 1939 and 1940 exposition seasons occurred when the Soviet Union decided not to continue its participation into 1940. Exposition managers determined to replace the Soviet building with an exhibit called the American Common. The brainchild of Robert Kohn, the American Common had explicit ideological aims. As one exposition news release explained:

"[Kohn] suggested that the space be used to demonstrate an idea dia-metrically opposed to the propaganda of the totalitarian states . . . [namely], that America's greatness springs from the free and democratic institutions that allow her individual citizens and cultural groups to pursue happiness in their own differing ways." To get this message across, Kohn ingeniously reached back into the history of American world's fairs and updated the tradition of special days that had been set aside for different ethnic groups. Rather than randomly scatter these celebrations throughout the duration of the fair, he made the American Common the focal point for week-long festivals by different ethnic groups and arranged for each group to "take over the giant band shell, the market-place, and the auditorium, and give its own distinctive 'county fair' with its own old-world bazaars and fiestas." To be certain that old world traditions did not simply reinforce old world loyalties, each day at the Common concluded "with a brilliant patriotic gather-ing." "Here," the publicity release intoned, "will be America in its rich-est mingled traditions. Here will be the most direct and powerful an-swer to the dictators who would mold all peoples into the same rigid pattern. At the center of the 'American Common', in almost the iden-tical spot where the red star of the Soviets stood last year, will be a 'Liberty Pole' carrying the highest flag in the Fair's whole 1,215 acres—the Stars and Stripes." [58]

Kohn's decision to highlight the plural traditions of the American "folk" instead of the techno-scientific possibilities of the future was brilliant but risky, given the hostilities between blacks and whites that lingered from the 1939 exposition season. What if African Americans boycotted the proceedings? Or, more threatening, what if African Americans again marched the picket line? To offset these possibilities, exposition authorities made clear that the purpose of the American Common was to "make loyalty to our country the only test of Christian or Jew, white or black, native or foreign born." Managers next ap-pointed prominent African-American civic leader T. Arnold Hill as Chairman of Negro Week festivities. Hill adroitly maneuvered through the sea of conflicting positions among African Americans about partic-ipating in fairs and enlisted the support of nearly one hundred and fifty prominent African-American men and women from around the coun-try, including Mary McLeod Bethune, Claude Barnett, Aaron Douglas, W. E. B. DuBois, Eugene Kinckle Jones, A. Philip Randolph, and Roy Wilkins. Many African-American leaders saw the American Common show for what it was: a loyalty test that would carry severe penalties for failure. And some, following in the tradition of Frederick Douglass, determined to seize the occasion to denounce white hypocrisy and to urge white Americans to live up to their ideals. As DuBois emphasized in a speech that opened the Negro Week celebration: "[African Americans] are in a position to help not only themselves but all America to realize the common democracy from which they themselves have been so long and widely excluded." [59]

That theme ran throughout the week-long event. Lawrence D. Reddick, curator of the Schomburg Collection at the New York Public Library, authored the text of the Negro Week souvenir program which concluded:

> And so today, the drive for liberty, security and for equality of opportunity is a broad struggle by and for the common man. Since the Negro, historically, has borne the brunt of these social denials, he, perhaps, more than any other, appreciates the value and meaning of them all. The American Dream is the dream of the Negro. The dream of the Negro is the dream of an America which guarantees, in the words of Douglass, "all rights for all."

These bold words echoed Douglass's speech at the World's Columbian Exposition in the previous century. But they failed to satisfy the concerns of many African Americans. Had African-American leaders, and their few white supporters, by lending their stamp of approval to the American Common, acquiesced too much? Editors of some African-American newspapers thought so and condemned Negro Week at the American Common in no uncertain terms, noting that employment for African Americans at the 1940 fair had remained insignificant and that African Americans had not been involved in major positions of responsibility. [60]

It was precisely this anger together with the growing clamor for equal rights by African Americans who participated in the fairs that prompted nervous United States government officials to act where private exposition corporations had failed. In 1940, with news of the war in Europe capturing headlines, federal authorities once again decided to lend assistance to a group of African Americans trying to organize an exhibition of African-American progress. With the cooperation of African-American exposition organizers, federal officials succeeded in turning Chicago's upcoming American Negro Exposition into a showcase for the Roosevelt administration's "new deal" in race relations.

In 1937, with Chicago's African-American community still smarting from the lack of African-American exhibits at the 1933–34 Century of

Progress Exposition and with the seventy-fifth anniversary of the Emancipation Proclamation on the horizon, a prominent African-American real estate developer, James Washington, began laying the groundwork for a diamond jubilee celebration. With the support of two African-American representatives in the Illinois legislature, Washington secured a state appropriation of $75,000 for an exposition. Despite this early success, Washington and his "Afra-Merican" Exposition Authority were bedeviled by problems of site location and charges that the exposition was being organized for private gain. In early 1940, plans for the exposition appeared to be in grave jeopardy. To save the exposition, prominent African Americans in Chicago replaced Washington with a young attorney, Truman K. Gibson, reorganized the corporation as the Diamond Jubilee Exposition Authority, and firmed up arrangements to hold the fair at the Chicago Coliseum.[61]

With less than four months remaining until the scheduled opening of the exposition, the board of directors followed the avenue pursued five years earlier in Dallas and turned to the federal government for assistance. A delegation of exposition sponsors, including perennial exposition booster Claude Barnett, met with F. D. R.'s Secretary of Agriculture, Henry Wallace, to secure government backing for their enterprise. Wallace listened sympathetically to their plans. After all, Wallace knew how New Deal agricultural policies had transformed the sharecropping system of the South and had forced many African Americans to migrate to northern cities. He saw in the exposition proposal a perfect occasion for showing how the Department of Agriculture was meeting this crisis of rural dislocation and how the federal government was attempting to solve African-American urban misery. Wallace's support was immediate and transformed the exposition from a dream to reality. The importance of his endorsement was not lost on the Chicago delegation: "From this meeting really evolved the Exposition, since it was there decided not only that the Department of Agriculture would participate, but Mr. Wallace's enthusiastic endorsement encouraged other Department heads to cooperate." Indeed, from the moment federal authorities came to the rescue of the American Negro Exposition, the imprint of New Deal planners overlay the stamp of local exposition officials.[62]

Once federal funds became available through congressional appropriation, government planning for the exposition moved quickly and threatened to leave local groups behind. The Federal Writers Project provided a staff to aid in the preparation of historical exhibits. The Department of Labor organized charts on African-American employment that showed how the number of African-American women professionals had increased in the 1930s. More compelling was the Department of Labor's talking robot that tried to assure visitors that machines would never displace workers. Other federal agencies also rushed displays to Chicago that emphasized the benefits of New Deal programs for African Americans. The National Youth Administration furnished guides and a clerical staff for the exposition and provided a children's choir as well as an amateur radio station for entertainment. The Federal Works Agency arranged an exhibit that emphasized its role in promoting "better housing facilities, increased recreational activities, an extended general health program and vocational and educational opportunities." Also on display were exhibits from the Social Security Administration and the Civilian Conservation Corps, with government lecturers informing visitors about the role of those agencies in promoting the welfare of African Americans. The Postal Service organized a booth that featured a new stamp commemorating Booker T. Washington, while the Civil Aeronautics Authority emphasized growing opportunities for African Americans in aviation, just as the country was "turning all of its avenues into the production of planes for national defense and to aid England in her battle to defeat invading forces." [63]

Not to be outdone by the federal government, state and city agencies contributed exhibits. The City of Chicago arranged an exhibit that included a model of the Ida B. Wells Housing Project and the Illinois exhibit emphasized the number of African Americans who had held state office and provided charts showing the percentages of African Americans employed in leading industries in Illinois. [64]

While federal, state, and city agencies were arranging displays designed to polish the image of the government's concern for African-American welfare, exposition organizers secured a range of exhibits designed to tell the story of African-American cultural and economic achievements and to underscore African-American patriotism. Just inside the main entrance to the Coliseum, exposition promoters installed a replica of Lincoln's tomb surrounded by dioramas showing significant events in African-American history, including depictions of the "loyalty and patriotism of the slave during the Civil War," the role of African Americans in the charge up San Juan Hill, and the "Negro's bravery in the World War as shown by the Eighth Regiment." Exhibits from churches and educational institutions emphasized the religiosity of African Americans and their struggle for self-improvement. The exposition also included an array of works by African-American artists and musicians and assembled one of the largest collections of African-

American literature, highlighted by the presence of leading authors, like Richard Wright, who autographed copies of their books.[65]

Equally impressive were displays from American corporations designed to illustrate their role in promoting African-American employment at home and abroad. Firestone Rubber Company built a miniature rubber plant as part of the Liberian national exhibit, while the Plymouth Automobile Company displayed photographs of African-American workers on its assembly line and in sales. And, for the first time at any exposition of this magnitude, a model kitchen provided by the Edison Company included African-American women as demonstrators and lecturers, not as maids. Other business concerns contributed $10,000 in door prizes, ranging from refrigerators to radios, that held out to African Americans the promise of future abundance if only they would renew their pledge of loyalty to American institutions.[66]

To emphasize the message that the future would be an improvement over the misery experienced during the depression, exposition managers turned for assistance to sociologist E. Franklin Frazier. He organized an exhibit that illustrated the basic argument of his book, *The Negro Family in the United States*. Through a series of dioramas, Frazier traced the development of the African-American family from slavery to the present. Under slavery, the dioramas stressed, the African-American family had been shattered, but in the present, according to a diorama entitled the "City of Re-Birth," plans to improve the urban environment would "improve the condition of the Negro family." [67]

With its emphasis on African-American achievements and on possibilities for African Americans to share in the future prosperity of the nation, the American Negro Exposition succeeded in attracting nearly 250,000 visitors—far below the expectations of its sponsors, but in keeping with the attendance at a similar exposition organized in Chicago just twenty-five years earlier to celebrate the fiftieth anniversary of emancipation. Like the separate Negro building at the Dallas fair and at the earlier generation of southern fairs, the American Negro Exposition raised the ire of critics. To some, the fair seemed like nothing more than another accommodationist sell-out. Especially jarring were the decisions by exposition organizers to grant the ice cream concession to a Chicago firm that refused to hire African Americans and to contract with a white-run firm for printing exposition programs. And many critics threw up their arms in despair when the exposition management caved into the Catholic Church's threat to withdraw from the event unless an exhibit devoted to birth control was removed. To these criticisms, a local Communist party publication, the *Fighting Worker*, added another:

The Exposition was arranged and financed by the New Deal and its Negro henchmen precisely in order to make palatable the War Deal role today in world politics. . . . The whole exposition was enveloped with propaganda for patriotism, for ideological war preparations to drag along the Negro masses into the white exploiters' robber war.

The *Fighting Worker* wished for a "real Negro Exposition" that would "smash the 'superior' theory (à la Hitler) of the white landowners in the South, that would reveal the hideous inequalities of Negro people and Jim Crowism," and that would include exhibits "on housing that would address those problems." [68]

Clearly, the American Negro Exposition failed to mount a radical critique of the dominant culture. If anything, the American Negro Exposition represented an effort by its organizers to negotiate for greater inclusion as full citizens in the culture of abundance in exchange for African-American support of the Roosevelt administration's war effort. African Americans no more had an option not to fight in the Second World War than they had to refuse to fight in the Civil War or First World War. Their choice was not whether to fight, but whom they would seek as allies to improve their position within American society.

At the American Negro Exposition, the federal government presented itself as a likely ally, especially in the person of its official representative, Henry A. Wallace. Wallace delivered the major address at the closing ceremonies. He was emphatic:

One of the most effective ways to fight fascism and nazism in this country is to fight class, religious and racial discrimination in the United States. . . . We accept the word of science that the world is round and that the earth revolves around the sun. I see no reason not to accept the word of science that there is no proof that one race is superior to another. If that is true—and, as I have said, I have no reason to doubt it—a lot of the responsibility that we have put on nature is our responsibility after all. And to accept our responsibility we must do all that we can to get rid of hatred and discrimination and to give human beings the opportunity to which they are entitled. There is no better way to rearm democracy.

On one level, Wallace affirmed that the American Negro Exposition had been about rearming African Americans to fight yet another war. But Wallace's address also gave evidence of the federal government's willingness to offer African Americans a "new deal" in the form of a commitment to condemning discrimination if African Americans renewed their pledge to fight in another world war. If Wallace's implicit guarantee was manipulative, it was also remarkable. A public declaration by a highly placed government official that echoed A. Philip Randolph's condemnation of scientific racism fourteen years earlier indicated that white supremacist policies, that had rested on the bedrock of government guarantees, were capable of shifting.[69]

The close of the 1940 exposition season left African Americans with many questions unanswered. Could the federal government be trusted to eliminate discrimination if African Americans once again joined an American war effort? Would the rhetoric of cultural pluralism at the American Common translate into equal economic opportunity and an end to segregation in America's postwar future? The fairs of the 1920s and 1930s had revealed persistent patterns of racial exclusion and discrimination. Barely welcomed as consumers and certainly not as citizens in these futuristic world's fair cities, African Americans had far less reason than whites to take at face value promises about the "dawn of a new day."

But through the fairs, many African Americans had succeeded in developing new tactics as well as a new front in their war of position for improved race relations and economic justice. They entered the Second World War determined to adopt tactics of civil disobedience to improve their position in the world of tomorrow if their new allies in the Democratic party let them down. At the century-of-progress expositions, African Americans, no less than whites, helped frame the world of tomorrow. They did so in full knowledge that the battle to improve black/white relations would continue well into the future.

CHAPTER SEVEN

The New Day Dawns: The American Pavilion
at the 1958 Brussels World's Fair

... the American way of life is about to be clobbered by alien
rivals from Andorra to Yugoslavia.
—Dillard Stokes, *Human Events*, 1958[1]

From the vantage point of the 1950s, the world of tomorrow forecast
by the century-of-progress expositions seemed remarkably predictive.
From plastics to television sets to superhighways, what had once
seemed like futuristic world's fair displays had become commonplace
features of what economist John Kenneth Galbraith described as an
"affluent society." But the future did not materialize in exactly the way
that world's fair planners had envisioned. Instead of realizing the promise of "peace and freedom," the theme of the 1940 New York World's
Fair, Americans found themselves ensnared in a cold war and leading
lives filled with deepening anxieties about nuclear conflagration and
racial conflict. Amidst renewed doubts about America's future, a generation of postwar political authorities and intellectuals became increasingly preoccupied with repackaging the modernizing visions of the
century-of-progress expositions in light of the changed geopolitical circumstances of the postwar period. Their thinking crystallized in plans
for the American Pavilion at the 1958 Brussels Universal and International Exposition, the first world's fair of the postwar period.[2]

In the spring and summer of 1958, the Atomium, "a gigantic jug-
gling act of silver spheres" arranged into a towering projection of an
iron molecule, beckoned more than forty million people to the Brussels
world's fair. The Atomium, like the dynamos that so intrigued Henry
Adams at the fairs that began the century, radiated the avowed theme
of the Brussels fair: a "new humanism" dedicated to the peaceful uses
of nuclear energy and to building better international relations. More
than fifty nations constructed pavilions at the fair as part of a broad
effort to project national images appropriate to the changed circumstances of the postwar period. Germany, for instance, tried to refurbish
its war-damaged reputation and project a new national self-image
through an official pavilion designed as a "necklace" of jewel-like ex-

193

hibition halls, a notable departure from Albert Speer's Nazi monumentalism at the exposition held in Paris twenty years earlier. The Soviet Union designed an imposing structure—it reminded western critics of an enormous refrigerator—that put on display models of the recently launched Sputnik satellites. Belgium, not to be outdone by its guests, organized a massive exhibit intended to renew international support for Belgian control of the Congo.[3]

From the American perspective, the Brussels world's fair gained increasing importance as government officials convinced themselves that an impressive representation of America's contemporary cultural landscape would increase America's prestige overseas, combat Soviet propaganda inroads in Western Europe, and assuage deepening popular concerns about the danger of nuclear power. With the assistance of an array of influential business figures, media executives, labor leaders, and intellectuals, government planners gave visible form to an ideologically supercharged cultural landscape that masked as much as it mirrored. The American Pavilion, while trumpeting the openness of American society and the material plenitude of American life, hid from public view the government's obsession with national security. By the time the exposition opened, the pavilion had been transformed into nothing less than a front for U.S. intelligence-gathering activities in Europe and a vehicle for monitoring political dissent at home.

Enthusiasm for American participation in the Brussels exposition built slowly, largely because of the costs of the Korean War. Once the U.S. government learned of Soviet plans to create a display as monumental as its exhibit at the 1937 Paris fair, the State Department moved quickly to launch plans for an American exhibit. In October 1956, the Office of the U.S. Commissioner General for the Brussels Exposition (BRE), was created as a "temporary arm" of the State Department. State Department officials immediately selected New York architect Edward Stone to design the American Pavilion. According to critic Thomas Hine, Stone's "strength"—on the basis of his designs of several university medical centers and of the American Embassy in New Delhi—"was packaging the United States." Three months later, President Eisenhower announced that Howard Cullman, head of the New York Port Authority, director of the Metropolitan Opera, and renowned Broadway "angel," would assume the post of the American commissioner general of the Brussels fair, with James Plaut, director of the Boston Institute of

Atomium, Brussels, 1958. Courtesy of the
Smithsonian Institution, National Museum of
American Life, Larry Zim World's Fair
Collection.

Contemporary Art, and Katherine G. Howard, former assistant administrator of Civil Defense, serving as his deputies.[4]

Faced with an exposition opening date of 17 April 1958, BRE exhibition planners turned to the task of constructing the intellectual scaffolding for the exhibit. Their first formulation suggested that the narrative structure of the pavilion stress "life, liberty, and the pursuit of happiness." But concerns that this slogan would seem "trite or 'corny' in the eyes of the modern, sophisticated American" convinced staff members to solicit the opinions of leading public figures about how America should be represented at the fair.[5]

Over the span of three months, members of the BRE committee on theme interviewed over fifty influential Americans, including heads of major corporations, leading intellectuals, entertainment moguls, labor leaders, foreign service specialists on American culture, and former ambassadors. Information gained from the interviews constituted a repository of concrete ideas for displays and an index to the cultural concerns of some of America's most influential thinkers. Thomas J. Watson, Jr., president of IBM, urged that the American Pavilion "emphasize productivity" and "point out that we have built the highest living standard in the world and show how we got that way." Another corporate giant, Walter Paepcke, chairman of Container Corporation of America, had a different idea: "The best exhibits would be American intellectuals in all fields, who could conduct seminars while the fair was in progress." Erwin D. Canham, editor of the *Christian Science Monitor,* also wanted living exhibits, not of intellectuals, but of workers and their families. Such a display, Canham believed, would demonstrate how "machines that are available to the farmer or to the housewife not only mean equality in standard of living, but equality in the community." Walter H. Wheeler, president of Pitney-Bowes Inc., stressed that the exhibit should underscore "that the American worker is a capitalist," while Victor Reuther, president of the AFL-CIO, urged a display that would stress the "individual freedom of American workers."[6]

Leading intellectuals also lent their weight to the project. Sociologist David Riesman believed that the exhibit should feature the latest assembly line technologies, while historian Arthur Schlesinger, Jr. advocated that "America should be presented in terms of the problems that it faces and the steps that are being taken to solve these problems." Above all, Schlesinger wanted an exhibit that would refute the argument that "Communism is the only way to master and apply the technical revolution to human life." Distilling these recommendations was no easy task, but a group of government planners concluded that the interviews yielded three important ideas: first, that "the U.S. exhibit should convey the feeling that in the USA there is a more equitable distribution of *all* the good things of life than anywhere else in the world"; second, that the exhibit should address "unfinished business" in the area of social problems, especially race relations; and third, that the pavilion be designed to "provide a spiritual and visual oasis" where the fundamental message "is put across by indirection," not "heavy, belabored and fatiguing attempts at 'propaganda.'"[7]

While valuable as a record of how leading public figures understood their culture and sought to combat communist propaganda, the interviews left BRE officials without a strong sense of thematic coherency for the exhibit. With the exposition's opening date rapidly approaching, panicky BRE officials sought advice from an institution that had been a major contributor to the Hall of Science at the 1933–34 Chicago fair and had been long established as a repository of wisdom about the intersection of science, technology, business, and American culture—the Massachusetts Institute of Technology (MIT).[8]

In late March 1957, BRE planners asked MIT to organize a small group of faculty to help illustrate the role of science and technology in creating "The American Way of Life." At the urging of its dean of humanities, John E. Burchard, MIT agreed to organize a three-day brainstorming session that would include BRE planners as well as prominent authorities in the sciences, humanities, social sciences, and engineering. With the assistance of historian Elting Morison and economist and former CIA assistant director Max Franklin Millikan, Burchard assembled an impressive group of intellectual underwriters for the American exhibit, including engineer Jerome Wiesner; physicists Victor Weisskopf and Martin Deutsch; political scientist Ithiel de Sola Pool; economist Walt W. Rostow; sociologist Wayne Kenodle; biologist Kenneth Thimann; CBS producer Ralph Hardy; and *Time* and *Life* editor Eric Hodgens. Significantly, just when a growing number of American intellectuals were celebrating an "end to ideology," MIT's working group set out, in a refrain heard throughout the symposium, to produce the "ideological glue" to hold the exhibits together in a coherent presentation of the American cultural landscape.[9]

The Cambridge Study Group for the Brussels Universal and International Exposition opened with BRE planners describing the spatial requirements of the pavilion and discussing exhibits that had already been decided upon, including a state-of-the-art IBM computer, atomic energy displays, and, at President Eisenhower's insistence, voting machines. Charles Siepmann, a Columbia University professor of education and consultant to the BRE, delivered the keynote address and, in words reminiscent of G. Brown Goode's delivered in the last century, hammered home the importance of exhibitions as a visual form of communication:

An exhibition is a kind of language, a distinctive and limited mode of communication. Much of our story cannot be told in it. The spoken word must be subordinate, and confined to special purposes. An exhibition is, essentially, an assault upon the eye. *It is for us so to organize the assault that, from a thousand visual impressions, the visitor gathers, and recalls, a total picture, the meaning of which transcends the sum of all the parts.* There must be more suggested to him, far more, than he sees.

Crafting a story about "the American way of life"—a phrase recurring throughout the symposium—that would be at once seen and unseen occupied the symposium for the next two days.[10]

To make their assignment manageable, symposium participants divided into five subcommittees organized around the following subjects: "Land and the People," "Life and Work," "American Idealism in Action," "Science and Technology," and "Culture." The extent to which these subcommittees brimmed to overflowing with the sticky substance of ideology became clear in their early deliberations. One participant envisioned the pavilion taking form around the slogan, "Technology a Friend not a Foe of Culture and Democracy," with exhibits designed to illustrate the following propositions: "science makes art the property of everyman; science abolishes classes; science at the service of peace; science makes the world one; science at the source of health; science abolishes the distinction between city and country." The idea of representing America as a classless society also led the subcommittee on "Life and Work" to flights of fantasy. This committee, chaired by Weisner, wanted exhibits to illustrate the proposition that "we have done for our people in practice that which the Communists have claimed as their goals and which they have not done." In particular, the committee wanted to emphasize that while the communists had set out to eliminate social classes, "America is this classless society." To get this point across, the subcommittee on "Life and Work" even suggested including a portrait of Karl Marx in the display. Not to be outdone, Hodgen's committee on "Land and People" suggested creating "islands of living" for American women that would feature "booths staffed by women answering questions on American life" supplemented by "booths in the ladies' rooms for more personal questions." As if to underscore the seriousness they attached to their ideas, Rostow's subcommittee on "American Idealism in Action" stressed that for any public display of America's efforts to grapple with poverty and desegregation, "the space must be right, soundproofed, and as solemn as a religious shrine." [11]

By the third day of the symposium, the coalition of government planners, media executives, and intellectuals had distilled innumerable suggestions into a proposal deeply rooted in the long-standing commitment of American intellectuals and social planners to using pragmatism as an organizing principle for American culture. A broad consensus finally emerged that "the dominant theme should be, simply stated, that the United States constitutes a society in ferment." As a BRE memorandum subsequently explained:

The idea was expressed at the M.I.T. conference that what we are dealing with is the phenomenon of continuous revolution, that the American people are dynamic, energetic, impatient and restless for change; that because of the vastness of our country, the diversity of our origins, and the free conditions pertaining to American enterprise, we are committed to a constant, unremitting search for an improved way of life. . . . Moreover, it is important to emphasize that the process is more important to Americans than the product, in other words, that the challenge of creation and achievement is still of central excitement in the American way of life.

Process elevated to a cultural ideal; revolution reduced to a quest for a paradise of mass consumption; culture armed for battle with communism—these were key ingredients in the ideological cement proposed by MIT planners for representing postwar American society. And BRE officials wasted no time instructing their exhibit designers to "attempt, wherever possible, to have the exhibits incorporate this point of view." [12]

While the BRE worked feverishly to implement the MIT blueprint for representing America as a "society in ferment," the Brussels world's fair suddenly rocketed into the American public's field of vision. In October 1957, the Russians launched the sputnik satellite that had the twin effect of sending Americans into orbit. Congress immediately began seeking ways to reallocate funds to the American space program and targeted the Brussels world's fair appropriation for a significant cut. Howard Cullman, the U.S. commissioner general, seized the offensive and informed Eisenhower: "With appropriate funds we can do a Sputnik culturally, intellectually, and spiritually for the nation I have the honor of representing." Furthermore, Cullman was convinced that the cultural landscape being prepared for display in Brussels was central to American foreign policy: "We have a great chance to tell the American story with complete truth, modesty, and conviction because we have nothing to hide. Properly handled, this could be a strong public relations weapon in combating Communist propaganda. With bungling, we could have a bombshell that could score a resounding victory for the other side. It seems to me it is vitally important to our whole foreign policy." The press agreed. "We'll go on Trial at the Fair," the *Saturday Evening Post* predicted. *Human Events* forecast the dire consequences of a poor exhibit: ". . . the American way of life is about to be clobbered by alien rivals from Andorra to Yugoslavia." And a Gary, Indiana, newspaper urged Congress to see the fair as a way to regain national self-confidence and international prestige after sputnik. These articles and others in a similar vein were read into the *Congressional Record* where they became rallying points for the pavilion's supporters, led by Senator Hubert Humphrey. "From what we know about Soviet plans," Humphrey declared, "there will be scarcely a credible Soviet theater group, ballet artist, musician, singer, dancer, or acrobat left in the Soviet Union if his services can be used in Brussels." The difficulty, as he understood it, was clear: "not enough Americans are willing to recognize that the Soviet Union has declared war on us." [13]

There was another difficulty as well. As plans for the American representation crystallized, the necks of southerners in Congress reddened at the thought of BRE plans to address the issue of desegregation in the form of the "Unfinished Business" exhibit first proposed by Rostow at the MIT symposium. "This exhibit could not have been more designed to reflect against the American Nation if it had been made in Moscow by the Kremlin," Senator Olin Johnston of South Carolina declared in a speech before Congress. Another representative from South Carolina vented his rage in a letter to the BRE, threatening that if the exhibit contained "anything which will cast the slightest reflection on our way of life—in any of its areas—you are going to hear plenty of reaction on the floor of the House. It is ridiculous to think that either you or anybody in authority would countenance such colossal and unimaginable stupidity." [14]

With Congress in turmoil over the appropriation, the State Department, having already determined that the fair would be an important source of information about the Soviet Union and its allies, decided that the only way to pressure Congress into restoring its appropriation would be to invoke the terms of the Mutual Security Act which authorized the expenditure of funds "when the President determines that such use is important to the security of the United States." The issue became so important that a deputy undersecretary of state informed Secretary of State John Foster Dulles that "the prestige of the President's office will be required" to secure the appropriation. In another move intended to apply pressure on Congress, the State Department issued a report claiming that the Soviet Union would be spending over $60 million on its representation at the fair and noting that the Russians had already set up a weekly newspaper, mischievously called *Sputnik*, in Brussels to influence European public opinion about Soviet technological and cultural progress. This information tipped the balance. In spring 1958, Congress restored most of the funds earmarked for elimination and brought the Brussels appropriation up to $12 million.[15]

Controversy would nevertheless continue to swirl about the American display as it became increasingly clear that the American Pavilion was not only a cold war battleground between the Soviet Union and United States, but a contested terrain over the transforming effects of the cold war on American domestic policy. Whether the ideological glue developed for BRE planners at MIT would withstand these pressures and prevent the fissures of racial conflict in the American cultural and political landscape from splitting wide open was put to the test when the pavilion opened on a site between the Vatican and Russian buildings, or as one pundit observed, "between heaven and hell."[16]

The site of the pavilion called to mind the cold war context of the world's fair and provided the opportunity for a powerful architectural statement about America. Architect Edward Stone, working closely with the BRE, seized the occasion to design a building that drew inspiration from Roman and British imperial precedent to suggest the legitimacy of America's rise to the status of world power as well as to demonstrate the strength and openness of American society. The clearest antecedent for the circular pavilion, Stone explained to a radio audience, was the Roman coliseum. But, as he proceeded to describe his creation, the coliseum idea was tempered by another: "Popularly described it is like a bicycle wheel with an outer rim and an inner rim with tension cables or spokes connecting them. Over this we have a plastic roof which allows the whole building to have light. . . . The walls will be of a metal mesh of clear plastic. So the whole building will be, you might say, the Crystal Palace brought up to date. All very light and airy and crystalline." True to its dual imperial origins, the dimensions of the building were heroic in scale. The pavilion covered 7.4 acres, stood 85 feet high, and boasted a diameter of 340 feet, thus making it one of the largest circular buildings ever built. Like the 1851 Crystal Palace, the interior of the American Pavilion also enclosed several large trees and was flooded with natural light. The effect, according to the official U.S. guidebook, was "expressive of the American spirit, with a feeling of openness and naturalness." Forty entrances and exits, in addition to the main entrance, were included in the pavilion to emphasize the openness of the American structure, while the ninety-ton roof, suspended by steel cables, conveyed the impression of hidden strength. According to one professional interior design journal, the building's design was wholly appropriate: its "merry-go-round shape, the turnbuckled rigging that yanks its umbrella roof taut, the lightness and translucency of that roof, its escutcheon-adorned walls of gilt mesh honeycombing—suggest play, joy in ornament, an idyllic humanism." Or, as the BRE design team, headed by government exhibition specialist Peter Harnden and MIT lecturer Bernard Rudofsky, put it: "The character of the American pavilion is that of a pleasure dome rather than of an exhibition hall." [17]

Within the pleasure dome, the transforming power of the cold war became apparent in a cultural landscape that enabled visitors to experience America simultaneously as Rome and, in the sarcastic words of a *Nation* correspondent, as "a Pompeii among nations, a huge holiday resort whence all care has been banished!" As Rudofsky explained, the focus of the exhibits, divided between the main floor and the balcony, was not so much with the American per se as with "his native environment, especially the man-made kind; his house and the objects he accumulates in his pursuit of happiness; his likes and dislikes as reflected in his surroundings, whether a town or a room; his interests and aspirations; his pet loves and pet hates; the things that make him laugh." To dramatize the "man-made" environment, Harden and Rudofsky developed a novel series of exhibits that avoided simple realism. Instead of incorporating model homes, the designers chose to highlight selected household technologies on display in compartmentalized interiors. Instead of building a "literal street in model form," Harnden and Rudofsky constructed a "streetscape" on the balcony that represented a pastiche of shopping streets across the country. Their vision of a "society in ferment," in short, was cinematic, inspired, as they explained, by the "loop film"—a short, repeating film shown as part of a particular dis-

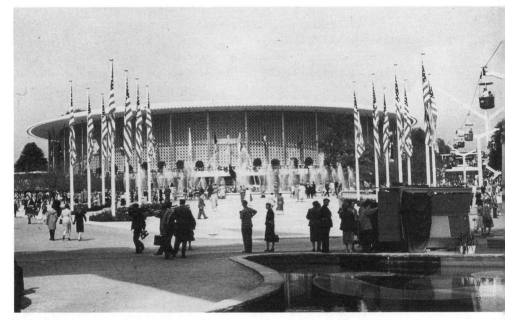

American Pavilion, exterior, Brussels, 1958.
Courtesy of the Smithsonian Institution,
National Museum of American Life, Larry
Zim World's Fair Collection.

play. The purposes of the loop films, Rudofsky explained, "is to produce a flash of insight, convey a flavor, a revelation—not to exhaust
any subject. Extremely important is their independence of captions and
other verbal crutches, their exploitation of the psychological advantage
of surprise. This is the key to the pavilion—the surprise of a crack train,
of Jones Beach on a crowded Sunday, of rush hour on the subway, of a
San Francisco Chinese restaurant, a Pizzeria, a kosher shop. . . ." By
bombarding visitors with unexpected and seemingly disconnected images, the designers hoped to shock fairgoers into seeing America as a
society where science and technology, in tandem with corporations and
the federal government, had refashioned anxieties about nuclear power
and automation into a dream world premised on the freedom to consume and spend time in the pursuit of leisure.[18]

Just inside the main entrance to the pavilion, designers arranged
their first surprise for visitors in the form of "The Face of America"
display that unfolded beneath a one-hundred-foot map of the United
States. The exhibit bombarded visitors with images of American diver-

sity. Tumbleweeds, jukeboxes, automobile license plates, a slab of California redwood, a 480-page Sunday edition of the *New York Times* and a football uniform were intended to present "a series of varied, largely unexpected and lasting impressions of Americana, the cumulative result of which will arouse the visitor's curiosity and create in his mind an intrigued sympathy with America and things American." [19]

Other exhibits followed suit. As visitors circumnavigated the main floor of the pavilion, they passed through a contemporary art exhibition, where the souvenir publication generated by the BRE assured them that American art forms, whether produced by American Indians or abstract expressionists, embodied universal concerns. From the art exhibit, fairgoers proceeded to a bizarre display entitled "Atoms Serving the Community," featuring mechanical hands that encouraged visitors to manipulate a radioactive sample as well as "an illuminated device showing a chicken consuming irradiated food which not only added to the strength and health of the fowl but increased the qualitative nature of the egg." From scrambled atoms, visitors were expected to head to an exhibit area devoted to the "continuing industrial revolution in America" and stressed the benefits of automation for improving America's standard of living. This display revolved around the enormous IBM RAMAC computer that answered historical questions in ten languages and was designed to show how computers were providing "more material abundance and more leisure for individual creative and recreational pursuits." To drive that point home, designers flanked the RAMAC display with a working television studio that introduced color television to European audiences and a music room that allowed them to select and play American popular music. As if to underline the pervasiveness of leisure in American culture, designers developed an exhibit that fused mass consumption and the political process. Eisenhower had insisted that the pavilion include voting machines; BRE designers transformed them into cultural vending machines. Visitors, some of whom mistook the curtained voting booths for toilet facilities, could actually "vote" for their favorite American president (Abraham Lincoln won), movie star (Kim Novak defeated Marilyn Monroe), and musician (Louis Armstrong won hands down).[20]

That postwar America had lived up to the expectations of century-of-progress exposition planners and become a paradise of mass consumption and entertainment was apparent in other exhibits as well. Walt Disney contributed one of the most popular features of the pavilion, Circarama, a motion picture tour of the United States which concluded with a chorus singing "God Save America." BRE designers also

American Pavilion, interior, Brussels, 1958.
Courtesy of the Smithsonian Institution,
National Museum of American Life, Larry
Zim World's Fair Collection.

included a fast-food restaurant that served hot dogs and a "Street-scape" consisting of a pastiche of display windows and an operating corner drug store. Live musical and theatrical performances in the pavilion's auditorium, featuring major symphonies (the Philadelphia Orchestra), theater groups (the Yale Drama Theater), and popular soloists (Harry Belafonte and Benny Goodman), further enhanced the message that atomic age Americans had become a "people of plenty."[21]

In their rush to put the best face on America, exhibit designers did not overlook the concerns expressed at MIT about America's social problems. Designers simply arranged exhibits that suggested that because problems of poverty and racial segregation were part of the American social fabric they were in the process of being solved. On the main floor, the BRE design team, in cooperation with the city of Philadelphia, constructed a scale model of Philadelphia with hundreds of moving parts showing how urban renewal programs were eradicating urban blight and solving housing problems. On the balcony, designers included a children's center to demonstrate the government's concern for the welfare of youngsters. But the centerpiece of the BRE's effort to show that solutions to America's social problems were just around the corner took form in an exhibit that originated in Rostow's proposal for a display devoted to America's unfinished business. Retitled "The Unfinished Work," after a phrase in Lincoln's "Gettysburg Address," the exhibit, funded by *Fortune* magazine, consisted of three twelve- by twenty-foot boxes constructed on stilts and joined by a ramp. Their form was peculiar and strikingly didactic. According to a prominent journal of design, the first box, called Chaos,

> is broken in outline, black and brown outside, lined with screaming newspaper clippings inside. It presents the unsolved problems. The second, Crystallization, more regular in shape, panelled in red, blue, and yellow outside, presents the progressive analyses and advances towards solutions of the problems. The third, Serenity, is regular in form, white, with a few poetic photographs, contains our hopes for final solutions.

Far from following in the footsteps of 1939–40 New York World's Fair planners and denying that racial conflict and urban poverty existed in the United States, exhibit designers enveloped these issues in crystalline shapes which suggested that social ills, once envisioned scientifically, could be solved.[22]

If the cultural landscape on view in the American Pavilion was crafted to convey the impression that in postwar America, as in the depression, social, economic, and political problems could be entrusted to expert planners, nowhere was this message made more clear than around the reflecting pool at the center of the pavilion where BRE designers drew together the threads of the Norman Bel Geddes's Futurama and Crystal Lassies shows as well as the World of Fashion display at the New York World's Fair and arranged hundreds of chairs for foot-weary tourists. As they sat in repose, contemplating contemporary America, visitors were invited to shift their attention from problems associated with nuclear conflict, automation, and poverty and watch models wearing the latest in American ready-to-wear women's fashions parade up and down a ramp from the "islands for living" exhibit on the balcony to a platform over the reflecting pool. Americans, it seemed, were uniquely blessed. Secure in their knowledge that science, technology, and corporate capitalism, under the benevolent guidance of the government, were propelling America forward toward utopia, they could relax and let the process take care of itself. But, as only a few individuals knew at the time, that process was hardly benign.[23]

By opening day, the American Pavilion had been molded into an

*Soviet Pavilion, exterior, Brussels, 1958.
Courtesy of the Smithsonian Institution,
National Museum of American Life, Larry
Zim World's Fair Collection.*

espionage weapon against the Soviet Union and its allies as well as a
vehicle for gathering information on alleged subversives in the United
States. This information was so sensitive that the State Department records of American participation in the Brussels world's fair remained
classified for thirty years after the close of the fair and remain so sensitive that to this day correspondence about the Brussels world's fair
between the FBI, CIA, Army Intelligence, State Department, and National Security Agency has not been declassified. But from records that
have been made public, it is clear that American intelligence agencies
determined that the fair would provide a bonanza of data about economic and political conditions behind the iron curtain. Army intelligence agents routinely photographed exhibits in the Soviet pavilion,
while State Department agents were told that Soviet exhibits "will be a
major target for the collection of factory markings." Intelligence agents
also kept their eyes on eastern European pavilions for clues to activities
that still remain mysterious. One agent reported: "Observation of

Czech World's Fair Pavilion on 3 occasions has not r[e]pea[t] not revealed guards wearing described uniform. Continuous observation will be made and info forwarded when received." There was, of course, nothing new about gathering information on foreign countries through the medium of international expositions. World's fairs had always afforded abundant opportunities for learning about product innovations and for gaining insights into particular national economic policies. What distinguished American actions at the Brussels fair was that formal, government-sponsored espionage activities were built into the structure of America's participation in the fair and, while unseen, were as much a part of the modernized American cultural landscape as computers, irradiated chickens, lounge chairs, and fashion shows. Indeed, seen in its totality, the cultural landscape that took form within the pleasure dome of the pavilion did nothing less than bring to life the world seen and lampooned by *Mad Magazine*. While BRE exhibit designers were arranging displays that lent substance to Alfred E. Neuman's perennial exclamation, "What, me worry?" government intelligence agencies were using the pavilion for their own dramatic rendering of "Spy vs. Spy"—a rendition that intertwined with political surveillance at home.[24]

Because the cultural landscape on display at Brussels was deemed so vital to America's national security, the government ran routine and extensive security checks on all Americans who participated as "living exhibits" in the display. Performers ranging from a Montana high school chorus to Harry Belafonte were carefully investigated to assure that they posed no security threat to the United States while performing for the government. Belafonte barely cleared the security process. "He can be very volatile and fear if we rejected him, he could create some adverse publicity," declared a cable to the secretary of state. Less fortunate was James A. Kershaw, a San Francisco union organizer and member of the Actor's Workshop theater group that had been contracted by the BRE to perform *Waiting for Godot*. The State Department never explained why it refused to allow Kershaw to perform, telling his lawyer only that it would be "inadvisable" to allow him to appear. In the matter of cultural representation, no less than with American life generally during the cold war, national security had become an obsession.[25]

It was precisely this attention to national security interests that led exhibition planners to refashion the "Unfinished Work" exhibit shortly after it opened to the public. Criticism of the display had become so severe that Dulles dispatched one of his assistants to investigate. Even before his arrival, the United States Information Agency (USIA) had decided that the newspaper "montage was far too specific" and made recommendations for changes. What bothered the government was the existence of "shots of mob violence at Cairo, Illinois, and Little Rock, and headlines, full and specific, such as WHITE PUPILS JEER NEGRO STUDENTS; LITTLE ROCK POLICEMEN DRAG A DEMONSTRATOR DOWN A STREET and WHEN A NEGRO FAMILY MOVED INTO CICERO ILLINOIS THE NATIONAL GUARD HAD TO BE CALLED OUT TO CHECK A MOB." This montage was so unacceptable to USIA authorities that they instructed BRE officials to eliminate the photographs and incorporate fragmentary headlines in the cubicle. Equally offensive in the eyes of the USIA were photographs of "mixed-groups of school children at work and at play," especially a photograph of "a colored boy dancing with a white girl," and a photograph of "the dome of the Capitol with three colored children in the foreground playing in a slum." These too were ordered removed and a guard was placed in front of the exhibit to prevent the press from witnessing the rewriting of American social reality.[26]

In this highly charged atmosphere that wedded a cultural landscape presentation to national security interests, other aspects of the pavilion, especially the exhibit of modern art, also attracted critical commentary. Shortly after the fair opened, a prominent Chicago business executive visited the fair and wrote a letter to Eisenhower blistering the pavilion as manifestly un-American. Several other visitors wrote letters in a McCarthyite vein to Congress suggesting that the art exhibit lent credence to Russian propaganda about the United States. A group of Republican senators met and condemned the exhibit sculpture as "right off a slag pile" and as "a modern question mark." These reactions distressed Eisenhower to such a degree that he sent George Allen, U.S. Information Agency director, to investigate the allegations. Allen's positive report about the pavilion, which concluded that the exhibit needed to include a few pieces of less abstract art and that the "Unfinished Work" exhibit include displays devoted to public health concerns, had the effect of mollifying Eisenhower and calling attention to the extent to which the American Pavilion had become a sensitive nerve ending for Americans anxious about the future in the brave new world of the cold war.[27]

Primed by the debate in the press about the quality and representativeness of the American display at Brussels, thousands of middle-class Americans joined with millions of Europeans to turn the Brussels fair into an atomic age mecca. Hundreds of American tourists shared their observations with congressmen, BRE officials, and the White House.

One American tourist informed Secretary of State John Foster Dulles that the exhibit left him feeling "immensely proud to be an American." A minister was pleased by the pavilion's equation of leisure and American political values: "Its atmosphere of leisure, which can only be explained in terms of liberty and freedom, makes for a very subtle yet telling story of our way of life." Another visitor was moved to write a lengthy memorandum defending the exhibit from criticism in the press. Not all American tourists, however, took pleasure from the pavilion. A visiting American Legion group condemned the pavilion as "unworthy and degrading," and other American visitors lambasted pavilion authorities for failing to represent American religious values and for playing into the hands of the Communists. While they disagreed about the merits of the pavilion and the exhibits it contained, visiting Americans did share a burning desire to find in the American Pavilion a common landscape that would at once serve to define American values and shield America from the threat of Communism.[28]

For European visitors, the American cultural landscape on display at the world's fair was equally significant. Queen Juliana of the Netherlands, like thousands of fairgoers to the American show, delighted in manipulating the mechanical hands in the atomic energy display. In a preview of the Nixon-Khrushchev "kitchen" debate at the American exhibition in Moscow the following year, Clement Voroshilov, president of the USSR, used the occasion of his private tour of the pavilion to debate Howard Cullman on the dangers of modern science. As one embassy official recounted the debate in front of the atomic energy display: "I believe [Voroshilov] said something to the effect that a scientist in a mad moment might even have the power to blow up the world all by himself. Mr. Cullman, in an exquisite rejoinder, said that while this was all very true, he was personally very happy about the invention of the electric razor. Voroshilov said that he had tried an electric razor several times himself but that he preferred the old-fashioned variety." That a highly placed American official could equate atomic dangers and the electric razor was absurd, but wholly in keeping with the tenor of the display. As a correspondent for a Brussels newspaper told his readers after his visit to the U.S. pavilion:

> The nuclear question, the birth, life and death of isotopes; everything is being presented like the manufacturing of chocolate . . . with that typical American easy-going style. In the Russian Pavilion, science is shown like it would be a problem that can be solved by the gods only. Here, a very amusing physic solves the biggest problems. You stand before the atomic pile like you would stand in front of a

jukebox; with the certitude of being the master of it thanks to a lever or a coin.

If this commentary was any indication, many Europeans left the American Pavilion less convinced by America's cultural prowess than by the discovery that chocolate-covered nukes were the perfect symbol for postwar America.[29]

A confidential USIA report confirmed that in the battle to win European hearts and minds, the U.S. exhibit won neither: "the U.S. exhibit at the Brussels Fair was outranked in audience preference by several of its competitors and in particular by the presentation of the Soviet Union." In their criticism of the exhibit, however, European commentators missed the full import of the display. In its pavilion, the American government and leading U.S. corporations had packaged American culture—*Pravda,* significantly, called the American Pavilion a "gilded candybox"—and signaled their commitment to exporting that culture to European audiences. While the pavilion, with its forty exits, gave European visitors the illusion that they could walk away from American culture, it also bore witness to the American cultural assault on Europe that would gain momentum over the next three decades and, because of its intensity and scope, be more difficult to escape.[30]

For Americans, the cultural landscape so carefully arranged in the American Pavilion held consequences no less profound. The American exhibit at the Brussels world's fair carried forward the cultural offensive launched at the century-of-progress expositions to give material shape to a vision of American culture as a paradise of mass consumption developing under the benevolent guidance of corporate capitalists, government authorities, and academic experts. Functioning as a cultural cyclotron, the American Pavilion bombarded European and American publics with thousands of images. In so doing, it accelerated the process of modernizing America and reconfiguring the culture of imperial abundance into the molten core of a value system that would define postwar America.

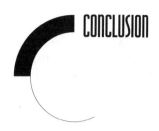

CONCLUSION

When planning began in earnest for the 1939 San Francisco Golden Gate International Exposition, Leland Cutler, newly appointed president of the exposition, and George Creel, the powerful California Democrat who had run the federal government's Committee on Public Information during the First World War, met at California's Bohemian Grove retreat for America's intellectual, political, and economic elites. As Cutler described their meeting: "I turned to Creel immediately, and, although the motto of the Bohemian Club is 'Weaving spiders come not here,' we had our first discussion of our problems of financing an exposition while at the Bohemian Grove." [1]

As this conversation confirms, the century-of-progress expositions were more than depression-era sideshows. These remarkably complex events were planned responses to the worldwide crises shaking the capitalist system. From the vantage point of America's elites, the magnitude of that crisis seemed to be growing at every turn. The Bolshevik Revolution, working-class revolutions in Europe, waves of strikes in major American cities in 1919—all these had shocked corporate executives and spurred government officials to take ruthless measures against strikers and alleged left-wing sympathizers. Then, just when the country seemed to be getting back to "normalcy," the bottom fell out of the economy and the Great Depression, a world depression, put the "modern world system" at risk. In the United States, corporate capitalists felt the ground quake beneath them as industrial unionism spread and major strikes hit automobile manufacturers, steel producers, and the city of San Francisco. These events terrified corporate and government leaders because of their scale and because of the disaffection of a growing number of Americans with the prevailing economic order. The century-of-progress expositions were calculated responses to these crises and presented Americans with blueprints for modernizing the United States—plans that, in the eyes of exposition organizers, would lead the nation out of the depression and place it on the road to future perfection.

Like the designs for the future laid down by an earlier, Victorian generation of world's fair builders, the century-of-progress exposition planners continued to exhibit a positivist faith in technology and unfolded blueprints for the future that were still flawed by racism. But the century-of-progress expositions were not carbon copies of their predecessors, as even the most cursory glance at their architecture and industrial laboratories reveals. What especially distinguished the century-of-progress expositions from the first generation of world's fairs was growing emphasis placed on entertainment as central to the modernizing strategies of the exposition promoters. To put this shift in perspective: if the 1893 Chicago World's Columbian Exposition represented a contest between the White City and Midway Plaisance for dominance in American culture, the American Pavilion at the 1958 Brussels fair reflected the triumph of the Midway as an organizing principle in American life.

That the century-of-progress expositions facilitated this transformation was no accident. By the 1930s, as historians Roland Marchand and David Nye have argued, American corporations—the primary financial underwriters and increasingly the primary exhibitors at American fairs—were responding "to the dictates of modern public relations" and were in the process of dissolving the boundaries that at earlier fairs had separated education from entertainment. The result, as expressed at Brussels, was a veritable cultural cyclotron that was constantly bombarding American and European audiences with images that equated better living with more entertainment and leisure.[2]

As compelling as this vision of the future may have been, the modernizing designs projected at the century-of-progress expositions were never so convincing that they encountered no dissent or resistance. As the actions of African Americans made clear, not all Americans agreed with the future imagined by world's fair promoters. But the presence of multiple and dissenting voices should not lead to the conclusion that the modernizing designs unfolded at these fairs for making America an ever more perfect realization of a dream world of abundance were so devoid of authority that they lacked effect. As political scientist Donald Horne has written: "some social groups have greater resources to define 'reality' than others." Precisely because of the asymmetry of power relations in American society and because the fairs incorporated the voice and authority of science into their presentations of social reality, the century-of-progress expositions helped secure the cohesion of national elites and middle-class Americans around a blueprint for the future that defined continued American progress as synonymous with material

growth, scientific and technological advance, and a continued acceptance of "empire as a way of life." [3]

The role of scientists in conceiving and lending legitimacy to this
ideological construct is clear. When Gerald Wendt ruminated about the
integration of science into everyday life through displays of science at
the New York World's Fair, the integration he envisioned was through
consumerism. Visitors to science exhibits at the fairs were not expected
to enter intellectually into science, but to become consumers of science
through mass production. By encouraging visitors to believe that any
application of science to the environment automatically leads to progress, scientists, in essence, were saying that judgments about these
matters were best left to themselves and their corporate patrons.

Therein lay a significant shift. The scientists primarily involved in
America's Victorian-era fairs had been anthropologists who had taken
the lead in constructing and displaying evolutionary ideas about racial
hierarchy among human beings. Their conceptualizations about race
had been crucial components in the ideological formulations presented
by the expositions' upper-class organizers. But, in a crucial sense, many
of these nineteenth-century scientists worked in a realm one step removed from the commercial and corporate elites who organized international expositions. By contrast, the scientists who became involved
in the century-of-progress expositions were chiefly "hard" scientists
whose professional identities were linked to corporate research laboratories or to university-based research programs sponsored by corporations. From their positions within or closely allied to corporations,
they helped develop a conceptual framework for the fairs of the 1930s
that not only helped rationalize the machine-age ethos on display at the
expositions, but, perhaps more importantly, lent legitimacy to claims
by corporation managers that they could be entrusted with planning
the future course of American society.

Through the efforts of scientists, architects, industrial designers,
and federal planners, the century-of-progress expositions outfitted
crisis-torn America with a cultural safety net that helped prevent the
nation's economic collapse from becoming a national free-fall. That
safety net consisted of many strands. Government planners developed
exhibits that put the redistributive policies of the New Deal on view
and refashioned the isolationism of the 1920s into a cultural national-
ism that permeated depression-era America. Federally-sponsored
world's fair exhibits complemented murals in New Deal–built post offices and visitors' centers at Tennessee Valley Authority and far-western
dams as part of a broad effort by the government to assure citizens of

215

the government's interest in their social welfare. Architects and industrial designers encouraged visitors to imagine a mass consumption-driven paradise if only Americans consented to modernize their lives along lines suggested by the fairs. As a result, there can be little doubt that the fairs shored up national faith in the government and in the fundamental rightness of the American economic order.

The American Pavilion at the 1958 Brussels fair revealed, in concentrated form, just how much America's future owed to the fairs of the depression era. In the ideologically supercharged American cultural landscape that took form in Brussels, science and technology were integrated into American life through consumerism. White supremacy, one of the crucial underpinnings of the century-of-progress expositions, continued to hold sway as African Americans were represented in an annex to the main pavilion as part of an "unsolved problem" in American society. In the representation of cold war America that took form in Brussels, body politics continued to dictate that women's bodies be modernized and designed along lines that were intended to reinforce women's subordinate role in American society. And the United States, by virtue of its triumph in the Second World War, had already moved beyond its secondary, supportive stance of coloniale moderne imperial relations to acting as an imperial broker in its own right. By 1958, the modernizing scaffolding for the world of tomorrow erected for the century-of-progress expositions had come down, the pleasure dome had been built, and the new day had finally dawned.

AN ESSAY ON ARCHIVAL SOURCES

The century-of-progress expositions, like their Victorian-era predecessors, left behind a stunning array of sources. In addition to hundreds of feet of manuscript materials, the fairs generated photographs, motion pictures, music, and souvenirs of the most entertaining sort (including souvenir pinball machines, television sets, and radios). This brief essay cannot do justice to all of the collections I have consulted, but if it illuminates the range and wealth of material available to researchers and thereby encourages additional studies of these fairs and the cultures in which they took form, I will have accomplished one of my chief aims in writing this book.

I first sketched out this study while working through a small—at least by world's fair standards—but invaluable collection at Yale University. The Century of Progress Collection, compiled initially by Yale librarian and future CIA officer Sherman Kent, and supplemented with materials gathered from the research office of the New York World's Fair, is a terrific collection of promotional materials developed by corporate exhibitors for the 1933–34 and 1939–40 fairs. Priceless as they are for the study of fairs, these materials are of inestimable value for researching the evolution of advertising and consumerism between the wars.

As my research developed, I was fortunate to have access to two collections acquired by the Division of Community Life at the Smithsonian Institution's National Museum of American History. One collection, the fabled Larry Zim collection of world's fair artifacts (including souvenir tables and chairs, full world's fair table services, buttons, badges, medals, posters, sheet music, and—you name it), provides an unsurpassed compendium of objects from fairs dating to the 1851 Crystal Palace Exhibition. The other collection, the Edward Orth collection, is more specialized, concentrating primarily on the 1939–40 New York World's Fair, but contains many photo albums and souvenir books assembled by fairgoers that open windows on the way different people choose to remember the fair.

As important as they are, the Smithsonian and Yale collections are summits in a larger archival landscape—a terrain that has its share of precipitous descents into deep valleys as well. Mercifully, some of this terrain has been mapped. See especially, John E. Findling and Kimberly D. Pelle, eds., *Historical Dictionary of World's Fairs and Expositions, 1851–1988* (Westport, CT: Greenwood Press, 1990); Brigitte Schroeder-Gudehus and Anne Rasmussen, *Les Fastes du progrès* (Paris: Flammarion, 1992); and my introductory essay to *Books of the Fairs* (Chicago: American Library Association, 1992).

There are several notable collections devoted to particular fairs that contain extensive internal records of exposition corporations, complete with incoming and outgoing correspondence, folders stuffed with information about exhibits, and revealing internal surveillance files about midway strip shows. Of particular importance are the records of the Chicago Century of Progress Exposition, on deposit in the Department of Special Collections at the University of Illinois, Chicago, and the records of the New York World's Fair corporation, on deposit in the Rare Books and Manuscripts Division of the New York Public Library. Both collections have been inventoried and include the original index cards developed by exposition officials for cross-referencing their own files. These cards may well be one of the most important and under-utilized body of sources for understanding the various strands that knotted the web work of American culture in the 1930s. Because these collections consume hundreds of feet of archival shelf space, researchers are well-advised to plan extended research stays.

Some historians are confronted by the problem of having too many sources; some have to make do with the opposite. I have experienced euphoria and frustration on both counts. While the Chicago and New York fairs left behind extensive internal files, other fairs, especially the San Francisco Golden Gate International Exposition and Cleveland Great Lakes and International Exposition, seem to have left virtually none of their internal records behind. I am cautiously optimistic that these records survive, unnoticed, in the vaults of banks or accounting firms for the simple reason that world's fair corporations had to save their records to fend off lawsuits by exhibitors, concessionaires, contractors, and shareholders. My optimism, however, may be misplaced. After all, most of the internal records of the 1893 Chicago World's Columbian Exposition have never surfaced, so it is entirely possible that the records of several of the smaller century-of-progress fairs were simply carted to the incinerator.

The archival record for the Philadelphia, Dallas, and San Diego fairs is mixed. Some internal correspondence survives, especially for the Sesquicentennial, in the City Archives of Philadelphia, and for the Texas Centennial Exposition, in the Dallas Historical Society. The San Diego Historical Society contains some surviving documentation from that city's fair and, like the other depositories, has invaluable scrapbooks of newspaper clippings.

As I tried to make clear in chapter 3, the century-of-progress expositions were the American version of a broader transatlantic exposition movement. Following the footsteps of American exposition planners to Europe led me to a variety of depositories. For information about the British Empire Exhibition, I examined records in the Wellcome Institute in London, the Public Record Office in London, and the Grange Historical Museum in Wembley. Official records from the French fairs of the period survive in varying quantities in the Archives Nationale in Paris, the Musée des Arts décoratifs in Paris, and the Archives d'Outre-Mer in Aix-en-Provence. The latter depository is a storehouse of information about colonial expositions. Scattered records of European fairs are also found in the City Archives of Amsterdam. The City Archives of Liège contains one of the most disheartening sights I have ever witnessed in my years of researching world's fairs—a large mountain of disintegrating manuscript and print material from fairs held in that city. Records from various fairs held in Brussels, including the 1958 exposition, are housed in Exposition Park, where the Atomium still stands. These records provide a great deal of insight into the changes that occurred in the Belgian exposition tradition as it evolved over the nineteenth and twentieth centuries and afford a great deal of insight into the political and cultural struggles of the Cold War.

Because of their national political and economic importance, world's fairs generated an extensive archival trail through the agencies of different governments. The National Archives in Washington, D.C. contains loads of information about government involvement in American and foreign fairs, especially in Record Groups 43 and 350. The Archives Nationales in Paris contains scattered holdings from French fairs in the 1920s and 1930s, while the Archives d'Outre Mer in Aix-en-Provence contains many records pertinent to the exploration of French colonial expositions, especially the 1931 extravaganza. For British fairs, especially British colonial fairs, the Public Record Office is a noteworthy depository.

Of all of these governmental records, one set, in particular, merits special mention. When I approached the National Archives to find out about holdings pertinent to the 1958 Brussels fair, I was pleased to learn that those records survived. But in my wildest dreams I never imagined that the U.S. government would have ever tried to classify its involvement in a world's fair as a state secret. That is exactly what happened with the American involvement in the 1958 fair. For reasons I explain in chapter 7, these records were classified in bulk. Mercifully, the staff of the Archives accomplished the "bulk declassification" in short order, leaving only a few documents still marked "secret." As of this writing, these documents remain under review by various federal intelligence agencies, including the CIA, the FBI, the National Security Agency, and various units of military intelligence. The final verdict on this fair will obviously have to wait.

In the first two chapters of this book, I make the argument that it is impossible to understand the world of fairs during the Great Depression and cold war without understanding the universe of fairs that came before. Abundant sources exist for the study of Victorian-era fairs and I refer readers to my introductory essay in *Books of the Fairs* (Chicago: American Library Association, 1992) for an introduction to relevant primary and secondary sources. Interested readers should also consult the works by Findling and Pelle and Schroeder-Gudehus and Rasmussen cited above.

No investigation of Victorian fairs or their century-of-progress successors would be complete without a visit to the Department of Special Collections in the Henry Madden Library at California State University, Fresno, where Ronald Mahoney, the head of that department, has turned the Donald Larson Collection of printed and photographic sources for the study of fairs into one of the premier collections of its kind in the United States.

In addition to the above institutions and collections, my work on fairs has led me to a number of libraries holding the papers of particular individuals and organizations that were involved in expositions. The bulk of my archival work on the eugenics exhibitions was conducted in the Charles Davenport papers at the American Philosophical Society, the Henry Laughlin papers, at Southeastern Missouri State University, and the Eugenics Records Office in London. For information on the involvement of scientists in the fairs, I consulted planning committee records in the archives of the National Academy of Sciences in Washington, D.C., the James M. Cattell papers in the Library of Congress, the Karl Compton papers at MIT, and the Henry Crew papers at Northwestern University. In addition to examining Yale's Century of Progress Exposition collection for information about corporate exhibitors at the fairs, I also conducted research in the Henry Ford Archives for information about the Ford Company's involvement in the century-of-progress expositions. The presidential libraries of Herbert Hoover in West Branch, Iowa, and Franklin D. Roosevelt in Hyde Park, New York, testify to the importance of world's fairs in the thinking of two important political figures. For additional insights into the political ramifications of the century-of-progress expositions, researchers should consult the George Creel papers in the Library of Congress. For materials concerning the involvement of African Americans in the century-of-progress expositions, researchers should begin with the records of the National Association for the Advancement of Colored People in the Library of Congress. The Claude Barnett papers in the Chicago Historical Society are also an important source of information on this topic as are the relevant files in the Records of the Texas Centennial in the Dallas Historical Society. For information on industrial designers, the collections of the Cooper-Hewitt Museum and Harry Ransome Humanities Research Center at the University of Texas, especially the Norman Bel Geddes papers, are invaluable.

This short research note does not begin to exhaust the possibilities available for the study of the century-of-progress expositions. In addition to oral interviews, I was fortunate to have access to the New York World's Fair exhibition at the Museum of the City of New York and to guest registration books that recorded the recollections of many people about their experiences at the 1939–40 fair. Images of these fairs have also been preserved on film. Home movies have survived as have films produced by corporations, the U.S. government, and Hollywood. Newspapers and magazines, of course, provided extensive coverage and reproduced millions of words of publicity releases and offered local commentary. No less important are surviving exposition structures themselves. The monumental structures that survive in Barcelona, Wembley, Brussels, Paris, and Dallas provide substantial testimony to the lasting effect of these fairs. So do museums, especially the Museum of Science and Industry in Chicago and the Musée National des Arts africains et océaniens, which owe the substance of their collections to the 1933 Chicago and 1931 Paris fairs respectively.

To sum up, archival records—not to mention the extensive body of printed sources and surviving world's fair buildings and museums that owe their origins to fairs—bear witness to the importance of the century-of-progress expositions. As these sources receive greater attention from scholars, there is every reason to believe that we will learn more about the struggles that gave meaning to modern times.

NOTES

Introduction

1. Merriam quoted in Charles S. Requa, *Inside Lights on the Building of San Diego's Exposition: 1935*, no imprint [1936?], frontispiece, Library of Congress.

2. America's interwar fairs drew approximately the same number of visitors as the fairs held in the forty years between the end of the Reconstruction and the First World War. See John Allwood, *The Great Exhibitions* (London: Studio Vista, 1977), 184; and John E. Findling and Kimberly D. Pelle, eds., *Historical Dictionary of World's Fairs and Expositions, 1851–1988* (Westport, CT: Greenwood Press, 1990), 376–381. In *Electrifying America: Social Meanings of a New Technology* (Cambridge, MA: MIT Press, 1990), 367, David E. Nye calls attention to the popularity of the Victorian- and depression-era fairs in Muncie, Indiana: "Just as Muncie residents had once flocked to the St. Louis fair and later to the dramatic illuminations of Niagara Falls, in 1933–34 they went to the Chicago Century of Progress Exposition, 250 miles away. . . . The railways provided special group rates; Sears sold tour packages that included hotel, meals, and entrance fees. The local automobile dealers attended, the town's Collins Boys Band was invited to play both in 1933 and 1934, and the Delaware County Legionnaires, with their wives and families, went en masse as part of Indiana American Legion Day."

3. Brock Brower, "1939: Now *That* Was a World's Fair," *Esquire*, 61, no. 4 (April 1964): 61–65, 159–60; Interview with Gertrude Saxton, March 1990; [Registration Books] from "Selling the World of Tomorrow," a 1989–1990 exhibition at the Museum of the City of New York; Lawrence Van Gelder, "New Yorkers, etc.," *New York Times*, 8 August 1979, C12; E. L. Doctorow, *World's Fair* (New York: Random House, 1985). An interesting assessment of Doctorow's novel is provided by Michael Robertson's "Cultural Hegemony Goes to the Fair: The Case of E. L. Doctorow's *World's Fair*," *American Studies* 33, no. 1 (Spring 1992): 31–44. For recollections of another fair, see Patricia F. Carpenter and Paul Totah, *The San Francisco Fair. Treasure Island, 1939–40* (San Francisco: Scottwall Associates, 1989).

4. Erik Orsenna, *L'Exposition Coloniale* (Paris: Editions du Seuil, 1988); Eduardo Mendoza, *La Ciudad de los Prodigios* (Barcelona: Seix Barral, 1986).

5. Robert W. Rydell, *All the World's a Fair: Visions of Empire at America's International Expositions, 1876–1916* (Chicago: University of Chicago Press,

1984); and Paul Greenhalgh, *Ephemeral Vistas: The Expositions Universelles, Great Exhibitions and World's Fairs, 1851–1939* (Manchester, U.K.: Manchester University Press, 1988), chap. 1.

6. Robert T. Small, "Calls Sesqui Last of World's Fairs," *Philadelphia Bulletin*, 29 November 1926, clipping, Sesquicentennial Scrapbooks, vol. 14, City Archives of Philadelphia, RS 232.22.

7. John MacKenzie, *Propaganda and Empire: The Manipulation of British Public Opinion 1880–1960* (Manchester, U.K.: Manchester University Press, 1985); and Greenhalgh, *Ephemeral Vistas*, provide useful introductions to British fairs. Catherine Hodeir and Michel Pierre's *L'Exposition Coloniale* (Paris: Editions Complexe, 1991) should inspire studies of other fairs held in Paris between the wars.

8. Warren Susman, ed., *Culture and Commitment, 1929–1945* (New York: George Braziller, 1973), 7, 10. See also William Stott, *Documentary Expression in Thirties America* (New York: Oxford University Press, 1973); Barbara Melosh, *Engendering Culture: Manhood and Womanhood in New Deal Public Art and Theater* (Washington, D.C.: Smithsonian Institution Press, 1991); Lawrence Levine, "Hollywood's Washington: Film Images of National Politics During the Great Depression," *Prospects* 10 (1985): 169–96; and, Alice G. Marquis, *Hope and Ashes: The Birth of Modern Times, 1929–1939* (New York: Free Press, 1986); Karal Ann Marling, *Wall-to-Wall America: A Cultural History of Post-Office Murals in the Great Depression* (Minneapolis: University of Minnesota Press, 1982); and, Marlene Park and Gerald E. Markowitz, *Democratic Vistas: Post Offices and Public Art in the New Deal* (Philadelphia: Temple University Press, 1984).

9. The best starting points for understanding the cultural significance of America's fairs between the world wars are Warren Susman's "Ritual Fairs," *Chicago History* 12, no. 3 (Fall 1983): 4–9; his *Culture as History: The Transformation of American Society in the Twentieth Century* (New York: Pantheon, 1984), esp. chaps. 10–11; Neil Harris, "Great American Fairs and American Cities: The Role of Chicago's Columbian Exposition," in his *Cultural Excursions: Marketing Appetites and Cultural Tastes in Modern America* (Chicago: University of Chicago Press, 1990), 111–131; and, Folke T. Kihlstedt, "Utopia Realized: The World's Fairs of the 1930s," in Joseph Corn, ed., *Imagining Tomorrow*, (Cambridge, Mass.: M.I.T. Press, 1986), 97–118. On the New York fair, in addition to Susman's essays, one should read Joseph P. Cusker, "The World of Tomorrow: The 1939 New York World's Fair" (Ph.D. diss., Rutgers University, 1990); Helen A. Harrison, ed., *Dawn of a New Day: The New York World's Fair, 1939/40* (New York: New York University Press, 1980); Marquis, *Hopes and Ashes*, 187–231; Robert A. M. Stern et al., *New York 1930: Architecture and Urbanism Between the Two World Wars* (New York: Rizzoli, 1987); Edward Tyng, *Making a World's Fair* (New York: Vantage Press, 1958). For the San Francisco fair, see Richard Reinhardt, *Treasure Island: San Francisco's Exposition Years* (San Francisco: Scrimshaw Press, 1973) and Jack James

and Earle Welleer, *Treasure Island* (San Francisco: Pisani Publishing Co., 1941). For the Dallas fair, see Kenneth B. Ragsdale, *The Year America Discovered Texas, '36* (College Station, TX: Texas A & M University Press, 1987). For the Chicago fair, see John Cawelti, "America on Display, 1876, 1893, 1933," in Frederic C. Jaher ed., *America in the Age of Industrialism* (New York: Free Press, 1968). For the Philadelphia fair, see E. L. Austin and Odell Hauser, *The Sesqui-Centennial International Exposition* (Philadelphia: Current Publications, 1929). For a detailed guide to the historiography of world's fairs, see my *Books of the Fairs* (Chicago: American Library Association, 1992). One should also consult John Findling, comp., *The Encyclopedia of World's Fairs* (Westport, CT: Greenwood Press, 1990), which contains a good bibliography of published literature about world's fairs as well as useful entries on the world's fairs of the period, and Brigitte Schroeder-Gudehus and Anne Rasmussen, *Les Fastes du progrès* (Paris: Flammarion, 1992).

10. "[Ripley's] Believe It Or Not," 15 July 1939, clipping, New York World's Fair Scrapbook, National Museum of American History, Edward Orth Collection, unprocessed. Kihlstedt, op. cit., 102–106, suggests that ideas for the theme exhibits at the New York World's Fair were also influenced by Age of Enlightenment architects and German expressionism.

11. Davidson quoted in Requa, 9.

12. Lawrence W. Levine, "American Culture and the Great Depression," *The Yale Review* 74 (1985): 223.

13. The centrality of asymmetrical power relations to ideological formulations is one of the subjects of John B. Thompson's *Ideology and Modern Culture* (Stanford, CA: Stanford University Press, 1990). My thinking has also been influenced by the lively debate about Antonio Gramsci's idea of cultural hegemony. For provocative explications of Gramsci's ideas, see: Eugene D. Genovese, *In Red and Black: Marxian Explorations in Southern and Afro-American History* (New York: Pantheon Books, 1971); Stuart Hall, "Cultural Studies: Two Paradigms," in Tony Bennett et al, eds., *Culture, Ideology and Social Process* (London: Open University Press, 1981), 19–37; and T. J. Jackson Lears, "The Concept of Hegemony," *American Historical Review* 90 (1985): 567–593. Critiques of hegemony theory include: James C. Scott, *Weapons of the Weak* (New Haven: Yale University Press, 1985), 304–350; esp. 320; Nicholas Abercrombie, Stephen Hill, and Bryan S. Turner, *The Dominant Ideology* (London: Allen & Unwin, 1980); E. P. Thompson, *The Poverty of Theory and Other Essays* (New York: Monthly Review Press, 1978), and Robertson, "Cultural Hegemony Goes to the Fair: The Case of E. L. Doctorow's *World's Fair*." My own view is that while world's fairs have lent a significant measure of legitimacy to the authority of dominant classes in American society and made significant contributions to reproducing dominant social relations, these fairs have always represented "contested terrains" or "sites of struggle" between dominant and subordinate groups. As Scott puts it: "Properly understood, any hegemonic ideology provides, within itself, the raw material for con-

tradictions and conflict." (Scott, *Weapons*, p. 336) Cultural hegemony, in other words, is always a matter of degree, never absolute, and always requires reformulation as historical circumstances change.

14. The influence of the 1925 Paris exposition on American culture has been amply documented. See, for instance, Richard Guy Wilson, Dianne H. Pilgrim, and Dickran Tashjian, *The Machine Age in America* (New York: Harry N. Abrams, 1986), 49–50 and accompanying notes.

15. Tony Bennett, "The Exhibitionary Complex," *New Formations* 4 (Spring 1988): 73–102.

16. Sidney W. Mintz, *Sweetness and Power: The Place of Sugar in Modern History* (New York: Viking, 1985), 157–158.

Chapter One

1. "President McKinley Favors Reciprocity," *New York Times* 25 September 1901: 1; R. F. Christian, ed., *Tolstoy's Diaries* (New York: Charles Scribner's Sons, 1985), 323. I am grateful to Elise Goldwasser for the latter reference.

2. On the reinvention of tradition, see Eric Hobsbawm and Terence Ranger, *The Invention of Tradition* (New York: Cambridge University Press, 1983). For an overview of scholarly literature about world's fairs, see my introduction to *Books of the Fairs: Materials About World's Fairs, 1834–1916, in the Smithsonian Institution Libraries* (Chicago: American Library Association, 1992); Walter Benjamin, "Paris, Capital of the Nineteenth Century," in *Reflections* (New York: Harcourt, Brace, Jovanovich, 1979), 151; Neil Harris, "Museums, Merchandising, and Popular Taste: The Struggle for Influence," in Ian M. G. Quimby, ed., *Material Culture and the Study of American Life* (New York: W. W. Norton and Co., 1978), 140–174; Rosalind H. Williams, *Dream Worlds: Mass Consumption in Late Nineteenth-Century France* (Berkeley: University of California Press, 1982), 58–106; Umberto Eco, "A Theory of Expositions" *Travels in Hyper-Reality* (1968; repr., New York: Harcourt, Brace, Jovanovich, 1986), 294; Burton Benedict, *The Anthropology of World's Fairs* (Berkeley: University of California Press, 1983); Warren Susman, "Ritual Fairs," *Chicago History* 12, no. 3 (Fall 1983): 4–9; Alan Trachtenberg, *The Incorporation of America* (New York: Hill and Wang, 1982), esp. 8, 208–234; and James Gilbert, *Perfect Cities: Chicago's Utopias of 1893* (Chicago: University of Chicago Press, 1991).

3. David M. Potter, *People of Plenty* (Chicago: University of Chicago Press, 1955); William A. Williams, *Empire as a Way of Life* (New York: Oxford University Press, 1980). American fairs were not unique. See John M. Mackenzie, *Propaganda and Empire: The Manipulation of British Public Opinion, 1880–1960* (Manchester: Manchester University Press, 1984).

4. Robert W. Rydell, *All the World's a Fair: Visions of Empire at America's International Expositions, 1876–1916* (Chicago: University of Chicago Press, 1984) examines the fairs as vehicles for popularizing scientific racism.

5. Ibid., 154–183; Henry Adams, *The Education of Henry Adams* (1907; repr. Boston: Houghton Mifflin Company, 1961), 466.

6. Richard Drinnon, *Facing West: The Metaphysics of Indian-Hating and Empire-Building* (New York: New American Library, 1980), 333–351; Rydell, *All the World's a Fair*, 154–183; William P. Wilson to Clarence Edwards, 21 October 1904, National Archives, Records of the Bureau of Insular Affairs, Record Group 350, General Classified Files, no. 6683-22.

7. See, for instance, *Official Catalogue: Philippine Exhibits* (St. Louis: Official Catalogue Company, 1904). The phrase "culture of abundance" is from Warren Susman, *Culture as History* (New York: Pantheon Books, 1984), xx.

8. Death and disease characterized many ethnological villages. See, for instance, "Hard on Eskimo," *Buffalo Commercial*, 8 May 1901.

9. Barbara Rubin, "Aesthetic Ideology and Urban Design," *Annals of the Association of American Geographers* 69, no. 3 (September, 1979): 339–361; Williams, *Empire*, 7.

10. Mable E. Barnes, "Peeps at the Exposition," *Mable E. Barnes Scrapbooks*, vol. 2, 8–22, Buffalo Historical Society.

11. Julian Ralph, "Exploiting the Great Fair," *Harper's Weekly* 36 (20 August 1892): 806; "Advertising the World's Fair," *Monthly Review of Reviews* 7, 40 (May 1893): 452–453.

12. J. W. Buel, ed., *Louisiana and the Fair* (St. Louis: World's Progress Publishing Company, 1905), vol. 10, 3769–3773.

13. [?] Wood to Ira Nadeau, 19 September 1907, University of Washington Archives, Edmund Meany Papers, Box 78, folder (hereafter f.) 12.

14. "The Tidings," *Pan-American Herald* 3, no. 2 (August 1900): 11; "Ten Mammoth Advertising Sign Boards," *Pan-American Herald* 1, no. 4 (October 1899): 9; "Bill Board Protests Numerous," *Seattle Times*, 18 January 1904, clipping, University of Washington, Northwest Collection, Alaska-Yukon-Pacific Scrapbooks; "A Little Boy From China," *Nashville Banner*, 30 June 1897, 1; Carl Abbott, *The Great Extravaganza* (Portland: Oregon Historical Society, 1981), 25; "Exposition Postage Stamps," *Omaha Bee*, 24 December 1897, 4; Robert Knutson, "The White City—The World's Columbian Exposition of 1893" (Ph.D. dissertation, Columbia University, 1956), 17.

15. Susman, "Ritual Fairs," 6; Harris, "Museums, Merchandising, and Popular Culture," 143; "Conference between F. J. V. Skiff, Esq. and the President and Directors of the Panama-Pacific International Exposition Company," 24 November 1911, vol. 4. Bancroft Library, Panama-Pacific International Exposition Collection, Box 3B/4A, f. 2.

16. Roland Marchand, *Advertising the American Dream* (Berkeley: University of California Press, 1985), 8–13; Raymond Williams, "Advertising: The Magic System," in *Problems in Materialism and Culture* (London: Verso Editions, 1980), 170–195. On advertising, one should also consult Richard Wrightman Fox and T. J. Jackson Lears, eds., *The Culture of Consumption* (New York: Pantheon Books, 1983), esp. ix–38.

17. "Movies to Invite the World to the Exposition," *San Francisco Bulletin*, 4 February 1915, 8. The relationship between fairs and the film industry has not received sufficient scholarly attention.

18. Robert Grant, "Notes on the Pan-American Exposition," *The Cosmopolitan* 31, no. 5 (September, 1901): 452; William Bittle Wells, "Our Point of View," *The Pacific Monthly* 7, no. 4 (March, 1902): 183.

19. "Kids Overrun the Exposition," *Omaha World-Herald*, 23 October 1898, 10.

20. The extent of these organizational activities is suggested by Jeanne M. Weimann, *The Fair Women* (Chicago: Academy Chicago, 1981), 125–140.

21. Dave Walter, "Montana's Silver Lady," *Montana Magazine* 76, 2, (March-April, 1986): 68–73.

22. Ibid. The vertical files in the Montana Historical Society (cited hereafter as MHS) contain extensive information on the silver statue controversy.

23. "Work for Our Women," newspaper clipping, MHS vertical files; Laura E. Howey to Walter Bickford, 12 August 1892; and L. G. Dawkins to Laura E. Howey, 22 August 1892, both in MHS, Chicago World's Columbian Exposition, Montana Board of Lady Managers Collection, folders D-G misc. and G-H misc.

24. Weimann, 332. On the pledge of allegiance, see Knutson, 55–56. Laura E. Howey, secretary of the Montana Board of Lady Managers, describes the content of the exhibit and makes clear that children were asked to contribute money. See her "Final Report of the Woman's Department of the Montana World's Fair Board," n.d., MHS, Montana Board of Lady Managers Collection, folder G-H misc.

25. "Ada Cast in Silver," *The Anaconda Standard*, 31 May 1893, 1; "The Montana Statue," *Helena Weekly Herald*, 19 January 1893, 5.

26. Walter, "Montana's Silver Lady," 73. On Montana's role as an "internal colony," see Michael P. Malone, "The Collapse of Western Metal Mining: An Historical Epitaph," *Pacific Historical Review* 55, no. 3 (August, 1986): 455–464.

27. Dave Walter, "Beautiful Columbia Gardens," *Montana Magazine* 73, no. 5 (September-October 1985): 22–27; Information is also available in Montana State University, Department of Special Collections, vertical files; John F. Kasson, *Amusing the Millions* (New York: Hill and Wang, 1978), 106.

28. *Montana at the World's Industrial and Cotton Centennial Exposition* (Helena: George E. Boos and Company, n.d.); *Montana: Its Progress and Prosperity, Resources and Industries. . . .* (St. Louis: [Montana World's Fair Commission], n.d.).

29. Rydell, *All the World's a Fair*, examines the relationship between fairs and the Smithsonian Institution.

30. Ruth H. Hunter's *The Trade and Convention Center of Philadelphia: Its Birth and Renascence* (Philadelphia [City of Philadelphia for Trade and Convention Center], 1962) and her *The Philadelphia Civic Center* (Philadel-

phia: City of Philadelphia for Philadelphia Civic Center, 1971) chronicle the history of the museum. One should also consult the annual reports from the Commercial Museum. Rydell, "The Open (Laboratory) Door: Scientists and Mass Culture," in *High Brow Meets Low Brow* (Amsterdam: Free University Press, 1987), examines the Commercial Museum's role in popularizing science.

31. Hunter, *The Trade and Convention Center of Philadelphia*, 4–5. The importance of the 1893 fair to the search for overseas markets is stressed in Justus D. Doenecke, "Myths, Machines, and Markets: The Columbian Exposition of 1893," *Journal of Popular Culture* 6, no. 3 (Spring, 1973): 535–549.

32. *Philadelphia Commercial Museums: Proceedings of the International Advisory Board* (Philadelphia: Press of the Philadelphia Commercial Museum, 1897), 47; *American Trade With Siam* (Philadelphia: Press of the Philadelphia Commercial Museum, 1898), in University of Pennsylvania, Van Pelt Library, Philadelphia, PA.

33. *Philadelphia Commercial Museums: Proceedings of the International Advisory Board* (Philadelphia [no imprint], 1897), 52, 71.

34. Rydell, *All the World's a Fair*, 168–169; Hunter, *The Trade and Convention Center of Philadelphia*, 22, notes the international prominence of the museum.

35. *National Export Exposition* (Philadelphia: National Export Exposition, Department of Promotion, 1899).

36. Hunter, *The Trade and Convention Center of Philadelphia*, 32–39.

37. Susman, "Ritual Fairs," 6.

38. E. L. Austin and Odell Hauser, *The Sesqui-Centennial International Exposition* (Philadelphia: Current Publications, 1929), 27. For an important discussion of the modularity of popular cultural forms, see John G. Blair, *Modular America: Cross Cultural Perspectives on the Emergence of an American Way* (New York: Greenwood Press, 1988).

39. Lizabeth Cohen, *Making a New Deal* (Cambridge: Cambridge University Press, 1990), 181–182.

Chapter Two

1. Florence B. Sherbon, "Popular Education," *Eugenics* 1 (October 1928): 33; Sinclair Lewis, *Arrowsmith* (1924; New York: New American Library, 1961), 239.

2. Histories of the eugenics movement include: Mark H. Haller, *Eugenics: Hereditarian Attitudes in American Thought* (New Brunswick, N.J.: Rutgers University Press, 1963); Kenneth M. Ludmerer, *Genetics and American Society: A Historical Appraisal* (Baltimore: The Johns Hopkins University Press, 1972); Hamilton Cravens, *The Triumph of Evolution: American Scientists and the Heredity-Environment Controversy, 1900–1941* (Philadelphia: University of Pennsylvania Press, 1978); Allan Chase, *The Legacy of Malthus: The Social Costs of the New Scientific Racism* (Urbana, IL: University of Illinois Press, 1980); Garland E. Allan, "The Misuse of Biological Hierarchies: The American

Eugenics Movement, 1900–1940," *History and Philosophy of the Life Sciences* 5 (1983): 105–128; Daniel J. Kevles, *In the Name of Eugenics. Genetics and the Uses of Human Heredity* (New York: Alfred A. Knopf, 1985); and Carl N. Degler, *The Search for Human Nature* (New York: Oxford University Press, 1991). Nearly all of these accounts discuss selected aspects of the eugenics exhibition movement. See also Madison Grant, *The Passing of the Great Race* (New York: Charles Scribner's Sons, 1916).

3. More is being written about the institutionalization of eugenics. See Randall Bird and Garland Allen, "The Papers of Harry Hamilton Laughlin, Eugenicist," *Journal of the History of Biology* 14 (Fall 1981): 339–353; and Garland Allen, "The Eugenics Record Office at Cold Spring Harbor, 1910–1940: An Essay in Institutional History," *Osiris* 2 (1986): 225–264. Allen's essay also contains important information about eugenics exhibits.

4. H. W. Waters, *A History of Fairs and Expositions* (London: Reid Bros., 1939), 5; Kevles, "Annals of Eugenics: A Secular Faith—I," *The New Yorker*, 8 October 1984, 60; Robert W. Rydell, *All the World's a Fair: Visions of Empire at America's International Expositions, 1876–1916* (Chicago: University of Chicago Press, 1984); Ralph W. Dexter, "Putnam's Problems Popularizing Anthropology," *American Scientist* 54 (1966): 315–332.

5. Burton Benedict, *The Anthropology of World's Fairs* (Berkeley and London: Scolar Press, 1983), 1–65; G. Brown Goode, "The Museums of the Future," in *Annual Report of the United States National Museum: Year Ending June 30, 1897* (Washington, D.C.: Government Printing Office, 1898), 243–262. On the exposition as "world's university," see J. W. Buel, ed., *Louisiana and the Fair* (St. Louis: World's Progress Publishing Co., 1904), vol. 1, introduction. I am indebted to Brian Durrans for suggestions concerning the effectiveness of the exhibition medium.

6. Rydell, *All the World's A Fair*, 224–226; *Official Proceedings of the Second National Conference on Race Betterment* (Battle Creek, Michigan: Race Betterment Foundation, 1916[?]), 6.

7. *Official Proceedings of the Second National Conference on Race Betterment*, 87, 50–52.

8. "Race Betterment, Burbank's Theme," *San Diego Union*, 9 August 1915, 12.

9. Frank Morton Todd, *The Story of the Exposition: Being the Official History of the International Celebration Held at San Francisco. . . .* vol. 4 (New York: G. P. Putnam's Sons, 1921), 38–40; *Official Proceedings of the Second National Conference on Race Betterment*, 145 ff.

10. *Official Proceedings of the Second National Conference on Race Betterment*, 5, 138–143.

11. Dexter, "Putnam's Problems Popularizing Anthropology," 315–332; *Official Proceedings of the Second Conference on Race Betterment*, 4–5.

12. John Higham, *Strangers in the Land: Patterns of American Nativism, 1860–1925* (New Brunswick, N.J.: Rutgers University Press, 1955), 151; Charles B. Davenport, "The Eugenics Programme and Progress in its Achieve-

ment," in *Eugenics: Twelve University Lectures* (New York: Dodd, Mead, and Co., 1914), 14; *Eugenical News* 5 (December 1920): 91–93; Harry H. Laughlin, "Historical Background of the Third International Congress of Eugenics," in *A Decade of Progress in Eugenics. Scientific Papers of the Third International Congress of Eugenics* (Baltimore: Williams and Wilkins, Co., 1934), 1–14; Kevles, *In the Name of Eugenics*, 63; and Charles Rosenberg, *No Other Gods: On Science and American Social Thought* (Baltimore: The Johns Hopkins University Press, 1968), 89–97.

13. Kevles, *In the Name of Eugenics*, 63; Allen, "The Eugenics Record Office at Cold Spring Harbor," 248–250; Chase, 165–166, 277–301. On the relationship between the American Museum of Natural History and the doctrine of Anglo-Saxon supremacy, consult: John Michael Kennedy, "Philanthropy and Science in New York City: The American Museum of Natural History, 1868–1968" (Ph.D. diss., Yale University, 1968); Charlotte M. Porter, "The Rise of Parnassus: Henry Fairfield Osborn and the Hall of the Age of Man," *Museum Studies Journal* 1 (Spring 1983): 26–34; and Donna Haraway, "Teddy Bear Patriarchy: Taxidermy in the Garden of Eden, New York City, 1908–1936," *Social Text* 11 (Winter, 1984–1985): 20–64. I am indebted to Ira Jacknis for calling my attention to these references.

14. "Preliminary Announcement of the Second International Congress of Eugenics," in Archives of the National Academy of Sciences, National Research Council, Div: Foreign Relations, International Congresses, f. "Eugenics;" and Kevles, *In the Name of Eugenics*, 76.

15. Ludmerer, *Genetics and American Society,* 87–119; Bird and Allen, 339–353; Chase, 289.

16. *Scientific Papers of the Second International Congress of Eugenics* (Baltimore: Williams and Wilkins Co., 1923), vol. 1, 1–4, 19; "Sees American Man Superior of Woman," *New York Times,* September 28, 1921, 11.

17. Harry Laughlin, *The Second International Exhibition of Eugenics . . . An Account of the Organization of the Exhibition, the Classification of the Exhibits, the List of Exhibitors, and a Catalog and Description of the Exhibits* (Baltimore, 1923), 1–60, esp. 13–18.

18. Laughlin, *The Second International Exhibition of Eugenics,* 18–60.

19. Laughlin, *The Second International Exhibition of Eugenics,* plate 24; *Scientific Papers of the Second International Congress of Eugenics,* I, pl. 18.

20. *Fifty-Third Annual Report of the Trustees of the American Museum of Natural History . . . May 1, 1922,* no imprint, 32–33, in American Museum of Natural History Library (cited hereafter as AMNH); Leonard Darwin, "Reports of the International Congress of Eugenics held at New York in September 1921," *Eugenics Review,* clipping, in Eugenics Education Society Library; Rob Kroes, *Naar het Beeld van de Vrijheld* (Amsterdam, 1986), 74–75. The importance of understanding popular events as organizing processes is suggested by David Matthews, "The Second Great Awakening as an Organizing Process," *American Quarterly* 21 (1969): 23–43.

21. F. A. Lucas to George Sherwood, memo, n.d., attached to Harry

Laughlin to Lucas, 16 June 1922, AMNH Archives, central files, folder 206; "The American Museum Invites Biology Teachers of Greater New York," September 1932, [press release], AMNH Archives, folder 1267t; "Report of H. H. Laughlin for the Year Ending 31 August 1922," American Philosophical Society, Charles B. Davenport Papers, Laughlin August–December 1922 folder (cited hereafter as Davenport Papers). See also, Kevles, *In the Name of Eugenics*, 96–104; and Allen, "The Misuse of Biological Hierarchies," 119–122.

22. *Report of the President of the American Eugenics Society, June 26, 1926* (New Haven, 1926), 2–9; and "The Eugenics Society of the United States of America," *Eugenical News* 10 (March 1925), clipping, in Northeast Missouri State University, Department of Special Collections, Harry H. Laughlin Papers, International Congress of Eugenics folder. On eugenics as "ruling class" ideology, consult Garland Allan, "Genetics, Eugenics and Class Struggle," *Genetics* 79 (June, 1975): 29–45. According to Allen, the founders of the eugenics movement were "wealthy businessmen, investors, the financial and ruling elite of America at the time."

23. Winona Evans Reeves, *The Blue Book of Iowa Women* (Mexico, MO: Press of the Missouri Printing and Publishing Co., 1914), 115–117; *History of Audubon, Iowa, 1878–1978* (n.p., 1978), 79–80; "Audubon Woman Gained Fame," *News Guide* (13 September 1951), in Iowa State Historical Society, vertical files; Mary T. Watts, "Fitter Families," *The Survey* 51 (15 February 1924): 517–518.

24. Kevles, *In the Name of Eugenics*, 61–62; Watts, "Fitter Families," 517; Florence Brown Sherbon to Irving Fisher, 9 December 1924, Davenport Papers, Sherbon folder; "Fitter Families and Psychological Tests," *Science—Supplement* n.s. 63 (29 January 1926): 32–34.

25. Mary T. Watts to Charles B. Davenport, 14 August 1923, Davenport Papers, Mary T. Watts folder; Watts, "Fitter Families," 518.

26. Watts to Davenport, 31 December 1924?, Davenport Papers, Mary T. Watts folder. For understanding vernacular culture as social text, see Dell Upton, "The Power of Things: Recent Studies in American Vernacular Architecture," *American Quarterly* 35 (Bibliography, 1983): 262–279.

27. "Eugenics Society Sends a Man to Watch 'Fitter' Families Contest at Fair," *Topeka Daily Capital,* 10 September 1924, 16; "Free Fair Fathers Move to Improve Breed of Men," *Topeka Capital,* 3 July 1920, clipping; "Fitter Families Eugenic Competition," *Journal of the Kansas Medical Society,* clipping; Ida Clyde Clarke, "Kansas Has a Big Idea," *Pictorial Review* 26 (January 1925), clipping, all in Kansas State Historical Society, vertical files. Frank M. Chase, "Kansas' Latest Challenge—'Fitter Families,'" *Dearborn Independent,* 18 December 1920, 11.

28. *Report of the President of the American Eugenics Society,* 26–29; Sherbon correspondence in Davenport Papers, Sherbon folder; *Thirty-Third Annual Convention of the International Association of Fairs and Expositions* (Sioux City, Iowa: Deitch and Lamar, n.d.), 66–70; *Thirty-Fourth Annual Meeting of*

the *International Association of Fairs and Expositions* (Oklahoma City: Oklahoma City Publishing Co., n.d.), 60–62; Watts to Davenport, 26 August 1925?, Davenport Papers, Mary T. Watts folder.

29. *Report of the President of the American Eugenics Society,* 25–27; Leon F. Whitney to Fair Associations, form letter; Sherbon, "Popular Education," *Eugenics* 3 (September 1930): 356–357; and, "The Fitter Families Eugenic Competition at Fairs and Expositions," both in Davenport Papers, Watts folder; Sherbon to Fisher, 9 December 1924, Davenport Papers, Sherbon folder.

30. Franz Boas, "Eugenics," *Scientific Monthly* 3 (November 1916): 471–478; Lewis, *Arrowsmith* chap. 23; Clarence Darrow, "The Eugenics Cult," *American Mercury* 8 (June 1926): 129–138; Ludmerer, *Genetics and American Society,* 82–83, 121–124; and Ludmerer, "American Geneticists and the Eugenics Movement: 1905–1935," *Journal of the History of Biology* 2 (Fall 1969): 337–361.

31. Kevles, *In the Name of Eugenics,* 169; *A Decade of Progress in Eugenics. Scientific Papers of the Third International Congress of Eugenics,* 486–509.

32. Laughlin to Sherwood, 10 September 1932, AMNH Archives, f. 1267t; Laughlin to Fay-Cooper Cole, 6 May 1932, Laughlin Papers, f. "Chicago Fair—Arrangements;" J. F. Pearson to Laughlin, 10 January 1933, Univ. of Illinois, Chicago, Dept. of Special Collections, Records of the Century of Progress Exposition, f. 1-8096. Postcard to Laughlin, Laughlin Papers, f. "Chicago World's Fair—Exhibit and Correspondence."

33. On the "typical American family" exhibit, see: Harvey D. Gibson to T. J. White, 12 March 1940, New York Public Library, Manuscripts Division, Records of the New York World's Fair (hereafter NYWF), Box 369, f. "W. F. Representatives"; G. W. Leete to Joseph M. Upchurch, 1 May 1940, NYWF, Box 371, f. Johns-Manville Company; "Questionnaire For Selecting the National Typical American Family," NYWF, Box 369, f. "National Typical Family;" "'Typical Arkansas Family' En Route to View Splendors of the World's Fair and of the Nation's Largest City," *Arkansas Gazette,* 13 September 1940, clipping, NYWF, Box 369, f. unmarked. In a speech on the occasion of the arrival of the first "typical" families, Gibson told them "that they were the people who make this country real." See "'Typical Families' Greeted by Mayor," *New York Times,* 12 May 1940, 42.

34. [Bonnie Yochelson], "Selling The World of Tomorrow: Section Labels" (unpublished script for an exhibition at the Museum of the City of New York). I am grateful to Dr. Yochelson for sharing this script with me.

Chapter Three

1. Leon Blum, "France is Putting Her House in Order to Welcome the World," *Paris 1937* 12 (May 1937): 3.

2. John E. Findling and Kimberly D. Pelle, eds., *Historical Dictionary of World's Fairs and Expositions, 1851–1988* (Westport, CT: Greenwood Press, 1990), passim.

3. On exoticism, see Edward Said, *Orientalism* (New York: Pantheon, 1978). My ideas about "coloniale moderne" have been influenced by Paul Rabinow, *French Modern: Norms and Forms of the Social Environment* (Cambridge, Mass.: MIT Press, 1989); Gwendolyn Wright, *The Politics of Design in French Colonial Urbanism* (Chicago: University of Chicago Press, 1991); and, by Marianna Torgovnick, *Gone Primitive: Savage Intellects, Modern Lives* (Chicago: University of Chicago Press, 1990). On the concept of habitus, see Pierre Bourdieu, *Outline of a Theory of Practice* (Cambridge: Cambridge University Press, 1977), esp. chap. 2, which suggests that habitus connotes that complex of cultural activities that bestow meanings of "sensibility" and "reasonableness" on particular practices.

4. William Appleman Williams, "The Legend of Isolationism in the 1920s," *Science and Society* 18 (1954): 1–20; Joan Hoff Wilson, *American Business and Foreign Policy, 1920–1933* (Lexington, KY: University of Kentucky Press, 1971); and Warren I. Cohen, *Empire Without Tears: America's Foreign Relations 1921–1933* (New York: Alfred A. Knopf, 1987).

5. Very little has been written about colonial fairs. Useful starting points are Findling and Pelle, eds., *Historical Dictionary, passim;* and Paul Greenhalgh, *Ephemeral Vistas: The Expositions Universelles, Great Exhibitions and World's Fairs, 1851–1939* (Manchester: Manchester University Press, 1988), esp. chap. 3.

6. Charles-Robert Ageron, "L'Exposition Coloniale de 1931: Mythe republicain ou mythe imperial?", in *Les Lieux de Mémoire,* ed. Pierre Nora (Paris: Gallimard, 1984), 1:561–591. On the 1922 fair, see Jean Angelini, *L'Exposition nationale coloniale de Marseille 1922: Son rayonnement local et national* (Ph.D. diss., Université d'Aix, 1971).

7. John M. Mackenzie, *Propaganda and Empire: The Manipulation of British Public Opinion, 1880–1960* (Manchester: Manchester University Press, 1984), 96–120; Mackenzie, "Wembley 1924–1925," in Findling and Pelle, *Historical Dictionary,* 235–238. See also, Sir Lawrence Weaver, *Exhibitions and the Arts of Display* (New York: Charles Scribner's Sons, 1925); and Clough Williams-Ellis, *Lawrence Weaver* (London: G. Bles, 1933).

8. "Engineering," *London Times,* 30 September 1924, supplement.

9. Charles Regismanset, *8 Jours à L'Exposition Coloniale de Marseilles* (Paris: Les Editions G. Grés, 1922). On French colonial fairs, see also Sylviane LePrun, *Le Théâtre des Colonies: Scenographie, acteurs et discours de l'imaginaire dans les expositions 1855–1937* (Paris: Editions l'Harmattan, 1986).

10. *Official Guide,* quoted in Mackenzie, *Propaganda and Empire,* 108; *British Empire Exhibition (1923). Handbook of General Information* (London: no imprint), 15; Mackenzie, "Wembley 1924–1925," 237; *British Empire Exhibition, Official Guide 1924* (London: Fleetway Press, 1924), quoted in Greenhalgh, *Ephemeral Vistas,* 95.

11. *British Empire Exhibition. The Business Man's Opportunity. Wembley 1925* [pamphlet]; "Pure Science," in *Guide to the Exhibits in the Pavilion of*

His Majesty's Government (n.p., n.d.), 61; *The British Empire Exhibition (1924) . . . Tropical Disease Section* (pamphlet); all in Grange Museum, Wembley. Several journals kept American scientists abreast of developments at Wembley. See for instance: "Exhibit of the Royal Society at the British Empire Exposition," *Science* n.s. 60 (19 September 1924): 261–262; "Popular Science Exhibitions; Royal Society's Exhibition of Pure Science," *Science* n.s. 60 (19 December 1924): 569–570; J. B. C. Kershaw, "British Empire Exhibition," *Scientific American* 131 (August–October 1924): 80–81, 168, 254.

12. "Minutes of an Extraordinary General Meeting of the British Empire Exhibition (1924) Incorporated," 10 November 1924, in Public Records Office, BT 60, f. DOT 1500; Mackenzie, *Propaganda and Empire*, 111–112.

13. On the importance of the 1925 fair, see: Alastair Duncan, *Art Deco* (London: Thames and Hudson, 1988); Alastair Duncan, *Encyclopedia of Art Deco* (New York: E. P. Dutton, 1988); Richard Guy Wilson, et al. *The Machine Age in America, 1918–1941* (New York: The Brooklyn Museum in association with Harry N. Abrams, Inc. 1986); Victor Arwas, *Art Deco* (New York: Harry N. Abrams, Inc., 1980); Yvonne Brunhammer, *1925* (Paris: Les Presses de la Connaissance, 1976); and, Frank Scarlett and Marjorie Townley, *Arts Décoratifs 1925: A Personal Recollection of the Paris Exhibition* (London: Academy Editions, 1975).

14. A. Maybon, "A l'exposition des arts décoratifs," *La Semaine Coloniale. Numéro special annuel,* 1925, 135–137, in Archives d'Outre-Mer; *Exposition internationale des arts Décoratifs et industriels modernes* (Paris: Librairie Larousse, [1925]), in Cooper-Hewitt Library, New York; and Guillaume Janneau, *Art et Décoration* (Paris: Librairie Centrale des Beaux-Arts, 1925).

15. Paul Greenhalgh, "Antwerp 1930 and Liège 1930," in Findling and Pelle, *Historical Dictionary,* 258–259.

16. The best starting points for understanding the 1931 Paris fair are: Catherine Hodeir and Michel Pierre, *Exposition Coloniale* (Paris: Editions Complexe, 1991); Charles-Robert Ageron, "L'Exposition Coloniale de 1931: Mythe republicain ou mythe imperiale?" in *Les Lieux de Mémoire,* ed. Pierre Nora (Paris: Gallimard, 1984), 1:561–591; Thomas August, "The Colonial Exposition in France: Education or Reinforcement?" *Proceedings of the 6th and 7th Annual Meetings of the French Colonial Historical Society* 7 (1980): 147–154; and Marc Lagana's "Paris 1931," in Findling and Pelle, *Historical Dictionary,* 261–265. On Lyautey, see Rabinow, *French Modern,* 15, 104–125; and Wright, *The Politics of Design,* 3, 75–89.

17. Catherine Hodier, "Une Journée à l'exposition coloniale, Paris 1931," *L'Histoire* 69 (1984): 41–48; André Castelot, "L'Exposition Coloniale," *Historia* 140 (1970): 1218–1222; Wright, 305–310; and, the five-volume general report edited by Marcel Olivier, *Rapport général* (Paris: Imprimerie Nationale, 1932).

18. Ageron, 571. See also: P. de Margerie, memo, 20 February 1931, Archives Nationale, F12 11890, file 2; and, "Anti-Imperialist Exhibit Arranged,"

Daily Worker clipping in "Rapport sur les activités du Comité americain," scrapbook, Archives Nationales, Paris f. 12-11894 (cited hereafter as Comité americain Scrapbook).

19. R. C. Dawes to C. G. Dawes, 11 March 1930, Univ. of Illinois, Chicago, Dept. of Special Collections, Records of the Century of Progress Exposition (cited hereafter as COP), General Files, f. 1-4348; "Charles Dawes Proves He's an Able Diplomat," *Chicago Tribune*, 15 February 1931; Sol Bloom, *The Autobiography of Sol Bloom* (New York: G. P. Putnam's Sons, 1948), 215–221; Karal Ann Marling, *George Washington Slept Here: Colonial Revivals and American Culture, 1876–1976* (Cambridge, Mass.: Harvard University Press, 1988), 325–327. Senator William Borah apparently was the one who insisted that the name "colonial" be dropped from the Paris fair before the U.S. would participate. See Marechal Lyautey to Charles Burke, 7 August 1931, National Archives (cited hereafter as NA), RG 43 Records of International Conferences, Commissions, and Expositions, Box 1, f. Bloom.

20. Herbert Hoover, "Address By Secretary Hoover at Exhibition Dinner," 20 January 1926, Herbert Hoover Presidential Library, Herbert Hoover Papers, Commerce Papers, Box 553, f. Sesquicentennial 1926 January-May; *Report of Commission Appointed by the Secretary of Commerce to Visit and Report upon the International Exposition of Modern Decorative and Industrial Art in Paris* (Washington, D.C.: Government Printing Office, 1926), 16; Marling, *George Washington Slept Here*, 325.

21. I am indebted to Mick Gidley for information about Burke. See also Kenneth R. Philp, *John Collier's Crusade for Indian Reform 1920–1954* (Tucson: The University of Arizona Press, 1977), 56–57; "C. Bascom Slemp," n.d., NA, RG 43, Box 1, entry 1317, f. French Colonial Exposition, Correspondence June–July 1931.

22. Marling, *George Washington Slept Here*, 325–327; William B. Rhoads, "The Colonial Revival and the Americanization of Immigrants," in Alan Axelrod, ed., *The Colonial Revival in America* (New York: Norton, 1985), 341–361.

23. The documentary record for the Mt. Vernon replica is contained in NA, RG 43, Box 1, f. Charles K. Bryant. Information on the construction of the building is available in the archives of the Sears, Roebuck & Co., Chicago. At the close of the fair, the building was reconstructed near a golf course in St. Cloud. See Maurice Durosoy, "Cinquantenaire de l'Exposition Coloniale Internationale de Vincennes," *Mondes et Cultures* 41 (8 May 1981): 389–392.

24. "Some General Remarks on the International Colonial and Overseas Exposition at Paris," n.d., NA, RG 43, Box 7, f. Fisher Report, pp. 21, 32.

25. On the Philippine reservation at the St. Louis fair, see Robert W. Rydell, *All the World's a Fair* (Chicago: University of Chicago Press, 1984), chap. 6. For descriptions of the colonial exhibits featured as part of the U.S. display at Paris, see "Some General Remarks on the International Colonial and Overseas Exposition at Paris," op. cit., passim.

26. Frank McIntyre?, memo, 23 October 1930, with 28349-6, NA, RG 350, Records of the Bureau of Insular Affairs; Thomas O'Brien, "Statement Re. Visit of the United States Indian Band to the International Colonial and Overseas Exposition," n.d.; Slemp to O'Brien, 26 February 1932 and attachments; all in NA, RG 43, Box 9, f. Indian Band.

27. [Radio addresses], 26 April 1931, NA, RG 43, Box 14, f. Radio.

28. "Some General Remarks on the International Colonial and Overseas Exposition at Paris," op. cit., 12–21.

29. Burke to George Akerson, 9 January 1931, NA, RG 43, Box 17, f. Sousa; "Some General Remarks on the International Colonial and Overseas Exposition at Paris," op. cit., 12–21.

30. "Some General Remarks on the International Colonial and Overseas Exposition at Paris," op. cit., 21.

31. [Le Consul de France à Porto Rico] à Ministre des Affaires Etrangères, 24 February 1931, Archives Nationales, F12-11890, f. 1; "Puertoriquenos Are Sensitive," (no title, ca. 19 January 1931), clipping; "Porto Rican Protest," *New York Herald Tribune,* 3 December 1930, clipping; "Llega a la Camara la protesta del pais contra la Feria de Las Colonias," *El Imparcial,* [August? 1931], clipping; all in NA, RG 350, file 28349–8. See also Ida Jewell D'Egilbert, "Porto Rico's Participation in the International Colonial and Overseas Exposition," NA, RG 43, Box 19, no folder.

32. "Bloc in Lower House Opposed to Islands' Participation in Colonial Exhibition," *Philippines Herald,* 1 October 1930, clipping; "La Exposición Colonial de Paris tiene tambien la enemigo de la prensa filipina," *El Imparcial,* 17 March 1931, clipping; both in NA, RG 350, f. 28349. Plans to include "native" demonstrators as part of the American exhibit are clear in Slemp to Ray Lyman Wilbur, 19 March 1931, NA, RG 43, Box 6, f. Exhibits for Hawaiian Islands.

33. [Excerpts from various registration books] attached to "Message from the President of the United States. . . ." U.S. Senate Document No. 74.; and, Laurence Hills to Slemp, 7 July 1931; both in NA, RG 43, Box 8, f. Final report.

34. Marcel Olivier, memo, 23 August 1930; George Harrison Phelps to Marechal Lyautey, 15 October 1930; both in Archives d'Outre Mer, Exposition Coloniale Internationale, Carton 27, f. Etats-Unis.

35. "Fashions to Go 'Colonial,'" unidentified clipping; "Clothes For Lounging," unidentified clipping; "Paris Bars Help Create New Thirst," unidentified clipping; "Dare Interprets the Mode," *Detroit News,* 4 February 1931; Elisabeth Hawey, "Algerian Motifs, Colors Inspire New Jewelry and Accessories," *New York World,* 16 February 1931; "Pajamas Now in Algerian Colors," *American,* 19 March 1931; "Must Be Beauty to Wear New Coolie Hat," *Sun,* 10 April 1931; all in "Rapport sur les Activités du Comité americain de l'Exposition Coloniale Internationale," Comité americain Scrapbook.

36. See for instance, "France and U.S. Will Honor Washington"; and, "*American Boy* offers Free Trip to Paris"; both in ibid.

37. Marling, 329; and, *History of the George Washington Bicentennial Celebration. Foreign Participation* (Washington, D.C.: George Washington Bicentennial Commission, 1932), 101–106.

38. "Visit of Mr. Burnham, Mr. Farrier and Mr. Tillson to Vincennes Exhibition," August 1931, COP, f. 1-8079.

39. "Report of D. H. Burnham on the Paris International Colonial Exposition," p. 40, COP, f. 1-8084.

40. Ibid., 5.

41. Charles Dawes to Lenox Lohr, 6 November 1931, COP, Confidential Files, Box 2, f. "Dawes."

42. John Stephen Sewell, "Project for an African Exhibit . . ." 17 February 1932, COP, General Correspondence, f. 1-192.

43. [Press Release], n.d., in ibid.; Sewall, ibid.

44. On the problems surrounding financing, see the correspondence in COP, General Correspondence, f. 1-190 and 1-191. On the controversy with the African-American community, see memo, 2 November 1932, f. 1-191, noting that African Americans "did not want their race represented" by a disreputable showman. For a fuller discussion of African-American representation at the fair, see chapter 6 below.

For a fine discussion of the "Darkest Africa" show, see Robert Bogdan, *Freak Show: Presenting Human Oddities for Amusement and Profit* (Chicago: University of Chicago Press, 1988), 195–197. Anthropologist Fay-Cooper Cole withdrew his endorsement of the Darkest Africa spectacle. Cole termed the show "a fraud from start to finish. They have not a single thing inside which they advertise on the outside. They have no pigmies, although they do have some dwarfs. I seriously doubt if any of their Negroes ever saw Africa. . . . There is nothing whatever to commend this show." See Cole to R. F. Moulton, 14 July 1933, COP, General Correspondence, f. 1-4823. What Cole wanted was an exhibit sanctioned by the appropriate colonial authorities. "I think it quite all right and desirable that other nations make exhibits of the inhabitants of their colonies," he explained. See Cole to Rufus Dawes, 7 August 1930, COP, Box 25, f. "SAC-Anthropology (Dawes Correspondence)."

45. Charles G. Dawes to Rufus C. Dawes, 19 May 1930, COP, Confidential files, Box 1, f. Dawes 16 May-December 1930; Charles G. Dawes to Lenox Lohr, 6 November 1931, COP, Confidential files, Box 2, f. Dawes.

46. George Creel, "Talk by George Creel Before Commonwealth Club," 26 August 1938, Library of Congress, Manuscripts Division, George Creel Papers, Box 5, f. Speeches 1938–40.

47. Gray Brechin, "Sailing to Byzantium: The Architecture of the Fair," in Burton Benedict, ed., *The Anthropology of World's Fairs* (London and Berkeley: Scolar Press, 1983), 94–113; Jack James and Earle Weller, *Treasure Island* (San Francisco: Pisani Publishing Co., 1941), 26; Richard Reinhardt, *Treasure Island: San Francisco's Exposition Years* (San Francisco: Scrimshaw Press, 1973), 83.

48. "San Francisco Golden Gate Exposition," *Architectural Forum* 70 (June 1939): 470; *Official Guidebook. Golden Gate International Exposition* (San Francisco: San Francisco Bay Exposition, 1939), 75, 101; Juliet James, *The Meaning of the Courts of the Golden Gate International Exposition, 1939* (Berkeley: Professional Press, 1939), 39.

49. "He Has Seen Them All," *Official World's Fair Weekly* 1 (May 27, 1933): 34–35; Leland W. Cutler, *America is Good to a Country Boy* (Stanford, CA: Stanford University Press, 1954), 210–232.

50. [French Consul General?] to [Minister of Foreign Affairs?], 25 March 1939, Archives d'Outre-Mer, FOM 492, dossier 111.

51. Miguel Covarrubias, *Pageant of the Pacific* (San Francisco: Pacific House, 1940), n.p., in California State University at Fresno, Department of Special Collections (cited hereafter as CSUF).

52. Creel, "In Honor of the American Indian," *Think* 4 (9 February, 1939): 10, 38; the importance of exoticism and "pay as you go" French colonies is noted in Thomas G. August, "Nineteenth-Century Exoticism in France: The Formation of French Colonial Attitudes," *Historicus* 1 (April 1979): 84. On Collier's interest in the European colonial experience, see Philp, *John Collier's Crusade*, 59.

53. *Official Guide Book*, 40, 61; "Today: Nicaragua's President Somoza Will Be Given a Rousing Reception at the Fair," *San Francisco Chronicle*, 2 June 1939, p. 1E; "President Somoza Wants Canal Built," *San Francisco Chronicle*, 30 May 1939, p. 8.

54. *Golden Gate International Exposition on San Francisco Bay, 1939*, pamphlet; and, *1939 World's Fair Progress* 1, no. 1 (1937): 14; both in CSUF.

Chapter Four
1. Rufus C. Dawes to Karl T. Compton, 23 July 1931, Massachusetts Institute of Technology, Institute Archives, AC 4, Karl Compton Papers, f. "Chicago World's Fair, February 1931–1934"; David Mamet, *The Water Engine* (New York: Grove Press, Inc., 1978), 16.

2. Bascom Johnson to Henrietta Additon, 13 July 1939, New York Public Library, Manuscripts Division, Records of the New York World's Fair (hereafter NYWF), Amusement Department, Drawer 5, f. "Nudity."

3. John G. Cawelti, "America on Display, 1876, 1893, 1933," in Frederic C. Jaher, ed., *America in the Age of Industrialism* (New York: Free Press, 1968), 317–363; Helen Harrison, ed., *Dawn of a New Day: The New York World's Fair 1939/40* (New York: The Queens Museum and New York University Press, 1980). I am also indebted to James Mann, "The Popularization of Science at the Chicago World's Fair, 1933–34," and Peter Kuznick, "The Mystification and Commodification of Science at the 1939 New York World's Fair," papers read at the 1985 meeting of the Organization of American Historians. See also Joseph P. Cusker, "The World of Tomorrow: The 1939 New York World's Fair" (Ph.D. diss., Rutgers University, 1990), 161–197.

4. Ronald C. Tobey, *The American Ideology of Science, 1919–1930* (Pittsburgh: University of Pittsburgh Press, 1971); Thomas Bender, "Science and the Culture of American Communities: The Nineteenth Century," *History of Education Quarterly* 16 (Spring 1976): 63–77; and Elizabeth Stong, "Science and the Early New Deal, 1933–1935," *Synthesis* 5, no. 2 (1982): 44–63. The "revolt against science" is illuminated by Daniel J. Kevles, *The Physicists* (New York: Alfred A. Knopf, 1978), 236–251; and Peter J. Kuznick, *Beyond the Laboratory* (Chicago: University of Chicago Press, 1987), esp. chap. 1.

5. Robert W. Rydell, *All the World's a Fair: Visions of Empire at America's International Expositions, 1876–1916* (Chicago: University of Chicago Press, 1984); and, A. Hunter Dupree, *Science in the Federal Government* (Cambridge, MA: Harvard University Press, 1957), 335.

6. David F. Noble, *America by Design* (New York: Oxford University Press, 1977), 152–156; Robert H. Kargon, *The Rise of Robert Millikan: Portrait of a Life in American Science* (Ithaca: Cornell University Press, 1982), 85–87; Daniel J. Kevles, "'Into Hostile Political Camps': The Reorganization of International Science in World War I," *Isis* 42 (1971): 47–60; and Kevles, *Physicists*, 102–138 (which describes the NRC as an "arsenal of science," 112). See also Vernon Kellogg, "The National Research Council" (1925), 2, ms. in Archives of the National Academy of Science (hereafter NAS), Washington, D.C. Useful studies of the Science Service are Paul A. Carter, "Science and the Common Man," *American Scholar* 45 (1975–1976): 778–794; and David J. Rhees, "A New Voice for Science: Science Service Under Edwin D. Slosson, 1921–1929" (M.A. thesis, University of North Carolina, 1979).

7. *Report of the President of A Century of Progress to Board of Trustees* (14 March 1936) (n.p., 1936), 28–34; [Dawes?] to Pupin, 3 February 1928, Univ. of Illinois, Chicago, Dept. of Special Collections, Records of the Century of Progress Exposition (hereafter COP), Box 22, f. SAC-misc. Dawes to W. A. Pusey, 31 May 1928, Executive Board Committee on Chicago World's Fair Centennial Celebration, 1928–1929 (hereafter Ex. Board Committee on CWF), NAS; Pusey to Dunn, 10 June 1928, ibid.; and "Report of the Permanent Secretary to the Executive Board," 9 October 1928, ibid.

8. "Report of the Permanent Secretary to the Executive Board," 9 October 1929; Albert L. Barrows to Gano Dunn, 21 August 1928; Dawes to George K. Burgess, 21 August 1928, attached to Kellogg to Members of the Executive Board, 1 October 1928; and Burgess to Frank B. Jewett, 19 October 1928, all in Ex. Board Committee on CWF, NAS.

9. [Dawes] to Trustees, 17 October 1928, COP, f. SAC-NRC October 16, 1928–32.

10. Burgess to Jewett, 19 October 1928, Ex. Board Committee on CWF; and Dawes as quoted in press release, f. "World's Fair, Chicago—1933–34"; both in NAS.

11. Jewett to Burgess, 18 December 1928, attached to NAS, Executive Board Minutes, 12 February 1929, f. "World's Fair, Chicago—1933–34."

12. "A Full Transcript of the Record Taken of the First Meeting of the National Research Council Science Advisory Committee to the Trustees of the Chicago World's Fair Centennial Celebration" (this and later minutes hereafter cited as "Full Transcript of the . . . Meeting of SAC"), 21 June 1929, Executive Board, Science Advisory Committee to Trustees of the Chicago World's Fair Centennial (hereafter Ex. Board, SAC), f. "Meetings, March 1930." See also the minutes for the second and third meetings of the SAC, and *Annual Report of the National Academy of Sciences, Fiscal Year 1929–1930,* pp. 51–52, all in NAS.

13. "Full Transcript of the Third Meeting of SAC," 28 March 1930, 4–5, in NAS, Ex. Board, SAC, f. "Meetings, March 1930"; and M. I. Pupin to Allen D. Albert, n.d., COP, Box 23, f. SAC-NRC Jan.–Oct. 1928.

14. "Full Transcript of the Third Meeting of SAC," 11–12; and "Full Transcript of the First Meeting of SAC," 7.

15. "Full Transcript of the Second Meeting of SAC," 20 September 1929, 6; and Pupin to Albert, n.d., op. cit.

16. James G. Mann, "Engineer of Mass Education: Lenox R. Lohr and the Celebration of American Science and Industry" (Ph.D. diss., Rutgers University, 1988); *Report of the President of a Century of Progress,* 34–35; "The Human View of Science," *World's Fair Weekly,* 13 May 1933, 5–7; and Henry Crew to James M. Cattell, 4 December 1931, Library of Congress (hereafter LC), James M. Cattell Papers, Box 162, f. AAAS (1931)–COP; and Cattell to Crew, 11 June 1932, Cattell Papers, Box 106, f. Crew; Henry Crew Diary, 14 October 1930, Northwestern University Archives, Henry Crew Papers. Doubts about Crew's abilities are apparent in the correspondence between SAC members and MIT President Karl Compton, MIT Archives, Karl Compton Papers, AC4, f. Chicago World's Fair, 1930–January 1931. Maurice Holland was especially concerned, noting that among Crew's associates there was "not an experienced exposition man or science showman in the group." See Holland to Compton, n.d., ibid. Disdain for Crew also permeated George K. Burgess's remarks to Compton: "as to the philosophy of the Research Council Group, to use an engineering illustration, the Science Advisory Committee may be considered in the nature of a designing organization, while Mr. Crew and his associates are the construction organization." See Burgess to Compton, 16 December 1930, ibid.

17. F. W. Tanner, "Our Secret Friends"; F. K. Richtmeyer, "How Light Puts Electrons to Work"; Maurice Holland, "Science in the Headlines." Transcripts of radio talks, all in LC, John C. Merriam Papers, Box 221.

18. *Official Guide: Book of the Fair 1933* (Chicago: A Century of Progress, 1933), 11; Lenox R. Lohr, *Fair Management* (Chicago: Cuneo Press, 1952), 197; "Starring A Star," *Literary Digest* 113 (7 May 1933): 24–26.

19. *Official Guide,* 22–23, 51, 121.

20. *Dedication Ceremonies of the Hall of Science, June 1, 1932,* in Yale University, Sterling Library, Manuscripts and Archives Division, Century of

Progress Expositions Collection, Box 3, folder 7; and "Fair Carillon Leads to South African Contract," *Progress* 4 (1 April 1934): 4.

21. *Dedication Ceremonies.*

22. S. L. Tesone, "Symbolism in Fair Sculpture," *World's Fair Weekly,* 15 October 1933, 33.

23. *Official Handbook of Exhibits in the Division of the Basic Sciences Hall of Science* (Chicago: A Century of Progress, 1934), 9–11, 17–19.

24. Ibid., 20, 30; and *Official Guide,* 39.

25. *Official Guide,* 59–66.

26. Lohr, *Fair Management,* 143; "Mass Measurements," *World's Fair Weekly,* 20 August 1933, p. 4; Helen M. Bennett, n.d., in COP, f. 15–155; "Indian Chants and Indian Footfalls," *World's Fair Weekly,* 30 July 1933, pp. 3–5; Fay-Cooper Cole to Lohr, 19 April 1933, COP, General Correspondence, f. 1-507; Cole to Director of Exhibits, n.d., COP, General Correspondence, f. 1-507; Cole to Matthew Sterling, 26 January 1933, assistant secretary in charge of the United States National Museum, Smithsonian Institution Archives, Record Unit 192, Box 395, f. 3; and Ralph W. Dexter, "Putnam's Problems Popularizing Anthropology," *American Scientist* 54 (1966): 315–332.

27. "Explanatory Notes on the General Layout of the Hall of Science for the Century of Progress," COP, Box 22, f. "SAC-misc. Aug.-Dec. 1929"; *New York World's Fair 1939* (New York: n.p., 1936), in New York Historical Society; see also Kevles, *The Physicists,* 252–266. The interest of Roosevelt and other New Dealers in the exposition movement of the 1930s is well documented in the exposition records of the Department of Commerce in the National Archives, Record Group 40, Box 640. See, for instance, Daniel Roper to Charles F. Kettering, 24 February 1938, RG 40, Box 640, f. 84608. See also Elizabeth Stong, "Science and the Early New Deal: 1933–1935," *Synthesis* 5, no. 2 (1982): 44–63. On the importance of science to other fairs, see: *The Cardinal,* 24 May 1935, San Diego Historical Society, Elaine Steele Scrapbooks, clipping; "General Motors Exhibit Attracts 127,645 . . ." clipping, 11 June 1936, Dallas Historical Society, Records of the Texas Centennial Exposition, unprocessed box of clippings; "Science," *San Francisco Chronicle,* 17 February 1939, 26E. The latter account notes how "[c]hemistry, the magical transformer of the sciences, is brought down to everyday language in the 'three-ringed circus' educational exhibit in the Hall of Science."

28. Gerald Wendt to Wayne M. Faunce, 7 July 1937, American Museum of Natural History Archives, General Files, folder 1276. The best analysis of the fair is offered by the essays contained in Harrison, ed., *Dawn of a New Day,* especially Warren I. Susman, "The People's Fair: Cultural Contradictions of a Consumer Society," 17–27.

29. Harold C. Urey to Grover Whalen, 31 January 1938, NYWF, Advisory Committee on Science, Drawer 225 (hereafter NYWF-ACS).

30. Joseph P. Cusker, "The World of Tomorrow: Science, Culture, and Community at the New York World's Fair," in *Dawn of a New Day,* ed. Har-

NOTES TO PAGES 108–114

rison, 13–15; "World's Fair to Display Progress in Research," *New York Times*, 16 January 1938, Sec. 2, p. 2; "New York World's Fair 1939, Inc., Members Advisory Committee on Science," n.d., NYWF-ACS; and Jewett to Samuel F. Voorhees, 1 March 1936, NYWF-ACS.

31. "Summary Report. Advisory Committee on Science," 3 March 1938, attached to Philip McConnell to Charles C. Green, NYWF-ACS.

32. [Waldemar Kaempffert?], "Science at the Fair," editorial, *New York Times*, 29 April 1938, clipping; and Kaempffert to Whalen, 29 April 1938; both in NYWF-ACS.

33. Kevles, *The Physicists*, 236–351; and Dupree, *Science in the Federal Government*, 344–368.

34. "New York World's Fair 1939 Advisory Committee on Science. Minutes of Meeting Held June 14, 1938"; and Wendt, "Science at the New York World's Fair 1939," 14 June 1938, both in NYWF-ACS.

35. [Wendt] to Einstein, 6 June 1938, attached to Wendt to Green, 6 June 1938; and Wendt, "Final Report as Consultant on Science," 24 June 1938; both in NYWF-ACS.

36. Wendt, "Science at the New York World's Fair 1939."

37. Wendt, *Science For the World of Tomorrow* (New York: Norton, 1939), 271, 13–15, 304–306. On scientific pragmatism, see David A. Hollinger, "The Problem of Pragmatism in American History," *Journal of American History* 62 (1980): 88–107.

38. Wendt, *Science For the World of Tomorrow*, 181–183.

39. Wendt, "A Proposal for a Daily Illumination Ceremony Utilizing Cosmic Rays," 29 December 1938, in NYWF-ACS; "Cosmic Ray Signal to Floodlight Fair," *New York Times*, 20 March 1939, 19; "Cops Yawn as Strip Dancer Seeks Arrest," *Daily News*, n.d., clipping in NYWF, Amusement Department, Drawer 3, f. Misc.; and Whalen, [dedication of Theme Center], typescript, n.d., in NYWF, Promotion and Development, Drawer 2.

40. Whalen, dedication of Science and Education Building, typescript, 26 May 1939, NYWF, Promotion and Development, Drawer 2; "The Progress of Science," *Scientific Monthly* 58 (May 1939): 471–475; "Proposal for a Focal Exhibit on Science and Education. Summary" [29 December 1938?], in NYWF-ACS; *Official Guidebook New York World's Fair 1939* (New York: Exposition Publications, 1939), 157–159; and "Science and Education Focal Exhibit, New York World's Fair 1939 Celebrates Opening," 26 May 1939, press release, NYWF, folder "Promotion and Development, Science and Education."

41. Quoting from "Progress of Science," 475. See also "Proposal for a Focal Exhibit on Science and Education, Summary"; and Wendt, "Science at the New York World's Fair 1939."

42. David F. Noble, *Forces of Production: A Social History of Industrial Automation* (New York: Alfred A. Knopf, 1984), 10.

Chapter Five

1. Walter Lippmann, "Today and Tomorrow," *New York Herald-Tribune,* 6 June 1939; *A Century of Progress. International Exposition, Chicago, 1933,* no imprint, Wellcome Institute Archives, unprocessed collection, Chicago Exhibition Box.

2. The phrase "dawn of a new day" gained currency from the song, "Dawn of a New Day," written for the 1939 fair by George Gershwin.

3. The militancy of workers during the 1930s is discussed in Irving Bernstein, *Turbulent Years* (Boston: Houghton Mifflin, 1970); "Interview with Fred L. Black," 10 March 1951, Ford Motor Company Archives, unprocessed collection, 192. On developments in Chicago, see H. L. Hollis to Frederic A. Delano, Franklin D. Roosevelt Library, Papers of Franklin D. Roosevelt, OF 275, Box 1, f. Century of Progress January–June 1933 (cited hereafter as FDR papers). Information about the intersection of the May Day and Preview of Progress parades is from "Red Light for Reds in May Day March," *World-Telegram,* 29 March 1938, clipping, New York Public Library, Manuscripts Division, Records of the New York World's Fair, Box 1053, f. Preview Parade Protests (cited hereafter as NYWF); and, "Divided Leftists in Quiet May Day," *New York Times,* 1 May 1938, 3. The quote by Whalen is from "Minutes of the Board of Directors. . . ." March 30, 1938, NYWF, Box 955, vol. 5, 266–267. See also, Whalen, "Selling the World's Fair to the World," n.d., NYWF, Promotion and Development files, Drawer 2, f. Advertising Club News. The idea of "selling the fair" was not unique to New York World's Fair promoters. See, Stanton Delaplane, "The Selling of a Fair," *San Francisco Chronicle,* 17 February 1939, E9.

4. "Interview with Fred L. Black," op. cit., 201.

5. On the "culture of production," see Richard Fox and T. J. Jackson Lears, *The Culture of Consumption: Critical Essays in American History, 1880–1980* (New York: Pantheon Books, 1983) and Warren I. Susman, *Culture as History* (New York: Pantheon Books, 1984).

6. On Roosevelt's involvement with earlier fairs, see Robert Rydell, *All the World's a Fair* (Chicago: Univ. of Chicago Press, 1984), 213. Roosevelt's complicated dealings with American business are the subject of several studies. See especially Steve Fraser and Gary Gerstle, *The Rise and Fall of the New Deal Order* (Princeton: Princeton University Press, 1989); and, Ellis W. Hawley, *The New Deal and the Problem of Monopoly* (Princeton: Princeton University Press, 1966).

7. John Stephen Sewell to General C. G. Dawes, 1 April 1931, University of Illinois, Chicago, Department of Special Collections, Records of the Century of Progress Exposition Confidential Files, Box 1, f. Dawes. See also Sewell's speech, "A Century of Progress," ibid, f. 15–125, where he declared: "Unquestionably we are heading for one of three alternatives: A) Either wise permissive legislation must be worked out and enacted which will enable business to regulate itself and get rid of unsound economic conditions, while protecting the

public against anything in the nature of monopolistic extortion, or B) We will have governmental regulation of all businesses without the benefit of participation by business itself, or C) the country will go bolshevik."

8. Information on the Dawes brothers is from Bascom N. Timmons, *Portrait of An American: Charles G. Dawes* (New York: Henry Holt, 1953), 110–111. On the capitalization of the fair, see: Charles Dawes to Herbert Hoover, 2 November 1929, Hoover Presidential Library, Herbert Hoover Papers, West Branch, IA, Box 94, f. Century of Progress, Chicago, 1929–1931.

9. "The World's Fair, Chicago, 1933" [precis of file]; and Sir E. Crowe, memo, March 1930; both in British Public Record Office (PRO), Board of Trade Records 60, f. 30485/1928; Godfrey Haggard to [?] Craigie, 5 June 1929, PRO, FO, 371, f. 13548 no. 197.

10. Information on Lohr is from James G. Mann, "Engineer of Mass Education: Lenox R. Lohr and the Celebration of American Science and Industry" (Ph.D. dissertation, Rutgers University, 1988), 46–74. The figure on the total cost of the fair is from John G. Cawelti, "America on Display: The World's Fairs of 1876, 1893, 1933," in Frederic Cople Jaher, ed. *The Age of Industrialism in America* (New York: The Free Press, 1968), 348.

11. "Big Value of Fair to Chicago is Told Centennial Chiefs," *Dallas News,* 1 September 1934, clipping, Dallas Historical Society, Texas Centennial Exposition Collection, Scrapbooks. Lohr would later claim that the fair generated a profit of $72,171. See Lohr to the editor, *Time,* 12 March 1962, University of Illinois, Chicago, Lenox R. Lohr Papers, f. 386. The details involved in organizing the Dallas fair are related in Kenneth B. Ragsdale, *Centennial '36: The Year America Discovered Dallas* (College Station, TX: Texas A & M University Press, 1987). On the San Diego fair, see Richard S. Requa, *Inside Lights on the Building of San Diego's Exposition, 1935,* no imprint, [1937?] Library of Congress. On the Cleveland exposition, see George Jackson, *History of Centennials, Expositions, and World's Fairs* (Lincoln, NE: Wekesser-Brinkman Co., 1939).

12. Leland W. Cutler, *America is Good to a Country Boy* (Stanford, CA: Stanford University Press, 1954), 186.

13. Whalen quoted in editorial, *Herald Tribune,* 3 May 1938, cited in "Minutes of the Board of Directors . . . May 25, 1938," NYWF, Box 955, vol. 5, 388–389; *$27,829,500 New York World's Fair Inc.* [pamphlet], NYWF, Box 959; "City Drive Opened for Bonds of Fair," *New York Times,* 24 November 1936, 1; "In Mr. Whalen's Image," *Time* 33 (1 May, 1939): 72.

14. Cawelti, "America on Display: The World's Fairs of 1876, 1893, 1933," 348.

15. Forrest Crissey, "Why the Century of Progress Architecture?" *Saturday Evening Post* (10 June, 1933): 63.

16. David Nye, *Electrifying America: Social Meanings of New Technology* (Cambridge, MA.: MIT Press, 1990), 353; Ibid., 17; Lenox R. Lohr, *Fair Management* (Chicago: Cuneo Press, 1952), 60.

17. Crissey, 16–17, 60–64; Hugh M. G. Gordon, "Color, Yes—But Ar-

chitecture?" *The Architect and Engineer* 114, no. 2 (August 1933): 21–23. Another critic called the architecture "three dimensional poster work." See "The Chicago Century of Progress Exposition, 1933," *The Architect and Building News* 134 (June 30, 1933): 392–397. And America's most famous architect, Frank Lloyd Wright, excluded from the fair's architectural commission, commented: "The 'public,' whatever that is, may be partially weaned from pseudo-classic only to find another 'pseudo' thrust into its arms." See, "Another 'Pseudo,'" *Architectural Forum* 59, no. 1 (July 1933): 25.

The full implications of architectural designs for the 1933 Chicago fair came to light in several Skidmore, Owings, and Merrill-designed buildings at the New York World's Fair. The architectural firm designed the RCA building as a giant radio tube, the Swift and Company Building as a frankfurter, and the Westinghouse Building as an enormous magnet. "We reverse the usual procedure and wrap the building around the exhibits," Skidmore explained. And, as a newspaper described their work, the architects no longer spoke of "designing" structures. Rather, they used the term "packaging." See "Buildings 'Package' Exhibits," *New York World-Telegram*, 4 February 1939, clipping, National Museum of American History, Smithsonian Institution, Washington, D.C., Edward Orth Collection, Scrapbooks, unprocessed.

18. *Freedom* [pamphlet], n.d., in Yale University, Sterling Library, Manuscripts and Archives Division, Century of Progress Collection (cited hereafter as Yale COP), Box 16, f. General Electric.

19. Brian Horrigan, "The Home of Tomorrow, 1927–1945," in *Imagining Tomorrow*, ed. Joseph Corn (Cambridge, MA: MIT Press, 1986), 137–163.

20. *Be Profit-Wise! Modernize!* [pamphlet], n.d., in Yale COP, Box 14, f. Formica.

21. "General Foods to Present 16 Shows at Century of Progress Exposition" [press release], n.d., in ibid, Box 16, f. General Foods. On the integration of education with popular entertainment in corporate exhibits, see Roland Marchand, "Corporate Imagery and Popular Education: World's Fairs and Expositions in the United States, 1893–1940," *Consumption and American Culture*, ed. David E. Nye and Carl Pedersen (Amsterdam: VU University Press, 1991), 18–33.

22. Stanley R. Edwards, "World's Fair; Psychology, Human Nature," *Telephony* 105, no. 21 (18 November, 1933): 10–14.

23. On architecture at the Texas Centennial, see Ragsdale, 174–207. Information about architecture at the San Diego fair is from Raymond Starr, "San Diego 1935–1936," in John E. Findling and Kimberly D. Pelle, eds. *Historical Dictionary of World's Fairs and Expositions, 1851–1988* (Westport, CT: Greenwood Press, 1990), 278–280. On the Cleveland fair, see: Eric Johannessen, *Cleveland Architecture, 1876–1976* (Cleveland: Western Reserve Historical Society, 1979), 190–194. On the cooperation between the rival San Francisco and New York exposition organizations, see Lawrence M. Hughes, "Many Major Advertisers Sign Years Ahead for Two World's Fairs," *Sales Management*, (15 January 1938), clipping, NYWF, Box 1050, f. financial.

24. *Official Guidebook. Golden Gate International Exposition* (San Francisco: San Francisco Bay Exposition, 1939), 41, 71–73 in California State Univ., Fresno, Henry Madden Library, Department of Special Collections, Expositions and Fairs Collection, (cited hereafter as CSUF); *World's Fair Progress,* I, 1 (1937), 7, in ibid.; "G. M. to Have Big Display in Vacation-land," *San Francisco Chronicle,* 8 January 1939, 18.

25. *Official Guide Book,* 72.

26. *1939 World's Fair. Preview Souvenir* [pamphlet], in CSUF; Angelo Rossi, "Fiesta Year in the West," *Think* 1, no. 9 (February 1939): 13.

27. George Creel, "Talk By George Creel Before Commonwealth Club," 26 August 1938, 3, Library of Congress, George Creel Papers, Box 5, f. Speeches 1938–40; Dean MacCannell, *The Tourist: A New Theory of the Leisure Class* (New York: Schocken Books, 1976), 186.

28. *New York World's Fair* (New York, n.p., 1936), in Cooper-Hewitt Museum Library; Langdon Winner, *The Whale and the Reactor* (Chicago: University of Chicago Press, 1986), 40–58.

29. The best account of industrial designers is Jeffrey L. Meikle, *Twentieth Century Limited: Industrial Design in America, 1925–1939* (Philadelphia: Temple University Press, 1979). See also Richard Guy Wilson, Dianne H. Pilgrim, and Dickran Tashjian, *The Machine Age in America, 1918–1941* (New York: The Brooklyn Museum in association with Harry N. Abrams, Inc., 1986); and, Miles Orvell, *The Real Thing: Imitation and Authenticity in American Culture, 1880–1940* (Chapel Hill: University of North Carolina Press, 1989), 188–194.

30. "News Release #225," 12 December 1937, attached to Perley Boone to Fiorello La Guardia, 10 December 1937, New York Municipal Archives, Fiorello La Guardia Papers, Box 852, no file; Rudoph Kagey, "Illustrated Lecture on the World's Fair of 1940 in New York," NYWF, Box 1051, f. Kagey.

31. *Official Guide Book. New York World's Fair, 1939* (New York: Exposition Publications, Inc., 1939), 27–29; Francis V. O'Connor, "The Usable Future: The Role of Fantasy in the Promotion of a Consumer Society for Art," in Helen A. Harrison, ed., *Dawn of a New Day* (New York: The Queens Museum, 1980), 62; [diary], Museum of the City of New York.

32. H. J. Brock, "Theatres for the Age of the Machine," clipping, The University of Texas at Austin, Harry Ransome Humanities Research Center, Theatre Arts Collection, Norman Bel Geddes Collection (hereafter Bel Geddes Collection), materials quoted with the permission of Mrs. Edith Luytens Bel Geddes, f. Chicago World's Fair Advisory, XH-1; Jennifer Roe Davis Roberts, "Norman Bel Geddes's Designs for Theatre and Industry" (University of Texas: M.A. thesis, 1979), 30–32. Norman Bel Geddes, *Horizons* (1932; New York: Dover reprint, 1977), 5, 289.

33. [Proposed Futurama Exhibit], n.d., Bel Geddes Collection, Box 19a, f. Proposal to Client; William S. Knudsen to Bel Geddes, 3 May 1938, Box 19a, f. Contract with Fair.

34. Donald J. Bush, "Futurama: World's Fair as Utopia," *Alternative Fu-*

tures 4 (1979): 3–20; Folke T. Kihlstedt, "Utopia Realized: The World's Fairs of the 1930s," in Joseph Corn, ed., *Imagining Tomorrow* (Cambridge, MA: MIT Press, 1986), 97–114.

35. Delwin W. Smith to Bel Geddes, 3 July 1939; William Adams Delano to Bel Geddes, 25 September 1939; Herbert Bayard Swope to Bel Geddes, n.d.; Leo Weiselberg to Bel Geddes, 21 October 1939; all in Bel Geddes Collection, Box 19b, f. Complimentary letters.

36. Bel Geddes, "Autobiography of Norman Bel Geddes," n.d., Bel Geddes Collection, AF-1.

37. *Variety*, clipping, n.d., Bel Geddes Collection, TH-13, Crystal Gazing Palace.

38. The best starting point for the study of erotic entertainment at world's fairs is Zeynep Çelik and Leila Kinney, "Ethnography and Exhibitionism at the Expositions Universelles," *Assemblages,* October 1990, 35–59.

39. *Webster's American Biographies* (Springfield, MA: G. & C. Merriam Co., 1974), 844; "Sally Rand, Whose Fan Dancing Shocked Country, Is Dead at 75," *New York Times,* 1 September 1979, 12; Studs Terkel, *Hard Times* (New York: Pantheon, 1970), 168–174.

40. Terkel, 168–174. On the subversive potential of popular culture forms, see John Fiske, *Understanding Popular Culture* (Boston: Unwin Hyman, 1989). For a specific discussion of the subversive potential of burlesque, see Robert C. Allen, *Horrible Prettiness: Burlesque and American Culture* (Chapel Hill: University of North Carolina Press, 1991), esp. 285.

41. Ragsdale, 217, 229; "Premiere. Sally Rand Will Ride in Fair Festival Parades," *San Francisco Chronicle,* 6 February 1939, 7. See also the cartoon in *The New Yorker,* 26 February 1937.

42. "Ballyhoo," in "Information Return From Applicants for Concession," 4 August 1938, Bel Geddes Collection, TH-13 Crystal Gazing Palace; Catharine A. MacKinnon, *Toward a Feminist Theory of the State* (Cambridge, MA: Harvard University Press, 1989), 195. MacKinnon's ideas have been the source of a lively debate. See Andrew Ross, *No Respect: Intellectuals and Popular Culture* (London: Routledge, 1989), 171–208; and Laura Kipnis, "(Male) Desire and (Female) Disgust: Reading *Hustler,*" in Lawrence Grossberg et al., eds., *Cultural Studies* (London: Routledge, 1992), 373–379.

43. Bel Geddes to W. Martin, 7 December 1938; [?] to Bel Geddes, 29 January 1940; Concession application, 15 July 1938; Contract, 8 April 1939; "Geddes Concessions, Inc. Report as at March 16, 1940"; all in Bel Geddes Collection, TH-13 Crystal Gazing Palace.

44. Concession application, 15 July 1938, ibid; "Click of the Year," *Look,* clipping, n.d., in ibid.

45. E. H. Bigelow, "Norman Bel Geddes' 'Crystal Lassies,'" 24 May 1939, NYWF, Box 383, f. Crystal Lassies; Contract with Eve Arden, 18 May 1939, in ibid; "Eve Arden's Other Selves," *Redbook,* clipping, March 1949, University of Texas, Austin, TX, Harry Ransom Humanities Research Center, Theatre

Arts Collection, Biographical files; [invitation telegram], n.d., in Bel Geddes Collection, TH-13 Crystal Gazing Palace.

46. *Goose-Creek News Tribune*, clipping, n.d.; Charles Grutzner, Jr., no title, *Brooklyn Eagle*, 30 May 1939, clipping; Marion C. Conger, no title, *Evansville Courier*, n.d.; all in Bel Geddes Collection, TH-13. Harry L. Bowlby to [exposition authorities], 8 May 1939, NYWF, Box 166, f. Criticisms.

47. Unidentified clipping, n.d., ibid; *New York Post*, n.d., clipping in ibid.

48. Policewomen Raleigh and Hickey, Memo, 9 October 1939, NYWF, Amusement Drawer 2, f. Enchanted Forest; "Notes Taken from the Field," 6 May 1939, ibid., f. Daily Report; [Report on Congress of Beauty], n.d., ibid., Drawer 3, f. Congress of Beauty; "Excerpts—Barking at NTG Shows," n.d., ibid., Drawer 5, f. Nudity. It is worth quoting from the concession contract for the Amazon Colony: "The women will be garbed as amazon warriors and gladiators, wearing gleaming plumed helmets, greaves in front of their shins, straps around the loins and will carry shields. There will be continuous variety of games and contests displaying the harmony of the perfect feminine physique in action. It is understood and agreed that one of the elements of the performances will be the exhibition of the physique of the performers in appropriate costumes, the exhibition to be in authentic period fashion and incidental to the portrayal of amazon skill." See Concession contract, in "Minutes of the Board of Directors . . . April 26, 1939," vol. 9, 780–781, ibid., Box 956.

49. For a brilliant description of the increasingly commonplace use of the phrase, "American Way of Life," see Warren I. Susman, *Culture as History* (New York: Pantheon, 1984), esp. chap. 9. In the same collection of essays, p. 223, Susman argues that the Crystal Gazing Palace posed a fundamental contradiction to the fair's overall theme. Robert D. Kohn, "World's Fair for Peace and Freedom," *The Synagogue Light*, n.d., clipping, NYWF, misc. clippings; "Click of the Year," *Look*, clipping, n.d.; and, "Fair Features Use of Mirrors in Architecture," *Tampa Tribune*, clipping, n.d.; both in Bel Geddes Collection, TH-13 Crystal Gazing Palace; MacKinnon, *Toward a Feminist Theory*, 214.

50. *Facts About Your Figure* [pamphlet], Yale COP, Box 14, f. Formfit. For an insightful discussion of fashion and politics, see Elizabeth Wilson, *Adorned in Dreams: Fashion and Modernity* (Berkeley: University of California Press, 1985).

51. "Hair Stylists Declare Garbo Bob is Unfair," unidentified clipping, 19 October 1938, NYWF, Box 1050, f. Fashion-female; "World's Fair to Get into Women's Hair," *New York Times*, 17 October 1938, clipping, ibid., f. Press clippings; "Experts Discuss Upward Coiffure," *New York Sun*, 17 October 1938, clipping, ibid.; [Script?], n.d., ibid., unfiled; "Be the First to Wear the Officially Licensed World's Fair Gala Dress," *Daily News*, 1 August 1938, advertisement, ibid., f. Press clippings.

52. "*Vogue* Presents Fashions of the Future," *Vogue*, 1 February 1939, 72, 137–146.

53. Alphonse Berge, quoted in [script?], n.d., NYWF, Box 1050, f. Televi-

sion Show; Lois W. Banner, *American Beauty* (Chicago: University of Chicago Press, 1984), 16.

54. J. H. Moore to Herbert Hoover, 17 March 1922; Hoover to Ernest T. Trigg, 5 June 1926; both in Herbert Hoover Library, Herbert Hoover Papers, Commerce Papers, Box 554, f. Sesquicentennial Herbert Hoover 1921–1926. See also, Hoover, "Address by Secretary Hoover at Exhibition Dinner," 20 January 1926, ibid, Box 553, f. Sesquicentennial 1926 January-May.

55. On Roosevelt's interest in continuing the Chicago fair into 1934, see Lohr, 148.

56. There is a vast literature on the New Deal. My own thinking on the Roosevelt administration's response to the economic crisis of the 1930s has been influenced by Barton Bernstein, "The New Deal: The Conservative Achievements of Liberal Reform," in B. Bernstein, ed., *Toward a New Past: Dissenting Essays in American History* (New York: Pantheon, 1968), 263–288; Paul Conkin, *The New Deal* (Arlington Heights, IL: Harlan-Davidson, 1975); Ellis W. Hawley, *The New Deal and the Problem of Monopoly* (Princeton, NJ: Princeton University Press, 1966); Steve Fraser and Gary Gerstle, eds., *The Rise and Fall of the New Deal Order* (Princeton, NJ: Princeton University Press, 1989); and Lizabeth Cohen, *Making a New Deal: Industrial Workers in Chicago, 1919–1939* (Cambridge: Cambridge University Press, 1990). Roosevelt is quoted from Franklin D. Roosevelt, "Address of the President by radio from Key West, Florida, on the occasion of the opening of the San Francisco Golden Gate Exposition, February 18, 1939," FDR papers, PPF, f. 3979, Golden Gate Exposition.

57. Frank G. Belcher to Joseph W. Hiscox, 20 May 1935, National Archives (hereafter NA), RG 40, Records of the Department of Commerce, Office of the Secretary, General Correspondence, file no. 84608/8; FDR [telegram], [November 1936?], in "Minutes of the Special Session Board of Directors . . . November 20, 1936," NYWF, vol. 1, Box 955. Roosevelt's message also appeared as the frontispiece to *The New York World's Fair and What It Will Mean to Business* [pamphlet], ibid, Box 959.

58. U.S. Congress, Senate Doc. 174, *A Century of Progress Exposition,* 73rd Congress, 2nd sess., 1–88, esp. 85–88; "Your Uncle Sam Thinks of Everything," *Official World's Fair Weekly* 1, no. 15 (12 August 1933): 6–8.

59. *A Century of Progress Exposition,* op cit., 61–62.

60. "Report of Department of Labor Exhibit at Texas Centennial Exposition," in Library of Congress, Prints and Photographs Division, Lot 2546 unsorted.

61. Theodore T. Hayes to Edward J. Flynn, 3 February 1938, NA, RG 148, Records of Minor Congressional Commissions, Box 4, f. Flynn, J.; Hayes to Carl Mittman, 15 November 1937, Smithsonian Institution Archives, RU 70, Exposition Records of the Smithsonian Institution and the United States National Museum, Box 94, f. New York World's Fair Exhibit Themes (Proposed); Nick [Eckhardt] to [?] Kerlin, 19 February 1939, NA, RG 40, Box 641,

f. 84608; "Nation's History in Art," *Mimeo Flashes* 19, no. 19 (October 1939), clipping, in ibid, Box 2, f. D.

62. On FDR's visits to various expositions see, for instance, G. Aubrey Davidson to Daniel Roper, 26 October 1935, NA, RG 40, Box 640, f. 84608; "50,000 Pack Bowl, Cheering Roosevelt at Every Pause," *Dallas Morning News*, 13 June 1936, clipping, Dallas Historical Society, Records of the Texas Centennial Exhibition, Scrapbook 4; "President Roosevelt Twice Guest of Expo and City," *Great Lakes Expo-nent* 2, no. 1 (December 5, 1936).

63. FDR's indebtedness to the iconography of the New York World's Fair was suggested to me by Rob Kroes and David Nye. Information about the "Four Freedoms" at the fair is from "Theme for Mall at Fair Acclaimed," *New York Times*, 1 December 1937, clipping, NYWF, Box 1051, f. "Mall"; and, [Press Release No. 581], ibid, Box 1014, unfiled.

64. The slippery slope of historical research into the way audiences responded to cultural texts is marked with an increasing number of cairns to help students find their way. Among the landmark works are Janice Radway's *Reading the Romance: Women, Patriarchy, and Popular Literature* (Chapel Hill, N.C.: University of North Carolina Press, 1984); Ien Ang's *Watching Dallas: Soap Opera and the Melodramatic Imagination* (1982; reprint London: Routledge, 1989); John Fiske's *Understanding Popular Culture* (Boston: Unwin Hyman, 1989); Andrew Ross, *No Respect;* and Grossberg et al., *Cultural Studies.* These works have provided an important corrective to the monolithic interpretation of mass culture forms as vehicles of ideological dominance offered by the Frankfurt School, especially as manifested in M. Horkheimer and T. Adorno's *Dialectic of Enlightenment* (1944; reprint New York: Continuum Publishing Company, 1987). But not everyone is convinced that "oppositional" or "counterhegemonial" readings of texts (including works of literature, fairs, television, etc.) have significantly altered prevailing power relationships. See, for instance, Donald Lazere, "Mass Culture and Its Audience," *Journal of Communication* 39 (Fall 1989): 131–133; Justin Lewis, *The Ideological Octopus: An Exploration of Television and Its Audience* (New York: Routledge, 1991); and Steven Watts, "The Idiocy of American Studies," *American Quarterly* 43 (December 1991): esp. 650–651.

For clues about the existence of surveys of world's fair audiences, I am deeply indebted to Roland Marchand's "Cultural History From Corporate Archives," *Public Relations Review* 16 (Fall 1990): 105–114, which called my attention to the existence of survey materials for the 1939–40 fair. I have tried to find similar detailed surveys in the official records of other expositions, including the 1933–34 Chicago fair, but was not successful. I want to emphasize, however, that such records may exist and that my search of New York World's Fair records for this particular information was guided more by serendipity than by that collection's inventory. The information cited is from: Sanford Griffith, "Sales Promotion Materials for World's Fair 1940," 24 October 1939, NYWF, Box 1051, f. "Market Analysts"; "[News Release No. BP2]," undated, ibid, Box 1029, unfiled; [Survey of World's Fair Visitors by Market Analysts, Inc.], 29 August 1940, ibid., unfiled; "Attendance and Amusement Area Survey of the New York World's Fair 1939 Incorporated," ibid., unfiled. Researchers should also consult Hadley Cantril and Mildred Strunk, *Public Opinion 1935–1946* (Princeton: Princeton University Press, 1951) for a more general survey of public opinion about the San Francisco and New York fairs.

Chapter Six

1. St. Clair Bourne, "Picket Fair as F.D.R. Speaks," *Amsterdam News,* 6 May 1939, 1, 3.

2. I am greatly indebted to the pioneering research by August Meier and Elliot Rudwick, especially "Black Man in the 'White City,' Negroes and the Columbian Exposition, 1893," *Phylon* 26 (1965): 354–361; "Come to the Fair?," *The Crisis* (March 1965): 146–150, 194–198; and "Negro Protest at the Chicago World's Fair, 1933–34," *Journal of the Illinois State Historical Society* 59 (Summer 1966): 161–171. For a different perspective that argues that the fairs really were showcases of African-American progress, see Christopher Robert Reed, "A Reinterpretation of Black Strategies for Change at the Chicago World's Fair, 1933–1934," *Illinois Historical Journal* 81 (Spring 1988): 2–12.

3. On the difficulties African Americans had experienced with the organizers of the nation's Victorian fairs, see my *All the World's a Fair* (Chicago: University of Chicago Press, 1984), esp. chap. 2–3.

4. Important studies of African Americans during the interwar period include: Nancy J. Weiss, *The National Urban League, 1910–1940* (New York: Oxford University Press, 1974) and *Farewell to the Party of Lincoln* (Princeton, NJ: Princeton University Press, 1983); John B. Kirby, *Black Americans in the Roosevelt Era: Liberalism and Race* (Knoxville, Tenn.: University of Tennessee Press, 1980); Harvard Sitkoff, *A New Deal for Blacks* (New York: Oxford University Press, 1978); Raymond Wolters, *Negroes and the Great Depression* (Westport, CT: Greenwood Press, 1970); Bernard Sternsher, ed., *The Negro in Depression and War: Prelude to Revolution, 1930–1945* (Chicago: Quadrangle, 1969); and, Andrew Buni, *Robert L. Vann of the Pittsburgh Courier* (Pittsburgh: University of Pittsburgh Press, 1974).

5. "Philadelphia to Witness Huge Klan Rally," *Philadelphia Inquirer,* 14 August 1925, clipping, City Archives of Philadelphia, Records of the Philadelphia Sesquicentennial (cited hereafter as RPS), Scrapbooks, vol. 5. Information about Klan activities is also loosely arranged in RPS, Box A-1484.

6. "Officials of Sesqui Ban Ku Klux Klan," *Philadelphia Record,* 23 June 1926, clipping, in RPS, Scrapbooks, vol. 10; "Treatment of Colored Citizens by Sesqui Officials Branded As Insulting, Grossly Unfair," *Philadelphia Tribune,* 13 February 1926, p. 9; "Fight on Real Representation at the Sesqui," *Philadelphia Tribune,* 20 February 1926, p. 1; "John C. Asbury Held High Tidewater Post, 1887–1891," unidentified clipping, Philadelphia Tribune Li-

brary, vertical files; "Asbury Makes Hot Reply to A.N.P. Charges," *Pittsburgh Courier*, 27 February 1926, p. 2.

7. Nahum D. Brascher to James Weldon Johnson, 3 February 1926, Library of Congress (hereafter cited as LC), NAACP Branch Files, Box G-187, f. "Philadelphia 1926"; "Dempsey-Tunney Fight," *Philadelphia Tribune*, 23 August 1926, p. 4; "Dempsey-Tunney 100 per cent Americans," *Philadelphia Tribune*, 9 October 1926, 16; "Sesqui Incomplete," *Philadelphia Tribune*, 30 January 1926, 4.

8. "Negro Exhibits in Palace of Agriculture at Sesqui Grounds," *Philadelphia Tribune*, 19 June 1926, p. 1; "The Sesqui Chorus," *Philadelphia Tribune*, 15 May 1926, p. 4; A. L. Sutton to Paul M. Winter, RPS, Box A-1484.

9. W. Freeland Kendrick to A. Philip Randolph, 22 May 1926, reprinted in *The Messenger*, 8 (June 1926): 190.

10. "42 Nations Join in Dedication," *Philadelphia Inquirer*, 1 June 1926; "Celebration in Honor of 150th Anniversary of Our Liberty Begins," *Philadelphia Record*, 1 June 1926, clippings, RPS, Scrapbooks.

11. "The Negro Faces the Future," *The Messenger* 8 (July 1926): 201–203; Blanche Watson to Mayor Kendrick, 6 June 1926, reprinted in *The Messenger*, 8 (October 1926): 317.

12. "The Negro Faces the Future," *The Messenger,* op cit.

13. "42 Nations Join in Dedication," *Philadelphia Inquirer*, 1 June 1926; "Orators, Cannon, and Pageantry Win Multitude," *Ledger and North American*, 1 June 1926, clipping, RPS, Scrapbooks; E. L. Austin and Odell Hauser, *The Sesqui-Centennial International Exposition* (Philadelphia, 1929).

14. "Randolph's Speech at Opening of the Sesqui-Centennial," *Pittsburgh Courier*, 12 June 1926, p. 1; "No White Man Can Boast of Longer Habitation in America Than Negro: Booker T. Washington's Theory. . . . ," *Philadelphia Tribune*, 12 June 1926, p. 15.

15. On Douglass's exclusion at the Centennial, see Rydell, *All the World's a Fair*, 28.

16. "Sesqui Committee," *Philadelphia Tribune*, 23 August 1926, p. 4; "Sesqui Exhibit Head Released by E. L. [*sic.*] Sutton," *Philadelphia Tribune*, 11 September 1926, p. 1; "Tunney and Dempsey Will Fight Here as Mayor and Clergy Play Turn About," *Philadelphia Tribune*, 21 August 1926, p. 1; "The 'Big Show' is Over," *Philadelphia Tribune*, 4 December 1926, editorial.

17. Meier and Rudwick, "Negro Protest at the Chicago World's Fair, 1933–1934," 161; Dewey R. Jones, "Race Aided in Making Fair History," *Chicago Defender*, 10 November 1934, p. 11; Harry Keene, "Indorse [*sic*] Defender's Plan Beautiful," *Chicago Defender*, 31 December 1932, p. 22; "Defender Launches Big World's Fair Contest," *Chicago Defender*, 28 January 1933, p. 1.

18. Dewey R. Jones, "Race Aided in Making Fair History," p. 1; Jones, "A Day at the Fair," *Chicago Defender*, 30 June 1934, pp. 11, 22; *Guide Memories* (Chicago, n.p., [1933?]), p. 172, LC.

19. [News Release], "Three States Have Negro Representation at World's Fair," 7 June 1933, Chicago Historical Society (cited as CHS), Claude A. Barnett Papers, Box 11, f. May 15–June 5, 1933.

20. [News release], "Old Mexico at World's Fair Raises Color Bar," 2 August 1933, CHS, Barnett Papers, Box 11, f. 2; "The Week," *Chicago Defender,* 12 August 1933, p. 10; Dewey R. Jones, "A Day at the Fair," p. 11; "Seen and Heard at the Fair," *Chicago Defender,* 24 June 1933, p. 15; Robert C. Miller to [Nathaniel?] Owings, 12 November 1933, University of Illinois, Chicago, Records of the Century of Progress Exposition (cited as COP), General Correspondence, f. 1-10356. Miller's partner, Paul F. Gaus, suggested a modification of the "African Dips" for the 1934 fair: "Instead of a man just falling into a plain water barrel, in my new game, the man would be snapped at by an alligator and it would be illuminated in colors." See Gaus to Century of Progress Exposition, 21 November 1933, in COP, General Correspondence, f. 1-10356.

21. Information on this concession is derived from Lou Dufour with Irwin Kirby, *Fabulous Years* (New York: Vantage, 1977), 68–69; F. M. Andrews to J. J. O'Donnell, 21 August 1933, and J. Riley to J. O'Donnell, 14 October 1933, in COP, General Correspondence, f. 1-4821; and Robert Bogdan, *Freak Show: Presenting Human Oddities for Amusement and Profit* (Chicago: University of Chicago Press, 1988), 195–197. The quotation from the *Chicago Defender* is from Charles M. Thompson, "The Century of Progress Closes," 10 November 1934, 11.

22. "DePriest Not to Take Part in 'Negro Day' Program," *Chicago Defender,* 5 August 1933, p. 2; "'Negro Day' To Be Gala Affair Here," *Chicago Defender,* 12 August 1933, p. 1; Dewey R. Jones, "A Day at the Fair," *Chicago Defender,* 26 August 1933, p. 10; Dennis A. Bethea, "More About 'Negro Day,'" 26 August 1933, "'Negro Day' at Fair Flops," *Chicago Defender,* 19 August 1933, p. 2.

23. [News release], "Citizens Demand Action By State. . . . ," 1 August 1933; "File Damage Suits," 21 August 1933; [News release?], "Case of Grand Jury World's Fair [*sic*]," October 1933; all in LC, NAACP Branch Files, Box G-51, f. Chicago, July 1933; and f. Chicago, October 1933.

24. On Roosevelt's intervention to reopen the fair, see COP, Confidential files, Box 8, f. 8-5 fair extension.

25. "House Bill 114," attached to A. C. MacNeal to Walter F. White, 25 May 1934, LC, NAACP Branch Files, Box G-52, f. Chicago, May 1934.

26. Jones, "A Day at the Fair," 5; [News release], "World's Fair Restaurant Refuses to Serve Social Worker," 1 August 1934, CHS, Barnett Papers, Box 14, f. August 1–27, 1934.

27. Kenneth B. Ragsdale, *The Year America Discovered Texas, Centennial '36* (College Station, Tex.: Texas A & M University Press, 1987), 65–66; "Bynum Says Press Printed Only Truth," *Houston Informer,* 18 July 1936, 1.

28. Ragsdale, 71.

29. Ibid; "Cline to Promise Negroes Building for Sale of Bonds," (uniden-

tified clipping), Dallas Historical Society, Records of the Texas Centennial Exposition (cited hereafter as DHS, RTCE), scrapbook clippings.

30. Rev. J. Raymond Huchinson[?], "History and Results of Negro Participation in the Texas Centennial," August 1936, DHS, RTCE, Box A-809; "Two-Day Barbecue Planned . . . to Inaugurate Centennial Bond Sale Among Negroes Boosting Exposition," *Dallas Journal,* clipping, 25 June 1934, DHS, RTCE, Buildings Clippings Box.

31. A. Maceo Smith to Eugene Kinckle Jones, 23 August 1935, DHS, RTCE, Drawer 21, f. Negro Participation.

32. Daniel Roper to William W. Sanders, 31 October 1935; Charles E. Hall to Daniel Roper, 14 July 1937; and A. Maceo Smith to W. B. Yeager, 7 September 1935, National Archives, Record Group 40, General Records of the Department of Commerce (cited as NA, RG 40), Box 683, f. 88449.

33. Weiss, *Farewell to the Party of Lincoln.*

34. Roper quoted in Jesse O. Thomas, *Negro Participation in the Texas Centennial Exposition* (Boston: Christopher Publishing House, 1938), 126.

35. On Thomas's background, see the preface to ibid, 7–8, by Booker T. Washington's longtime confidante, Emmett J. Scott.

36. Jones, quoted in ibid, 53, 55–56; "Argument Rages Between Jesse O. Thomas and Editor," *Houston Informer,* 18 July 1936, 2.

37. Thomas, 8, 73–74; George Dahl to W. B. Yeager, 17 July 1936, DHS, RTCE, drawer 21, f. Federal Negro Building; Ragsdale, 177; "The Centennial," *Houston Informer,* 8 February 1936, p. 8; "Negro Progress—The Centennial," *Houston Informer,* 18 April 1936, p. 10; Claude C. Tedford, "The Texas Centennial Exhibit," 7 August 1936, [News release], CHS, Barnett Papers, photocopies in DHS.

38. John L. Blount, "Blount Puts 8 Queries on Dallas Expo," *Houston Informer,* 6 June 1936, p. 1; "Argument Rages Between Jesse O. Thomas and Editor," *Houston Informer,* 18 July 1936, p. 1.

39. Thomas, *Negro Participation,* 71–85; "Argument Rages Between Jesse O. Thomas and Editor," and "Blount Puts 8 Queries on Dallas Expo."

40. Thomas, *Negro Participation,* 25–44; Tedford, "Hall of Negro Life," [News release], CHS, Barnett Collection, photocopy in DHS.

41. Thomas, *Negro Participation,* 27; Roscoe Dunjee, "Here's A Laugh," [News release], Barnett Collection, photocopy in DHS.

42. "Officials Expect 1,000,000 Negroes Here During Fair"; and "For Juneteenth," 18 June 1936, DHS, RTCE, misc. clippings; "Dr. A. S. Jackson Flays Insults to Negro in Centennial Parade," *Houston Informer,* 13 June 1936, 1–2; Thomas, *Negro Participation,* 83; "Negroes Stage Big Juneteenth at Centennial," *Dallas Morning News,* 20 June 1936, DHS, RTCE, Scrapbooks, vol. 2.

43. Benjamin Dillard to Frank Watson, [March 1937], DHS, RTCE, drawer 37, f. Negro Participation; "Negroes and Centennial Posts," *Houston Informer,* 2 May 1936, clipping, DHS, RTCE, drawer 21, f. Negro Participa-

tion; "Centennial Insults," *Houston Informer*, 20 June 1936, p. 4; "Duke and Cab Booked for Texas Centennial Meet," *Chicago Defender*, 2 May 1936, p. 8; Thomas, *Negro Participation*, 96; Thomas to Ned Blaine, 22 October 1936, DHS, RTCE, drawer, 21, f. Negro Participation.

44. Thomas, *Negro Participation*, 84–85, 147.

45. Ibid, 117–124.

46. Ibid.; Thomas to Barnett, 2 February 1937, CHS, Barnett Collection, Box 311, f. 311–312.

47. Thomas, *Negro Participation*, 149.

48. Michael L. Gillette, "The Rise of the NAACP in Texas," *Southwestern Historical Quarterly*, 81 (1978): 393–416.

49. For a good account of African-American buildings at southern fairs, see Ruth M. Winton, "Negro Participation in Southern Expositions, 1881–1915," *Journal of Negro Education* 16 (Winter 1947): 34–43.

50. Grover A. Whalen, *Mr. New York. The Autobiography of Grover A. Whalen* (New York: Putnam, 1955), 183–186. I am indebted to Peter J. Kuznick for this reference.

51. Meier and Rudwick, "Come to the Fair?," 196; [Roy Wilkins?] to Arthur Spingarn, 7 March 1939; "Memorandum on Conference with Mayor LaGuardia . . . 29 April 1939"; [Walter White] to Grover Whalen, 20 October 1937; all in NAACP Administrative Files, Box C-481, f. World's Fair, LC.

52. Thomas Donovan to Walter White, 26 October 1937; Karl N. Llewellyn, "Notes on World's Fair Situation," 1 May 1939, both clippings in ibid.

53. "Memorandum on Conference with Mayor LaGuardia . . . 29 April 1939," ibid. See also, John H. Johnson to Mayor LaGuardia, 2 December 1937; and, "Data from Lee for Mr. Kohn," n.d., both in New York Public Library, Records of the New York World's Fair (cited as NYWF), f. A-4, Negro Policy.

54. Arthur Spingarn to Grover Whalen, 23 May 1938, NYWF, f. PR2.28, Interracial Advisory Committee.

55. I am grateful to David E. Nye for calling my attention to Anderson's performance at the fair; Robert Kohn to Farrow R. Allen, 3 May 1939, NYWF, f. A-4, Negro Policy.

56. Rev. John H. Johnson to Mayor LaGuardia, 2 December 1937, New York City Municipal Archives, Fiorello LaGuardia Papers, Box 26, f. 2, World's Fair; G. P. Wylly, memo, 13 April 1939; Adam Clayton Powell, Jr., to Grover Whalen, 4 April [1938?]; both in NYWF, f. A-4, Negro Policy: "St. Clair Bourne, Picket Fair as FDR Speaks," *Amsterdam News*, 6 May 1939, pp. 1, 3; Meier and Rudwick, "Come to the Fair?" pp. 196–197.

57. John Allwood, *The Great Exhibitions* (London: Studio Vista, 1977), 148; Warren I. Susman, "The People's Fair: Cultural Contradictions of a Consumer Society," in Helen A. Harrison, ed., *Dawn of a New Day: The New York World's Fair, 1939/40* (New York, 1980), 3–15.

58. "World's Fair Bulletin No. 1," n.d., Yale University, Sterling Library, Century of Progress Collection (cited hereafter as Yale, COP), Box 38, f. 11.

59. "The American Declaration of National Unity," n.d., rough draft, NYWF, American Commons Exhibit Drawer, f. Misc.; W. E. B. DuBois, "The Negro in American Culture," Schomburg Library, Negro Week Collection, Box 1, f. 6.

60. Reddick, quoted in *Negro Week on the American Common* . . . , no imprint, in Yale, COP, Box 38, f. 12; "Fair Discrimination," *Amsterdam News*, 27 April 1940, p. 14.

61. *American Negro Exposition*, no imprint, CHS; Truman K. Gibson, Jr., "Memorandum" n.d., CHS, Barnett Collection, Box 366, f. 3.

62. *American Negro Exposition*, 8–10.

63. Ibid., 16–27; "Department Exhibit at the American Negro Exposition"; and, "The Skill of the Craftsman"; both in CHS, Barnett Collection, Box 369, f. 1.

64. *American Negro Exposition*, 25.

65. Ibid., 17, 22.

66. Ibid., 25, 34.

67. Ibid., 23–24, 38.

68. Ibid., 37–38; H. Geo. Davenport, "The Negro in Chicago," clipping, CHS, Barnett Collection, Box 369, f. 3; "Cancels Exhibit on Birth Control," *New York Times*, 8 July 1940, clipping, CHS, Barnett Collection, Box 369, f. 3; Frank Marshall Davis to Roy Wilkins, 7 January 1941, CHS, Barnett Collection, Box 368, f. 6; "Negro Exposition Front for New Deal War Plans," *Fighting Worker*, 1 October 1940, p. 3, University of Michigan, Labadie Collection.

69. "Wallace Attacks 'Scapegoat' Idea," *New York Times*, 3 September 1940, p. 7.

Chapter Seven

1. Dillard Stokes, "Bureaucrats and the Brussels Fair—Why America Is Slated for Humiliation," *Human Events*, reprinted in *Congressional Record Appendix*, vol. 104, 85th Cong., 2nd Sess., A3430.

2. John Kenneth Galbraith, *The Affluent Society* (1958; repr. Boston: Houghton Mifflin, 1984); David M. Potter, *People of Plenty* (Chicago: University of Chicago Press, 1954). Useful surveys of postwar American life include: Paul Boyer, *By the Bomb's Early Light: American Thought and Culture at the Dawn of the Nuclear Age* (New York: Pantheon, 1985); Spencer R. Weart, *Nuclear Fear. A History of Images* (Cambridge, MA: Harvard University Press, 1988); Thomas Hine, *Populux* (New York: Alfred A. Knopf, 1986).

3. *This is America* (Washington, D.C.: n.p., 1958); John Allwood, *The Great Exhibitions* (London: Studio Vista, 1977), 153–158; H. de Meyer and P. H. Virenque, *Brussel '58 in Cijfers* (Antwerp: De Nederlandsche Boekhandel, 1959); "Bilan du monde pour un monde plus humain," *Objectif 58* no. 9 (November 1955), in Archives of the Brussels World's Fair, Tentoonstelling Parc du Bruxelles (cited hereafter as TPB); "Architecture at Brussels: Festival of Structure," *Architectural Record* 123 (June 1958): 163–170; "Best at Brussels," *Ar-*

chitectural Forum 108 (June 1958): 78–86; "The U.S. at the Fair," *Newsweek* 51 (14 April 1958): 53; "Un editorial de M. A. Buisseret," *Objectif 58* (October 1956): 3–31, in TPB. For a brief overview of the fair, see Robert W. Rydell, "Brussels Universal and International Exposition," *Historical Dictionary of World's Fairs and Expositions, 1851–1988,* ed. John E. Findling and Kimberly D. Pelle (Westport, CT: Greenwood Press, 1990), 311–318.

4. Fernand Baudhuin, *Histoire économique de la Belgique, 1957–1968* (Brussels: Establissement Emile Bruylant, 1970), 213–221; *Exposition de Bruxelles 1958. Les Participations étrangères et belges* (Brussels, n.p., 1958); "President's Special International Program," National Archives, RG 43, Records of Minor Congressional Commissions (cited hereafter as NA, RG 43), box 15, black binder; Hine, *Populuxe,* 160; Edward D. Stone, *The Evolution of an Architect* (New York: Horizon Press, 1962); Elmer Cox, "Article for the American People's Encyclopedia"; "Howard S. Cullmann . . . ," attached to Gerson Lush to Elmer Cox, 5 January 1959, both in NA, RG 43, Box 1, f. Admin.-12. For a good overview of American cultural concerns in the postwar period, see Lary May, ed., *Recasting America: Culture and Politics in the Age of Cold War* (Chicago: University of Chicago Press, 1988).

5. "Theme Development. Staff Discussions, November 6, 1956," in MIT Libraries, Institute Archives and Special Collections (cited hereafter as MIT), Max Frank Millikan Papers, MC 188, f. 119.

6. Transcripts and summaries of interviews are all in ibid.; United States Information Agency, "Proposed Thematic Treatment for United States Exhibit at Brussels World [*sic*] Fair," n.d., in ibid., f. 120.

7. Ibid., f. 120.

8. Robert Warner to Elting Morison, 5 April 1957, ibid., f. 119.

9. "Questions to be Presented at Meeting with Massachusetts Institute of Technology Faculty Members," 22 March 1957, MIT, Office of the Dean Records, AC 20, Box 1, f. 27; "M.I.T. Conferees and Interviewees Who Aided in the Formulation of U.S. Theme," n.d., NA, Box 20, f. American Theme; "[Informal Summary of Discussion]," n.d., MIT, Ithiel de Sola Pool Papers, MC 87-54, Box 5, f. World's Fair Brussels 1957.

10. Robert Warner to Elting E. Morison, 23 April 1957, MIT, MC 87-54, Box 5, f. World's Fair Brussels 1957; Charles Siepmann, "1958 Brussels Universal and International Exhibition," n.d., MIT, AC 20, Box 1, f. 27.

11. "Subcommittee Reports Presented at the Final Meeting of the Cambridge Study Group for the Brussels Universal and International Exhibition, 1958," 28 April 1958, MIT, Collection 87-54, box 5, f. World's Fair, Brussels.

12. "Memorandum of Theme and Exhibits Program," 6 May 1957, NA, RG 43, Box 8, f. BRU-24.

13. Howard Cullman to Eisenhower, 12 November 1957, NA, RG 43, Box 22, f. Brussels Fair '57; Marguerite Cullman, *Ninety Dozen Glasses* (New York: W. W. Norton, 1960), 59–60; "The Brussels Fair," 23 January 1958, *Congressional Record,* 85th Cong., 2nd Sess., 104: 828–829, reprints "We'll

Go on Trial at the Fair"; "Bureaucrats and the Brussels Fair—Why America is Slated For Humiliation," *Congressional Record Appendix,* 85th Cong., 2nd Sess., 104: A3430, reprints Dillard Stokes's article from *Human Events;* 9 January 1958, *Congressional Record,* 85th Cong., 2nd Sess., 104: 195.

14. "United States Exhibit at Brussels World's Fair," *Congressional Record,* 85th Cong., 2nd Sess., 104: 11869–70; "The Brussels Fair," ibid., 5541–5542; L. Mendel Rivers to Gerson Lush, 25 April 1958, NA, RG 43, Box 12, f. Exh. 414.

15. John Foster Dulles, "Memorandum for the President," n.d., NA, RG 43, Box 22, f. Brussels Fair; Mr. Murphy to the Secretary, 2 November 1957, NA, RG 43, f. Brussels Fair; 26 February 1958, *Congressional Record,* 85th Cong., 2nd Sess., 104: 2914; "Pennypinching at the Fair," ibid., A1321.

16. "Brussels '58," *Interiors* 117, 2 (September 1957): 128–141.

17. "A Report of the Brussels World's Fair," 16 September 1957, NA, RG 43, Box 14, f. PA-20; *This is America,* 8; "Brussels '58," *Interiors* 117, 2 (September 1957): 128.

18. Philip Siekevitz, "The Decadent Pavilion," *Nation* 187, 11 (October 11, 1958): 211–213; "Brussels '58," *Interiors* 117, 2 (September 1957): 139–140.

19. Peter G. Harnden Associates, "United States Pavilion of the Brussels Universal and International Exposition, 1958. Draft Working Script," 1 July 1957, NA, RG 43, Box 18, Program binder.

20. Cullman, "The United States at the Brussels Universal and International Exposition 1958," NA, RG 43, Box 20, f. unmarked; "Nuclear Energy," ibid., f. 9b-Science; *This is America,* passim; "United States Has It, Soviets Do Not, at Brussels," *Congressional Record Appendix,* 85th Cong., 2nd Sess., 104: A6562; [press release?], n.d., in NA, RG 43, Box 12, f. Exh.

21. Cullman, "The United States at the Brussels Universal and International Exposition 1958," NA, Box 20, f. unmarked; David M. Potter, *People of Plenty* (Chicago: University of Chicago Press, 1954).

22. *This is America,* passim; "The Philadelphia Model (draft)," n.d., NA, RG 43, Box 20, f. Philadelphia Story; Judith P. Murphy, "Fortune's Pavilion at Brussels," NA, RG 43, Box 12, f. Exh.-414; "Brussels '58," *Interiors* 117, 2 (September 1957): 141.

23. Howard Taubman, "Brussels: American Mistakes and Lessons," *New York Times Magazine,* 1 June 1958, 11.

24. "Foreign Service Despatch 483," 4 November 1958; "Department of State Instruction to American Embassy, Brussels," 25 November 1957; both in NA, RG 43, Box 5, f. BEG-401; "Confidential Message," no. CX-5, June 1958, ibid., f. BEG-40.

25. Cullman, "The United States at the Brussels Universal and International Exposition 1958," NA, RG 43, Box 20, f. unmarked; Brussels to Sec. of State [telegram], 26 March 1958, NA, RG 43, Box 4, f. Adm.-77; Ernest Besig to Sec. of State, 13 October 1958, NA, RG 43, Box 15, f. unmarked; "Conver-

sation by telephone between Mr. Lush and Jules Irving," 4 September 1958, NA, Box 15, f. unmarked.

26. Burke Wilkinson to Andy [?], 28 April 195[8], NA, RG 43, Box 15, f. Brussels Fair—1957 general.

27. "Our Image at Brussels," *Life* 45, no. 2 (14 July 1958): 44; Lush to Thurston Davies, 18 June 1958, NA, RG 43, Box 14, f. PA-21; "United States Exhibit . . ." *Congressional Record,* 85th Cong., 2nd Sess., 104: A5828.

28. William F. Fay to Dulles, 20 September 1958; Rev. T. James McNamara to Louis Widmer, 11 August 1958; Leo Cherne, "Memorandum on the U.S. Exhibit at the Brussels Exhibition;" all in NA, RG 43, Box 11, f. BRU-00 Popular Comment Favorable; [Telegram] to Ralph Yarborough, 23 June 1958, NA, RG 43, Box 11, f. BRU-00 Popular Comment Unfavorable.

29. Cullman, "The United States at the Brussels Universal and International Exposition 1958," NA, RG 43, Box 20, f. unmarked; William A. Buell, "Visit by Voroshilov to the United States Pavilion," NA, Box 5, f. BEG-401; Hugh Vehenne, "A Visit to the U.S. Pavilion," *Le Soir,* 23 April 1958, clipping, NA, RG 43, Box 14, f. PA-21. For a good overview of efforts by the American government to mask the dangers of nuclear energy, see Catherine Caufield, *Multiple Exposures: Chronicles of the Radiation Age* (New York: Secker and Warburg, 1989), esp. chap. 15.

30. "Program and Media Studies . . . Visitor Reaction to the U.S. versus Major Competing Exhibits at the Brussels International Fair," July 1958, NA, RG 48, Box 11, f. BRU-001; "The Brussels Fair in Soviet Propaganda," 2 May 1958, ibid. For a good summary of U.S. government efforts to promote American culture overseas, see Reinhold Wagnleitner, "The Irony of American Culture Abroad: Austria and the Cold War," in *Recasting America,* 285–301.

Conclusion

1. Leland W. Cutler, *America is Good to a Country Boy* (Stanford: Stanford University Press, 1954), 182–206.

2. Roland Marchand, "Corporate Imagery and Popular Education: World's Fairs and Expositions in the United States, 1893–1940," in David E. Nye and Carl Pedersen, eds., *Consumption and American Culture* (Amsterdam: VU University Press, 1991), 29; David Nye, "Synthetic Sublime: The New York World's Fair of 1939," unpublished paper. It is also worth noting that not all world's fair authorities made this transition in their thinking about fairs. Mayor Fiorello H. La Guardia, for one, called the 1940 New York fair "one of the greatest educational enterprises of the modern world." See La Guardia to Harvey Gibson, 10 October 1940, New York Municipal Archives, Fiorello La Guardia Papers, Box 2600, f. WF3.

3. Donald Horne, *The Great Museum: The Re-Presentation of History* (London: Pluto Press Ltd., 1984), 256.

INDEX

References to illustrations are printed in boldface type. World's fairs are listed by city.

51
52
53
54
55
56
57
58
59
60
61
62
63
64
65
66
67
68
69
70
71
72
73
74
75
76
77
78
79
80
81
82
83
84

378
379
380
381
382
383
384
385
386
387
388
389